Walled In
Walled Out

A Young American Woman in Iran

Mary Dana Marks

A PEACE CORPS WRITERS BOOK

WALLED IN, WALLED OUT:
A YOUNG AMERICAN WOMAN IN IRAN

A Peace Corps Writers Book

An imprint of Peace Corps Worldwide

Printed in the United States of America
by Peace Corps Writers of Oakland, California.

For more information, contact peacecorpsworldwide@gmail.com.
Peace Corps Writers and the Peace Corps Writers colophon are trade-
marks of PeaceCorpsWorldwide.org.

Book design: Jim Bisakowski www.bookdesign.ca

ISBN-13: 978-1-935925-82-8

Library of Congress Control Number: 2017936077

First Peace Corps Writers Edition, July 2017

For Richard

Walls are meant to block views, but they block only the view of the eye—the ocular view—not the imaginative view. When the eye scans a certain barrier, the imagination tends to go beyond that barrier. Walls reveal more things than they hide. —*El Anatsui*

v

CONTENTS

Map by Tom Klobe, adapted from his book *A Young American in Iran*.

Prologue

January 1966

The taxi screeched to a halt in front of a low-slung building, part of a government complex in this provincial capital on the high Iranian plateau. While I seldom visited this part of town, the neighborhood looked very familiar: shops abutting each other; tall adobe walls barricading unseen households; a barefoot young boy herding a flock of thick-fleeced sheep down the paved road. Men pedaled bicycles, their dark suit jackets flapping as they wove between taxis and animals. A few women hurried about, their heads down, flower-printed chadors tenting their bodies.

The occasion was a celebration of the Day of Freedom for Iranian Women. Mrs. Nouri, the president of the women's association, led me into an elegant hall where we were seated in the prestigious third row, a compliment to my hostess and her foreign guest. A slight murmur rose when the wife of the governor general, a model of modernity in an elegantly tailored suit, was escorted to her place of honor in the first row.

"Exactly what is the Day of Freedom?" I asked. Mrs. Nouri paused to pat her dark hair, her elaborate gold rings reflecting circles of light from the crystal chandelier above.

"It was this day," she began. "Oh, my English is not good enough. It was on this day, thirty years ago," she continued in Farsi, "that Reza Shah forbade Iranian women to wear chadors ever again."

I glanced around the room. The guests—wives of the city's dignitaries, government employees, school teachers like me—were wearing smartly cut two piece suits, high heels, and sheer stockings. Not even a headscarf could be seen. In my plaid wool skirt and brown sweater, I was woefully underdressed. Usually when Reza Shah, the current shah's father, was mentioned, it was with a hint of scandal. Unapologetic about his pro-German sympathies, he had been forced by the Allies to abdicate in 1941. Among Iranian women, however, he was infamous for his heartless manner in banning the veil.

"Soldiers ripped my mother's chador from her body," I remembered a friend saying. "After that, she refused to go outside. She felt naked." Yet on this day we were paying official homage to Reza Shah's vision of a westernized, secular Iran.

The mistress of ceremonies, Mrs. Moaveni, who often addressed assemblies like this one, took the stage, standing next to a gilt bust of Reza Shah mounted on a stand, a black drape hanging from its shoulders. Strains of the Iranian national anthem rang out from an unseen tape recorder, and the audience rose to face the red, green, and white flag, stage left.

When the music ended, we settled back in our chairs to listen to Mrs. Moaveni praise the wisdom of the former shah in releasing the women of Iran from the constrictions of the chador, adding: "Because of Reza Shah's foresight and determination, with the edict of *kashf-e hijab* Iran became the first Muslim country to ban the wearing of the veil." She went on at length, in formal Farsi, about how all in this room should be grateful that this symbol of the confinement of Iranian women had been abandoned. The audience members nodded their heads solemnly in agreement with her emphatic rhetoric.

When Mrs. Moaveni had finished her remarks, the wives of the governor general and the city's mayor approached the bust of Reza Shah, placing a huge wreath of greenery at the foot of the pedestal to an enthusiastic round of applause. As the national anthem played, we stood again facing the disgraced shah, saluting his efforts for women.

The music stopped, the program was over. Standing, I pulled on my coat as the women filed out of the building. Pausing at the door, these wives and teachers, Mrs. Moaveni in the lead, unfolded their chadors and draped them carefully over their heads. Wrapping these long veils closely around their bodies, they hailed the taxis that would take them home.

1

I JOINED THE PEACE CORPS!

I am going out to find myself, but if I return before I get back, please hold on to me until I get there. —Calvin and Hobbes

Hell

The scene was a lake in Michigan in a town called Hell, on a cold, drizzly day in August 1964. In the water, bobbing up and down, raising their heads only to breathe, eighty Peace Corps trainees were treading water. I was one of them. Nearing the end of our training program for Iran, we were in the lake to demonstrate our stamina and character, while Freddy Lanoue, the expert imported from Georgia Tech to teach us drownproofing, his life-saving technique, shouted encouragement from the dock. We'd been floating upright here for three hours; it seemed Hell would freeze over before he let us out of the water.

Housed in University of Michigan dormitories for most of the summer, we had to make room for arriving freshmen as two weeks of training remained. Crowded buses had transported us to the camp in Hell where rustic cabins, lumpy cots, and Half Moon Lake awaited us. I wondered what I was doing there.

No one in our group had grown up wanting to be a Peace Corps volunteer. In this summer of 1964, the idea of the Peace Corps was just three years old. During his campaign for the presidency, John F. Kennedy had challenged young Americans to serve their country overseas. Thousands answered his call, though for me, what I could do for our country was a minor aspect of what impelled me to sign up.

In February I had filled out the Peace Corps questionnaire at the University of Illinois as a fall-back plan, but one by one other options faded. Losing out on a fellowship to study Chinese history was the final blow. The Peace Corps was welcoming, offering a spot in a training program for Iran, and a much-needed stipend. At the end of my service, it promised a readjustment allowance of more than $1000, enough for at least a semester of Chinese history. My short answer to "Why did you volunteer?" was "for the money."

But there was a long answer, too. For as far back as I could remember, I had pictured myself somewhere else: on a mission of mercy in an African country whose name I barely knew; in a Paris garret, writing a novel, of course; or bringing hope to China's downtrodden, like Luise Rainer in the film *The Good Earth*. The missionary tinge had faded by the time I got to college, but the desire to be part of the larger world, somewhere utterly different from the places I called home—Illinois, New Jersey, and West Virginia—was still compelling. I majored in international relations and political science at the University of Illinois, ignoring the impracticality of such study for a young woman. Determined to live abroad, I envisioned myself the perfect foreigner, fluent in the language and embracing the local culture—a most un-ugly American. But first, I had to get through summer training.

Shahla, my roommate that hot Ann Arbor summer, was an "informant," the Peace Corps' peculiar title for the Iranian students hired to teach trainees the Persian language and impart cultural tidbits as the summer progressed. She helped me practice the many unfamiliar sounds. I couldn't wait to show off when I produced my first rolled "r."

"Shahla, listen! I can do it! *Tehran, meeram, Rasht!* Just hear those 'r's!"

"*Bah, bah, bah!*" ("Good for you!"), she said, her dark curls bouncing with approval.

After conquering the rolling "r," I mastered more unfamiliar Persian sounds, like the "kh" in *khanum* and the "q" in *qanat*. The Peace Corps promoted me to "A," the fastest language class, with volunteers I didn't know well. Lynn, a quick-witted brunette with flashing eyes, was from Kentucky, and of Lebanese descent. Eden, an Assyrian woman (Syrian with an ass, she said) had been born in Iran and was the best in Persian by far. John, a shy, bespectacled Harvard grad, could parrot back Farsi phrases with the accent of a native speaker.

The A class ripped through Persian lessons at warp speed. Ahmad, the instructor, peppered us with a barrage of commands and queries in Farsi that the others grasped and shot back before I even understood the drill. The thrill of mastering new sounds and speaking a few sentences vanished. I dragged myself to the class of stars each morning and afternoon.

"Where did you go? Why did you go there? Who did you see?" Ahmad directed a fire of Farsi at me one muggy afternoon.

"I went... I saw... I don't know. I can't do this."

Unable to stifle the sob of frustration and embarrassment welling in my throat, I ran out of the classroom, tears streaming down my face. But a final exit was unthinkable. I showed up for class the next morning.

"You're slowing us down, Mary," Lynn said a few days later. "Ahmad's afraid he's going to make you cry."

"You think I want to cry? I can't go at his pace."

I wasn't among the stars for long. The Peace Corps demoted me to the B class, where I rolled my r's under a lot less pressure.

"Deselection," the Peace Corps' term for rejecting a trainee, shadowed us throughout the summer. After we'd been at the University of Michigan for about a month some of our group were called into the counselor's office and told to go home. We never learned why that dozen or so were deselected. Was it the psychological tests we took, classroom performance, language skills? With more deselections to come, my future as a volunteer remained precarious.

Sucked into the vortex of Peace Corps training, where the single goal was to be selected for service, I was determined to succeed, to be chosen to go to this country that was a mere blip in most Americans' awareness in 1964. "I'm going to Iran—or is it Iraq?" a volunteer for Iran's first group announced to a friend before heading off for training. It was only when I dragged out a huge atlas in Illinois' graduate library that I placed Iran with certainty in its Middle Eastern context: Iraq and Turkey to the west, the Soviet Union to the north, Afghanistan and Pakistan along its eastern border, and the Persian Gulf to the south.

But after weeks in muggy classrooms, Michigan's Near East history professors and our Persian language instructors had fleshed out the complex realities of this country. I sensed a different worldview from the one I embraced. Poetry, almost absent in my life, was a shimmering thread in the fabric of Iran. In any given situation, verses from Sa'adi, the thirteenth century bard, or Hafez, who flourished a hundred years later, rolled in sonorous tones from our trainers' lips. "Mention no ill of anyone to me and you will prevent my thinking ill of you," a diplomatic informant quoted Sa'adi, when I complained about a fractious trainee. An iconic poet from 700 years ago—and I thought Shakespeare was an old guy. My sense of the world, firmly anchored in western tradition, was beginning a perceptible shift toward the east.

The subdued role women played in Muslim Iran, however, complicated this new understanding. Lying on our beds in West Quad dormitory, Shahla and I discussed it.

"What do girls do for fun in Iran?" I asked.

"Well, we visit relatives, play volleyball at school, go to the cinema with our brothers. You know, stuff like that."

"Do you go shopping?"

"Sure, when I need cloth for a dress, my mom will take me to the bazaar."

"How about parties?"

"We get together with our girlfriends all the time, and we go on picnics with our families on our days off," she said.

"Can you just hang out at a luncheonette, or someplace like that?"

"Oh no, that wouldn't be proper. Girls in Iran don't go out in public by themselves."

I wondered what I would do with my spare time. Had I been so busy trying to impress the Peace Corps that I had forgotten to consider if Iran was really the right place for me?

The difficulties of melding Iran's poetic past with the modern twentieth century reached far beyond the role of women. Rich in oil, it remained a monarchy whose tradition extended to its pre-Islamic roots. The Iranian elite, epitomized by the royal families of the past and present, controlled much of the country's wealth. As large landholders, their power was felt across the Iranian economy. The government was parliamentary in form only, existing to rubber stamp the policies of Shah Mohammad Reza Pahlavi. Dissent was dangerous, leaving few options for those who advocated a true democratic system of government, or wished to address the problems of poverty, health care, and education in rural areas.

"I thought the shah had implemented land reforms," I said to one of our professors after class.

"He did, but only under great pressure from his opposition, particularly the clerics," the professor said. "It's too soon to know how real the reforms are, or if he's managed to placate the mullahs."

"If Iran has so much money," asked another trainee, "why does it need the Peace Corps?"

"That's a good question." The professor's cheeks reddened as he studied his feet. "One could argue that the shah's close relationship with the United States government is a factor."

The shah's control reached into Peace Corps training. "Be careful what you say around Mehdi," warned one Iranian teacher. "They say he's on SAVAK's payroll." The influence of Iran's much-feared secret police, the *Sāzemān-e Ettelā'āt va Amniyat-e Keshvar* (the Organization of Intelligence and National Security), stretched from small Iranian villages and towns to university campuses in the United States and Europe. Reports of the imprisonment, torture, or even death of those who opposed the shah and his policies stifled dissension in Iran and abroad. Still, many of the Iranians training our Peace Corps group in Ann Arbor were outspoken in their opposition to the current regime.

Ahmad, my former teacher, was one of them. Several train-ees gathered on the lawn of the university's law school, lis-tening as our Iranian informants aired their frustrations about their country and mine. Ahmad took the lead.

"I thought freedom of speech was important to Americans," he said, stretching his long legs out on the grass. "How can your government support a dictatorship where people die for complaining about the royal family's corruption?"

"Why should you wonder? You know the American gov-ernment always sides with oil," said Iraj, a student of political science when he was not working for the Peace Corps. "Look what happened in 1953 when Mossadeq nationalized Iran's oil industry. He was our democratically elected prime minister, for God's sake!"

We knew that history had revealed the true story. Mossadeq's actions would have been a triumph for democ-racy if the Americans hadn't butted in. The shah had already decamped to Italy when the CIA trucked in suitcases full of dollars, bribing the religious men of the bazaar to protest. The bazaaris, believing Mohammad Mossadeq was a godless sinner, held huge demonstrations and trashed the prime minister's office. There went democracy, just like that. When the shah returned, the western oil industry heaved a huge sigh of relief. Nothing would change after all.

"There's no doubt about it. The Americans meddle," said Mehri, another Persian teacher. "Is that why you volunteers are going to Iran, to meddle? And if that's not the reason, why are you helping the shah's government?"

"Come on," said my roommate Shahla. "They're not meddling, and they're not helping the government; they're teaching Iranian kids English. You know that's different."

I couldn't do anything about Iran's political situation; many countries welcoming Peace Corps volunteers were equally compromised. I was not going to Iran to interfere, nor did I plan to abet its government. Shahla was right. I was going to teach real people, high school students, English.

Teaching English, a language I already knew, was a realistic option for me, and for the rest of Iran 4. We were in a TEFL program, Teaching English as a Foreign Language, which espoused a new way of language learning, the aural-oral method. Rather than burying their heads in a book, our students would listen, then repeat.

"But Iranians already study English for six years in high school," more than one trainee said.

"By practicing patterned language structures verbally, students learn to reproduce them at will, just like you're doing in your Persian language classes," our instructor answered. There was something to this. After studying French the traditional way for three years, I couldn't order a meal in France.

We developed our teaching skills in front of groups of foreign students who were learning English at the university during the summer. My knees were shaking the first time I stood before a class. The students looked up at me expectantly.

"Good morning, class." My voice trembled. "I am Miss Beckett."

"Good morning, Miss Beckett," the class chorused, smiles on their faces. Their enthusiasm was contagious. By the time I finished the day's lesson on countable and uncountable nouns, (the apples are on the table, but the flour is in the jar), my nervousness was forgotten. That summer I loved being in front of the class, on stage, the center of attention. And I was elated whenever a reluctant student mastered a new sentence pattern. Maybe teaching English was not going to be so dull after all.

Would I have a chance to find out? The Peace Corps' deselection criteria seemed so arbitrary. Those administering the psychological tests had never been to Iran. The trainees who were sent home had little in common so far as I could see.

My time in Hell was almost over. Either I would be going home for good or I would be going to Iran. If they deselected me, what would I do next?

One after the other, unfortunate trainees were summoned into the office on our last day. I busied myself with packing, praying I would not hear my name. When the last unhappy reject stowed his suitcase in the belly of the waiting bus and climbed aboard, the remaining volunteers emerged from the dim corners where we had waited out this final ordeal. Congregating in front of the mess hall, our faces mirroring relief, we broke into applause. We were going to Iran.

Getting There

Years later, staring at that group photograph taken at Kennedy Airport before we boarded the airplane for Frankfurt, the first leg of our journey, I smile at the faces of the seventy-five Iran volunteers who made the cut. Fresh, youthful, they show no strains of apprehension, no hints of indecision. The "boys" in ties and jackets, the "girls" in nylons and heels, we're ready for anything Iran can offer.

I'd had ten days to collect everything I would bring to Iran: forty pounds of essentials would continent-hop with me from Chicago to Tehran; sixty pounds would fly after in my airfreight allotment. The things that would make Iran seem like home—the short wave radio; a year's supply of Tampax; photographs of Mother, Daddy, brother Don, and our dog Spike—were stowed in a large trunk, scheduled to make a leisurely journey by land and sea to my final destination. Mother and I scoured Rau's Department Store, looking for clothing that would last the duration. Just how much underwear, or how many pairs of stockings would I need? Tehran had everything, they said, but how about the rest of the country? "I won't go naked," I assured my mother, who was alternating between being proud of her daughter and terrified about this unknown adventure. "Iranian women manage to dress themselves just fine."

We boarded the plane in New York that early September evening too excited to sleep. But twenty hours later, crammed into a Pan Am flight that was hopping eastward from Frankfurt, to Munich, to Istanbul, exhaustion engulfed our group. By the time we got to Beirut, the last stop before Tehran, I had abandoned all efforts to be pleasant. Curled up in my seat, ankles swollen to three times their normal size, I didn't believe we'd ever arrive.

"Ladies and gentlemen. Please fasten your seatbelts. We are approaching Mehrabad Airport in Tehran." The flight attendant's voice resounded shrilly over the loudspeaker. Mehrabad Airport of Persian lesson fame. Mark, a volunteer who oozed confidence, stood:

"Okay, Iran 4, you know what to say. On the count of three..." He waved his arms like he was conducting a symphony orchestra. "One, two, three!"

"*Hala beh foroudgahye Mehrabad recedeem*" ("Now we've arrived at Mehrabad Airport"), we chanted, the line from our Persian language textbook eliciting a laugh from our fellow passengers.

It was after one a.m. when we got through customs and spilled out into the hot desert air. Clambering onto a waiting bus, we headed for Alborz College where we would stay for the next few days. Wide awake now, I peered out the window. The paved streets leading into the city were lined with long, high walls and two or three-storied mud brick buildings. Running along the edge of the road on either side were *jubes*, the defining characteristic of any Iranian city. All summer long, we had heard about these trenches, about eighteen inches wide and two feet deep, that channeled water through the city. In some places, there were sycamores planted by these waterways, but trees were not plentiful. At this hour, no one was up and about, but we passed occasional sleeping men stretched out on the cool cement sidewalks.

Our dormitory room at Alborz College had four beds; a single light bulb hanging from a wire in the middle of the ceiling illuminated the sparsely furnished quarters. Bare windows lined the white-washed walls on two sides. My roommates and I tossed our suitcases on the floor, pulled on our nightgowns, and passed out almost immediately on the tops of our cots.

Morning arrived with the clang of a loud bell the minute I closed my eyes. "Look out, Mary," said Nancy, one of my roommates. "There's a bunch of men on the roof staring into our room." Sure enough, six men in baggy white pants were gaping at us from the flat roof next door. Throwing a sheet around my body, I grabbed some clothes from my suitcase and headed for the bathroom. It was 7 a.m., time for breakfast.

At first glance, the dining hall could have been in any college in the world. Long Formica tables and folding chairs were spaced around the room, the tables brightened by small vases of pink plastic roses. Nancy and I joined others for breakfast.

"*Befarmayeed*" ("Help yourself"), said the waiter, a slight, apron-clad man with a three-day stubble of beard, who was offering me a large glass of tea, bread, butter, and jam. Flat with long raised ridges, the bread was oven-warm. *Noon-e barbaree* the waiter called it. He added some additional commentary, but my Persian wasn't up to his rapid speech. Undeterred, I pointed to the thin red jam that had lumps of an unknown hard fruit.

"*In chee-eh?*" ("What's this?"), I asked in my best classroom Farsi.

"*Morabayeh beh*," the waiter answered, whatever that was. Quince jam, someone told me.

My stomach had no idea it was breakfast time, so I didn't eat much. I was apprehensive; soon I would find out where in Iran I would spend the next two years, and who would be with me.

The remains of breakfast were vanishing into the kitchen when the Peace Corps/Iran staff began to arrive. Two field officers, both former volunteers, circulated around the room. Each responsible for half the country, they would make onsite visits to volunteers to offer support, trouble-shoot, and negotiate with government authorities. They were men, of course.

None of us would have expected a woman to hold this job. The Peace Corps doctor, an intense, dark-haired man, was the next to make the rounds. "Expect to get sick," he said. "Everyone does, even in Tehran." Dr. Dorry, a no-nonsense older woman who headed the English teaching program, and Hussein, a handsome Iranian who was the liaison with the shah's government, followed soon after. The arrival of Cleo Shook, the director of Peace Corps/Iran for the past two years, signaled the start of our meeting. He banged on the table to get our attention.

I shifted in my chair, only half listening as Mr. Shook went through the steps necessary to get us out into the provinces. The residence permits required to live and work in Iran were underway, he said, now that the staff knew which volunteers had shown up. The director reiterated that none of us was to work for the CIA, or any other covert agency. We did not have U.S. Commissary privileges, nor were we to acquire supplies from those who did. And if any one of us ran afoul of the law, that person was in big trouble; Peace Corps volunteers lacked diplomatic immunity. While we could listen sympathetically to political debates, under no circumstances were we to criticize the shah's government publicly. I'd heard all this before, and wished he'd get on with volunteer assignments.

The field officers unfurled a large map of Iran and hung it on the wall. The country looked huge. I could be stationed hundreds of miles from anyone I knew. Dots scattered around the map indicated where volunteers now lived or would be placed. Mr. Shook and Hussein sat behind a table in the front, shuffling pieces of paper. Hussein cleared his throat and began calling volunteers forward one by one. I didn't know what to hope for, except that they'd speak Persian in my town—not the Turkish or Kurdish of northwestern Iran. "Mary Bac-katt,"

Hussein called. Beckett, I thought, Beckett. Cheeks flaming at the momentary attention, I made my way to the front to claim my assignment. 'Mary Beckett,' my slip of paper read. 'Kerman, with Betsy Burlingham and Tom Sisul.' Thank goodness I wouldn't be there by myself. Just where was Kerman? As Hussein worked his way down the roll of volunteers, I joined the crowd at the map, locating my new home in the southeastern part of the country.

"It's a great place," said a voice in my ear. "That's where I was a volunteer. You'll love it." I turned to see Don Croll, one of the field officers, smiling at me. He didn't look much like a boss. His rumpled blue shirt was coming untucked, his light brown hair still had impressions from his pillow, and he hadn't wiped the dusty outdoors off his black shoes, as I'd watched Hussein do.

"It's a good place to learn Persian," he continued, "and Kermanis are very hospitable."

"How big is it?"

"It's a provincial capital. At last count, I think it had about 65,000 residents," Don said.

"Where will we live?"

"We're not certain. There's a volunteer there now. He's looking into it for us. We think you and Betsy will do great things together."

I glanced around the room, looking for my future roommate, a tall, stocky New Englander. When I caught her eye, she grinned, giving me the high sign. Tom Sisul, six feet five inches tall, was easy to find. When I waved my assignment paper at him, he reddened. Kerman would be home to two American blushers. A flicker of a smile crossed his face as he looked away.

I spent the next few days in Tehran untangling the unfamiliar. First, there was the twist in my diet, with carbohydrates comprising most of what I ate—bread for breakfast, rice with some kind of light-on-the-meat stew for the main meal at noon, the crusted bottom-of-the-pot rice in lieu of dessert, and sandwiches (or yet more rice) for dinner. At this rate, they would have to roll me out of Iran at the end of two years.

Then there were those jubes. Narrow water trenches edging the streets, they added a layer of complexity to crossing Tehran's broad avenues. On most corners, they were bridged, allowing pedestrians to traipse across into the intersection. But should one carelessly move a little this way or that to avoid a bus careening through a red light, a backward step could send her plunging two feet into the channel. Iranians were unfazed by this obstacle, parking their cars with alacrity just inches from the jube's edge, or adroitly hopping across the waterway to forge forward into oncoming traffic.

And the traffic! It was unrelenting and unpredictable. The only way to get from one side of the street to the other was to join a crowd, forming a wedge to defy the cars, trucks, buses, and bicycles approaching the intersection at breakneck speed, oblivious to the color of the stoplight. The leader of the pack, a brave, assertive individual who detected a weakness in the traffic flow, would step into the fray, resolutely ignore oncoming automobiles, and charge across the street, the rest of us following as quickly as we could.

Some of the Iranians carving a pathway across these perilous thoroughfares were women, hurrying to their destinations dressed in somber suits and sensible heels, their long black hair wound up in French twists, or turned under at the shoulders. Scarves covered the heads of others, hiding their hair so it would not tempt the men passing by. Still others were enveloped in dark *chadors*, half-moon shaped pieces of cloth that draped from the top of the head, over the shoulders, to the ground. When grasped at the chin, it obscured all of the woman but her face. Sometimes, even this was too bold and the chador would be pulled forward over the brow and held across the bridge of the nose so only the eyes were visible. Although we had discussed this modest attire in training, the large number of women that shopped, hailed taxis, and jumped jubes wearing chadors surprised me.

That first week in Tehran, the unfamiliar was spiced by the unexpected. Three of us were muddling around a small grocery store, trying to compute the price of a box of Kleenex in dollars and cents, when a well-dressed customer inquired in the Queen's English if he could be of assistance. "We speak a little Persian," I said in my best Farsi. After a short conversation—in English, because we'd run out of the right Persian words—Mr. Ablee led us to his nearby office in the executive suites of the Iran Oil Company to discuss the Peace Corps and its relevance to Iran. If Mr. Ablee was a typical Iranian, this country did not need us. He was erudite, wealthy, and well-traveled. Sipping my third glass of tea, I was spellbound as he laid before us his dreams for his country, the best place in the world he believed, and his conviction that we, as volunteers here, could contribute to its future.

"You have a marvelous opportunity to bring the ideals of the west to the corners of Iran," Mr. Ablee said. "Your efforts will help our country defeat complacency and backwardness." Looking directly at me, he continued: "As a modern woman in a conservative city like Kerman, your very presence will signal its girls that they, too, have a role in transforming our society. We Tehranis are educated and well-versed in the philosophies of the West. We're proud of the important role Iran played historically, and committed to restoring its prominence in the world. There is such beauty here. With our vision and your help, we can transform this land of poetry and wisdom into a modern country."

As his words flowed, I observed modern Tehran. Inside this modern building, men in ties and coats hurried up and down the halls. Across the way, two women sat behind desks typing—one covered by a chador, the other bareheaded and dressed in a business suit. Through his office window, the sidewalk stretched below, piled high with dirt and bricks for a building under construction nearby. In the other direction, nestled behind a high wall, was the company's courtyard, an Eden of trees, rosebushes, and spraying fountains. Was this the Iran he loved, this hodgepodge of the old and the new, the plain and the lush?

Amid the tangles of this burgeoning city, poverty flourished, with scores of unfortunates pleading for money anywhere I went. In the suburbs of 1960s America, I had never seen a beggar, never been accosted by the drug dazed specters who in later years would wave paper coffee cups jingling with coins in my direction. Our nation, the richest in the world, had yet to empty its asylums onto city streets, denying the mentally ill a roof over their heads. So, beggars in Iran—wretched women in torn chadors pulling on my arm, pleading for money, or small children with twisted limbs blocking my path—shocked, confused, and irritated me. When I gave a coin to one, ten others took her place. I tried jerking my head upwards and clicking my tongue, a firm Iranian no, as I said "I don't give" in Persian. I didn't know what to do. How could a *rial* or two, less than five cents, make any difference? What was my responsibility?

As I roamed the streets of Tehran those first days in Iran, the shah was there, too—his image filling a banner over the road leading into the city, or smiling out from a colored photo in a silversmith's shop in the bazaar. His visage guarded the counter in the grocery store where we met Mr. Ablee; Pahlavi Boulevard, a major thoroughfare, bore the name of his family. But it was on Ferdowsi Street that the shah himself, Mohammad Reza Pahlavi, the king of kings, made a personal appearance. Named after the author of the *Shahnameh,* Iran's epic poem, Ferdowsi Street was an important north-south artery, with hundreds of shops full of antiques and gorgeous carpets at its northern end, and a nest of government buildings further south.

I was looking at an expensive flowered silk rug in a shop window when a murmur coursed through the crowd. All eyes turned toward the road where a long line of black limousines was creeping toward us. Men in scruffy suit jackets sprang up from nowhere to line the sidewalks, brandishing small red, white, and green Iranian flags. Curious, I waited in the background. "Long live the shah!" the crowd chanted in Farsi. I stood on my tiptoes. Could it really be the shah? It was. A small man ensconced in the seat of honor of the luxury limo, His Majesty in profile was unmistakable. He waved slightly to the assembled throng.

"Who's with him?" I tried out my Farsi with the chadored woman standing next to me.

"Haile Selassie, the emperor of Ethiopia."

"Where are they going?"

"To the Bank-e Melli. He always takes visitors to the national bank to see our country's treasures."

My arms were all goosebumps. A king was in my sights—a king seeking to impress an emperor with incomparable jewels and finely woven carpets, the wealth of his nation. I was in the presence of royalty.

Soon they were gone. The flags were collected, and crowd dispersed. During dinner with the volunteers that evening, I was off-handed about my encounter: "Yeah, I saw the shah on Ferdowsi today. He's smaller than I expected."

Members of our group began filtering out to their sites during the next few days. I couldn't believe they were leaving, that our life as a group was over. Kerman, the capital of Iran's southernmost province, was a real outpost. In Kerman, I would be dependent on Americans I barely knew; I would rely on the kindness of Iranians I had yet to meet.

Tom, Betsy, and I were the last to leave Tehran, opting for one of the two weekly flights to Kerman in lieu of a nineteen-hour bus trip. I stared out of the window of the DC 6 that was transporting us to our final destination. From high in the cloudless blue sky, I could see dusty adobe villages dotting the barren, brown land. Peering down, I saw what looked like lines of huge molehills, starting at the bases of nearby mountains, and converging at village hubs, where a hint of green in the outlying fields tinged the desolate scene.

"What do you suppose those things are, Betsy?" I asked my seatmate.

"They are called qanats," a nearby passenger chimed in. "You know this country is very dry. Ancient Iranians dug underground tunnels like these more than a thousand years ago to channel water from the mountains to the villages, and they're still used today."

"But what are all those holes with the piles of dirt around them?" Betsy asked our expert.

"They're entrances for the workers who maintain them. It's a very dangerous job. It's so dark many of the laborers go blind." An incongruous image of the sprinklers on my dad's verdant lawn popped into my head. Turning on a faucet was taking on new meaning.

The flight attendant began her announcement. First in Persian, then French, and finally English: "Ladies and gentlemen. Please fasten your seatbelts. We are arriving at Kerman airport." I looked at Betsy. She sat straight, exuding a confidence I didn't feel. Tom blinked his eyes open and smiled. The airplane hit the dirt runway and bumped to a stop.

I hesitated at the head of the airplane stairs, blazing rays of the hot noonday sun obscuring any textures, any relief in the brown landscape below. A shiver trailed down my spine as I followed Tom and Betsy toward a sallow, low building, the only one in sight, Iran Air's Kerman terminal.

Our welcoming committee of two waited in the shade near a sign announcing "Baggage Claim" in English. It was easy to pick out Fred Jones, the Peace Corps volunteer. Clad in khaki pants and an olive green wash-and-wear sports jacket, he sported a reddish-brown, Iranian-style mustache. His middle-aged companion, Ahmad Sayeed- Nejad, stood very erect, his expression stern. Supporting his slender body were hand-high crutches, the right pant leg of his dark business suit swinging loosely with the breeze. We introduced ourselves and went inside to claim our luggage.

Suitcases collected, Mr. Sayeed-Nejad and Fred climbed into the front seat of the Office of Education jeep, while Betsy, Tom and I squeezed into the back. In the intimacy of the car, Mr. Sayeed-Nejad's features relaxed when he turned to explain that he was the liaison between the volunteers and the Office of Education. Betsy and I were going to share a room at the *daneshsera*, the teachers' training school for young women.

When school started later this month we would eat our meals with the students who boarded there.

Knowing Iranians protected their women, I had hoped that Betsy and I would live alone. Surely, at ages twenty-one and twenty-two we were adult enough to be on our own. But it was not to be. I stared out the window, finding little in the drab, dusty landscape to divert me as we bumped down the packed dirt road leading to Kerman. The distant outline of the city grew larger as the jeep approached. Just as Fred announced, "You're here. This is Kerman," we hit smooth pavement.

The city was a medley of drab browns: mud brick shops, high adobe walls, dusty roads, bare mountains in the background. Slowing to navigate his way through donkey carts and an unruly gaggle of goats, our driver almost collided with a bicyclist weaving through the traffic. Swerving, the cyclist narrowly avoided the water-filled jube running along the side of the road. Unfazed, the driver shrugged: "*Dast-e khoda.*" "It's in the hands of God," Fred translated as I caught my breath.

It didn't take long to get to the teachers' training school. Turning into the driveway of the daneshsera, the driver stopped at its imposing red metal gate and beeped his horn. Mr. Sayeed-Nejad chatted briefly with the woman who opened the gate. "This is Kobra-*khanum*," he said, introducing Betsy and me. "She's the caretaker's wife. She'll let you in when you come home." Iranians, I knew, tack the Persian version of "miss" or "mister" on to the end of first names. And with a name like Kobra, she would be unforgettable. Loosening her grip on her dark flowered chador, Kobra grinned, the gold in her teeth gleaming as Betsy and I greeted her with awkward Persian pleasantries.

The jeep moved slowly through the grounds of the school, picking up a trail of teenage girls clad in gray school uniforms and colorful headscarves. We passed several buildings and a small grove of trees next to a volleyball court before we stopped in front of a small sandy brick structure—a single room—its roof domed, with a set of French doors at either end. This was it. This would be home for the next two years.

"Hello. How are you?" chorused the girls as the driver unloaded our suitcases and carried them into the room.

"*Bachaha*" ("children"), Mr. Sayeed-Nejad said, "the teachers haven't even seen their room. There will be plenty of time to talk later."

"Will we be teaching classes here at the daneshsera?" I asked.

"These girls have finished high school. They're preparing to be elementary school teachers so they don't have to study English. You'll be working in the public high schools where English is required, but maybe you can have a class here for those who want to learn."

"Do all the daneshsera's students live here?" Betsy asked.

"Oh no. Just the girls from towns so far away they can't go home at night."

"Is this a private school?" I asked.

"No. The government supports it, although the students pay some fees. Elementary school is now mandatory for Iranian children. We need more teachers, especially for the girls."

Soon, the jeep carrying Mr. Sayeed-Nejad, Tom, and Fred was gone. We were to join them later at the volunteers' house in the bazaar. "Mr. Jones will meet you at the entrance at four o'clock," Mr. Sayeed-Nejad had said, hopping into the front seat and stowing his crutches next to the door. "You can get a taxi outside the school gate. Tell him *Maidun-e shah*, Shah Square. You must each pay the driver a *toman* (thirteen cents)."

Standing in the doorway, I surveyed our room. A good size, it was rectangular in shape, with natural light streaming in through the doors at either end. A bare light bulb hung by a long cord from the domed ceiling. Two cots, their thin mattresses on metal springs, were at one end, and a small gray metal table and two folding chairs anchored the other. A narrow shelving unit was propped up against one wall. Betsy set to work, pulling sheets and a blanket onto her bed. "Let's make a list of the things we need," she said. Now here was something we could do. I liked this girl already.

We spent the next couple of hours getting situated. "*Mostarah kojust?*" ("Where is the toilet?") I asked one of the many girls lurking outside our doors. Giggling, she pointed to a building sixty yards across the courtyard. Midnight runs were going to be challenging. Mohammad-*agha*, Kobra's husband, brought us tea. He was followed by the assistant principal, whose name I promptly forgot. When he asked if we had everything we needed, Betsy didn't skip a beat, informing him we could use a closet, a small table to go between the beds, and a lamp for reading at night. The assistant principal said he'd look into it, and would we mind tape recording some dialog so he could improve his English?

Right about then, I wanted to close the doors and bury my head in a mystery story. Reality was exhausting. Instead, we padlocked our door, and made our way to the gate of the daneshsera, engulfed in a swarm of students.

"Where are you going?" asked one in halting English. Before I could answer, another told me she wanted to go to America. I was absorbing this when a third asked me if I missed my mother. The crowd melted away as Kobra-khanum banged the gate closed. We had barely stepped on the pavement outside when a taxi pulled to a stop in front of us. The driver, like many others, I'd learn, had personalized his cab, the results brightening the drab browns of the city. Draped around his windshield was a vivid red fringe, a picture of Ali swung from the rear view mirror, and a vase of faded plastic flowers adorned the dashboard. "Maidun-e shah," I directed, and minutes later we pulled into the square in front of the bazaar where Fred stood waiting.

The square was a busy place. Vintage buses painted with exuberant vines and flowers in gay colors were unloading scores of villagers; men in gray felt caps and baggy trousers staggered under bundles piled high on their backs; women, loosely wrapped in light-hued chadors, sat cross-legged on cloths of indeterminate color, tall mounds of flat bread heaped next to them. "Bread fresh from the country, baked today," I understood one to call as we passed. Donkeys harnessed to carts loaded with merchandise lumbered into the shadows of the covered marketplace, the bazaar.

And there was so much more that I wasn't absorbing in this place where the montage of life was not at all familiar. I had seen most of the pieces. I knew what a donkey looked like, but I had never heard one bray; never heard the god-awful racket one of them was making right there. I thought Oriental carpets were beautiful, but I had never seen a man's back so burdened with rugs his head almost touched his knees. My overloaded senses were having trouble putting it all together.

The dark recesses of the domed bazaar provided immediate relief from the scorching sun and hubbub of the square. Betsy and I followed Fred through the entrance, shaking off a group of beggars congregated there. It took a minute for my eyes to adjust to the bazaar's cool shadows, its wide, packed dirt walkways illuminated by light wells at the top of each high dome. We passed stall after stall of merchants selling similar items, the pungent odors of unfamiliar spices permeating the air. Fred nodded to many of the men behind their counters, responding to their greetings. Physically, with his pale complexion and blue eyes, Fred would not be mistaken for an Iranian. But somehow he seemed more Persian than American as he sauntered through the bazaar toward his house. "*Salaam alaikum, hal-e shoma khoobeh?*" ("Hello, how are you?") he said, the Farsi words rolling off his tongue as if he had been speaking to these men all his life.

We had walked less than a block when Fred turned left, leaving the spice sellers behind and entering the realm of the coppersmiths. What a racket they made, perched on short legged stools, anvils in front of them, fires to the side, hammering the cooling metal into vessels for the kitchens of Kerman. The smiths smiled, nodding their heads as Fred and his entourage of two young women passed by. The pathway of the copper bazaar headed off to the right. Fred turned left, and Betsy and I followed him several steps to a scarred green door.

Stepping through the short hallway into the courtyard, the din stopped, the house's thick mud walls muffling the clanging, banging coppersmiths just yards away. As courtyards go, I would learn, this one was typical. Oblong in shape, it was covered with paving stones, except for a narrow band of dirt that surrounded a raised, empty fountain in the center. A water faucet stuck up through the pavement at one end. Here, squatting on her haunches, Fatimeh, Fred and Tom's live-in servant, would wash their dishes and scrub their clothes. Individual rooms lined all four sides of the courtyard, with the kitchen opposite the entryway.

The place was barely furnished. "I like it that way," Fred said. "We'll buy a big kilim and some cushions for the living room, and that will be it. We'll just have to be happy on the floor." I had met this man just hours earlier, but I knew he had an opinion about everything. He had been in Iran for six months, starting as a community development volunteer in the northern city of Rasht near the Caspian Sea. Something had not clicked, and the Peace Corps had transferred him to Kerman to teach English. He loved it here, and we would too, if we had any sense. And no, he didn't know what had happened to Mr. Sayeed-Nejad's leg. It would be rude to ask.

Rooftop view of Kerman's bazaar and Peace Corps guys' courtyard.

"Our house is actually part of the bazaar," Fred said. "From the roof you can see how we're connected." With that, he unlocked a door next to the kitchen and we scrambled up the steps to get a better view.

From our perch at the top of the stairs, I looked out on dome after dome of the bazaar roof cutting a broad swath across the center of the city. The merchants, Fred told us, hired guards to patrol the miles of roof, but I didn't see any. In the late afternoon sun, the craggy bare mountains surrounding the city glowed in startling pink hues, their shadows adding welcome texture to the arid landscape. Peering down into the adjoining courtyard, I saw two goats and a camel, the camel's mangy fur worn out at the knees. Sprawled on its side on the hard paving stones, it looked more like an exhausted beast of burden than an exotic ship of the desert.

Standing there on the steps, quiet for the first time that day, my head cleared. Life would play out differently here, I was certain. For that moment, looking out over the mud domed bazaar, a camel in the courtyard, the melodic ringing of the coppersmiths' hammers in the background, and stark mountains in the distance, I was exactly where I wanted to be.

Reality Strikes

Journal entry

> It looks like Betsy and I will starve to death before we even set foot in a classroom. Either that, or I'll drown in tea.

The tranquility of that moment on the roof during our first afternoon was soon overwhelmed by the reality of being new in town. Those first days in Kerman, our mentor, Mr. Sayeed-Nejad, shepherded Betsy and me from tea party to teachers' room to bazaar. Nothing either of us did escaped his notice. We wondered how he had spent his time before we arrived.

"You paid ten tomans for that?" Seated behind his desk at the Office of Education, Mr. Sayeed-Nejad was incredulous. Had I really spent $1.30 on a simple blue plastic shopping bag? "Everyone knows they cost seven tomans. You must bargain. You can't let the merchants take advantage of you like this. I thought one of the English teachers volunteered to go shopping with you."

He was right. Our colleagues had been very polite as we sipped tea in the teachers' rooms, not yet invited to their classes. Not just one, but every teacher we met had offered to protect Betsy and me from the greedy men of the bazaar. But it wasn't practical. I couldn't wait until tomorrow afternoon at three when I needed the makings for today's lunch. For the past few days, Betsy and I explored the bazaar's cool passages, shopping for necessities, searching for familiar food. The green leaves in that basket were spinach? At home, Birds Eye frozen spinach is clearly labeled in rock-hard boxes. Succulent chops like my mom used to broil were somewhere on the headless lamb carcasses strung up in the outdoor meat market —but on which part of the beast? It was easier to settle for simpler fare, like pistachios and dates, treats that were plumping out my cheeks, waist, and hips.

We bargained in familiar Farsi phrases, but the merchants weren't fooled. The teachers, Mr. Sayeed-Nejad, everyone, grilled us about our final purchase prices. At home we didn't talk about how much we paid for things; here, a good deal was a badge of honor, a bad one an embarrassment. Already, I was shaving tomans off the amount I spent. The ten tomans I confessed to paying for that blue plastic bag? Actually fifteen, twice its true cost.

But I loved the bazaar. Outside the marketplace, Betsy and I stood a head above everyone, our uncovered brown hair and bare legs the subject of stares and comments. Although the bazaar, with its nearby mosque, was a center for religious con-servatives, it was also the most diverse place in town. There, we mixed with white turbaned Baluchi tribesmen from Iran's southeast; dark-skinned merchants from the Persian Gulf; vil-lage women wearing their fortunes in gold coins strung across their foreheads; brown robed mullahs; and Kerman's own pop-ulation—men in shapeless suit jackets and chador-draped women, all going about their business.

A main street in Kerman. Note the jube (water channel) running alongside the road.

In some parts of the city, Kermanis shopped for fruit, vege-tables, and bread close to home. But there were no stores along wall-lined Zarisse Street, the upscale neighborhood that was home to the daneshsera, so Betsy and I took turns buying our food in the bazaar. Without a refrigerator, this was a daily task. In Kerman less than a week, I rang the bell at the school's gate as I shifted my bag of groceries from one hand to the other in the noon-hot sun. Kobra-khanum, her chador thrown over her flowered dress and pajama pants, answered. She closed the gate behind me, shutting out the world, shutting in the school's students and teachers. Within these walls, young women walked, studied, played, or dined protected from curious out-siders. Chadors were left folded by desks while their owners strolled the grounds or participated in class. And behind these walls, these teachers-in-training had found a new source of entertainment: Betsy and me.

"Hello, Miss Mary. What did you buy?" A tall girl with a thick, long braid called out to me in English. Her friends hid their giggles behind cupped hands.

"I bought tomatoes and cheese and some bread."

"What's 'cheese?'" one girl asked another in Persian.

"*Paneer*," I said, proud to understand the question and know the answer.

"Where is Miss Betsy?"

"Inside. She is waiting for lunch," I said in slow, deliberate English, pointing to our French doors, opened wide onto the courtyard.

"We are hungry," the tall girl said, a gleam of laughter in her voice.

"Befarmayeed" ("Be my guest"), I said, offering my bag of groceries.

"Oooh, she's making *ta'arof*," another said in Persian. She was referring to the Iranian system of manners that can involve a lot of offers and refusals. *Befarmayeed*, the most ubiquitous example, carries a host of meanings. I was reluctant to insist again.

"Uhh, goodbye," I said, my cheeks burning. A burst of laughter from the assembled throng followed me through the doors.

Betsy sat cross-legged on her bed, hemming dark blue drapes to cover the windows. Thank heavens she knew how to sew. Curtains had sprung to the top of the must-buy list our very first morning when we awakened to the sound of laughter. Rubbing my eyes, I'd squinted at the alarm clock: 6:00 a.m. A montage of faces, teenage girls, was smashed up against the glass panes of our doors peering in at the pajama-clad foreigners. "Hello, meeses. Vat ees your name?" their voices rang out. Now, days later, I wondered if the thin panels of navy blue cotton would protect us from curious eyes inside the danesh-sera's walls. Only at night. In this hot weather, the doors to our wall within a wall had to be open if we were to breathe.

I slung the shopping bag up on the gray metal table, shooing away the cloud of flies that settled on my purchases. What a nuisance they were. We'd swatted at them, we'd sprayed them with Pif Paf, but the survivors just sent for reinforcements.

"I got tomatoes, Betsy. I guess we'd better soak them." Betsy slid off her bed and filled our bucket part way with water from the large tin drum that sat on a low chair. I dug into a small paper sack and dropped tablespoons of tiny purple crystals, permanganate, into the bucket. Betsy plunged our two perfect, ripe tomatoes into the mix.

"How long should they soak?" she asked.

"Mr. Sayeed-Nejad said half an hour." I glanced at my watch, then out the door where the group of girls was watching our every move. Permanganate was the Kermani answer to purifying uncooked fruits and vegetables. The Peace Corps wanted us to boil our water and skip anything that could not be peeled or cooked. Betsy and I were compromising, buying drinking water like everyone here did.

"*Ob-e Hussein abad*" ("water from Hussein's spring"), the stooped vendor would call, leading a horse-drawn wagon loaded with a large tank of water into the daneshsera's courtyard. Hauling ten-liter tins into our room, he poured the water into our drum. Each tin cost two rials, about three cents. No one tipped him. We hoped the purple powder we added to soak fruits and vegetables would kill microbes unfriendly to our digestive systems—a bit of wishful thinking.

Chatter drifted in from the courtyard as I pulled plates off the shelf and put bread and cheese on the table.

"I'm starving. The bugs must be dead by now," I said, pulling the tomatoes out of the solution. Betsy joined me at the table, and soon we were munching to the background of ongoing commentary outside our open doors.

"You eat very little for lunch," said one member of our audience.

"You should have rice," said another. "We eat cheese and bread for breakfast."

"You'd think they'd get bored with this," I said to Betsy. "It's like we've got our own Greek chorus."

But the girls were right. Bread and cheese weren't enough for the main meal of the day. After our first supper of stale bread, melon, and too many pistachios, I had confronted Mr. Sayeed-Nejad:

"All we've got is a single kerosene burner. I can boil water, or fry an onion. I can't do both," not adding that I didn't know how to cook much more than that.

"And we don't have any place to keep things so they don't spoil," Betsy said.

"In Kerman we shop every day," Mr. Sayeed-Nejad said. "Food that's been refrigerated tastes stale. Why don't you ask the teachers about meals? I've heard some of them are wonderful cooks."

Well, at least it would be something we could discuss with them. I cornered Mrs. Nahidi, an English teacher about my mother's age, in the teachers' room of Parvin Etesami High School.

"I'm trying to learn to prepare Iranian food," I said. "Can you tell me how to make chicken kabob? We had some the other day that was delicious."

Mrs. Nahidi took a deep breath. "Well, first you go to the bazaar. Pick out a plump chicken. Get one that's active, they're the best. If you don't have a servant to kill it, you can pay a few rials to the merchant's helper. He'll grab the chicken by the neck and offer it a drink of water."

"Then what?"

"He'll face its head toward Mecca, and slit its throat."

Trying to keep a neutral expression on my face, I asked, "What do I do next?"

"You take it home and dip it in a pot of boiling water to loosen its feathers. Pluck it, and save the feathers for a pillow. Be sure you get all the quills out of the chicken's skin. Then you clean the inside…" At this point my attention wandered. Obviously, this wasn't a lunch-hour task. Chicken was out. I'd known it the minute we faced its head toward Mecca.

Back to Mr. Sayeed-Nejad. This time he was more conciliatory. "I'll see what I can do," he said. "Maybe Kobra-khanum can prepare something for you. The school's not ready for you to eat with the girls."

A day later, Kobra was cooking our supper. Betsy and I strolled home in late afternoon from the guys' house, wondering if she would fix something like the soup Fatimeh was preparing for their dinner, with big pieces of chicken and thin noodles simmering in a broth seasoned with dried lemons and tomatoes. It was dusk when Kobra's husband Mohammad rapped at our door.

"Come in," Betsy called in Persian.

"Here's your dinner," he said, waiting outside to hand her a tray holding two covered plates, along with a dish of pickled vegetables, a small bowl of yogurt, and several pieces of thin bread.

"Just put the things outside the door when you're finished," Mohammad said, hurrying away.

What was that strong, fatty odor? Betsy put the tray on the table and lifted the cover from one of the dishes. Three cigar-shaped kebabs of ground meat rested on a plateful of glistening white rice, dusted with sumac, a pungent, rust-toned spice. The meal looked innocent enough.

"What on earth is that smell?" I asked.

"Dinner. What did Mohammad do to this kebab?"

"I have no idea. I suppose we'd better try it."

One spoonful was enough. Did people really eat this? There was no way our noses could get around the odor, and the mouthful I tried to swallow was steeped in oil. (We would learn later that the unidentified odor was lamb's oil, rendered from its fatty tail, and poured over rice to give it a rich flavor.) We put the offending plates as far away from the table as possible, and wolfed down the bread, yogurt, and pickled vegetables. Bread and greasy rice, starch on starch, was this any way to live? Why was life here so easy for Kermanis but so hard for me?

The night was pitch black, the courtyard deserted, when Betsy and I strolled to the bathroom building, each carrying a toothbrush and glass of water in one hand, a bowlful of food concealed by a large towel in the other. We peeked in the door. The building was empty. Hurrying to the stalls, we bolted the doors and dumped dinner into the toilet, washing down the evidence with pitchers of water. At the communal sink, we rinsed the telltale bowls and brushed our teeth. Towels slung over our shoulders, we headed back to our room, worried that regular meals would be a challenge as long as we lived at the girls' school.

The Ground Shifts

"Hello, meeses," "I love you," had echoed in our wake when Betsy, Mr. Sayeed-Nejad, and I entered Parvin Etesami High School for the first time. It was named after a woman, a famous Iranian poet, I learned, as the three of us sat in the principal's office sipping tea.

Tea! Tea! Tea! Over the past week, we had drunk more tea than I had had in the whole of my life. Glasses of tea sweetened each encounter, lubricated every introduction, but we couldn't get beyond the teachers' rooms of the girls' high schools. The visit with Mrs. Khosrovi, Parvin Etesami's principal, was typical. After "hello, how are you's" in English, the conversation reverted to Persian for the more flowery expressions of her delight in meeting us. Taking ladylike sips, Betsy and I tried to appear engaged although we understood barely a word. What I did pick up—Betsy and I were *khaylee ghashang* ("very beautiful")—had little to do with teaching.

As we left the school, Mr. Sayeed-Nejad recapped the conversation:

"I explained that you want to visit the English classes and help the teachers with conversation and pronunciation."

"It took all that time to say that?"

"When can we start visiting classes?" asked Betsy.

"Soon, soon. But you can drop in anytime to chat with the English teachers during their mid-morning breaks."

English wasn't flowing at the nursing school the afternoon Mr. Sayeed-Nejad introduced Betsy and me to Fatimeh and the other live-in teachers at this two-year, post-high school program. In the school's formal reception area, we sat on straight-backed chairs lined up against the wall, trying not to drop crumbs of sandy rice cookies on the flowery Persian carpet. Balancing our glasses of tea, we strained to decipher Fatimeh's English as she spoke with authority about the life of American women in Kerman.

Fatimeh was an expert because Barbara Smith, Kerman's first female Peace Corps volunteer, had lived with the nurses for a short while. She hadn't stayed long, but her memory lingered, shining brighter each time one of her amazing feats was recalled: "Miss Barbara spoke Farsi very well.... Miss Barbara was such a good teacher.... Miss Barbara would never go to the bazaar by herself.... Miss Barbara always wore stockings...."

Sight unseen, I hated her. "Maybe she was perfect," I said to Betsy later, "but I notice the nurses didn't ask us to live with them." Certain we could do anything the sainted Barbara could do, we agreed to teach the second-year nursing students three afternoons a week.

"When should we start?" Betsy asked the head nurse.

"I'm not sure. We'll let you know."

Accompanied yet again by Mr. Sayeed-Nejad, we paid a call at Bahmanyar High School, whose principal, Mr. Tavanah, spoke English in eloquent, Churchillian tones. This visit was different; we could have a direct conversation with this charming, snowy-haired gentleman, who suggested we hold a late afternoon English class at his school, for women in the community.

Leaving, Betsy and I danced down the steps to the street. "A class of our own," she said. "I'd be glad to teach it."

"Oh, no you don't. We'll share the teaching. But you can do the first lesson."

Later that week I shifted about on an uncomfortable chair in a Bahmanyar High School classroom, waiting for Betsy's class of ten women to start. Seated in the back, next to Mr. Sayeed-Nejad, was a surprise visitor, the school's principal—I had forgotten his name.

Betsy began: "Hello, class. My name is Betsy Burlingham. I am an American teacher. I come from the state of Maine. Please tell me your names, where you are from, and your occupation."

A murmur of "I don't understand," and "What did she say?" bounced around the room in Farsi, but soon, one by one, the women answered: "I-am-a-teacher-from-Kerman," or "I-am—how do you say housewife?—oh, I-am-a-housewife-from-Kerman," and the lesson was underway. Admiring Betsy's poise and ease, I had started to relax when the principal cleared his throat.

"Yes, Sir?" said Betsy. Our distinguished visitor stood.

"I believe that the pronunciation of that word is 'cahn't', not 'can't'," he said, striding to the front of the room. "Our students are accustomed to British pronunciation. The English were here in Iran for so long, they taught so many of us, we prefer to speak the way they speak. 'I cahn't go' is correct." He turned and addressed our students: "Repeat after me, 'I cahn't go.'"

"I cahn't go," echoed the women.

What's she going to do? How awkward! How rude! Mr. Sayeed-Nejad cleared his throat. Betsy appeared unfazed.

"I know the British pronounce some words differently," she said, "but native English speakers understand either pronunciation. Now let's get back to our lesson."

The principal went back to his seat. A few minutes later, nodding to Betsy, he left the room. She taught the rest of the class in standard American English.

"The nerve of that principal," I said after the last woman wrapped her chador tightly around her body and departed into the warm fall evening. "You really kept your cool."

"Mr. Sayeed-Nejad, do you think he's going to make trouble for us?" Betsy asked.

"Now, now, don't fret. You have a meeting with the director of education on Thursday. Everything will be all right."

The day of our meeting started early. Days always began early for Kermanis, who rose at dawn to pray. A little before seven, Betsy and I hailed a taxi in front of the daneshsera. I was determined to be patient, as Mr. Sayeed-Nejad advised, assuming not much would come from this meeting. We would drink tea, understand only a few words of the conversation, and end up just where we started—nothing decided and little to do.

The taxi driver sped along Zarisse Street, already crowded with donkeys, bicycles, sheep, and taxis. Turning down the music blaring on his radio, the driver peppered us with questions in slow, deliberate Farsi. Yep, I miss my mother, I thought, before he even asked the question. By the time he pulled up in front of the Office of Education, we had covered our nationality, occupation, marital status and, of course, missing mom.

"*Salaam alaikum*" ("peace be unto you"), we greeted Hassan-agha, the office factotum, who was standing at the building's door, just as he was every day when we picked up our mail. "Has Mr. Manucher arrived?" This kind of Farsi was getting easier and easier.

"The director has been here for more than an hour. You may see him in his office."

Hassan-agha led the way down the hall, opening the door to a large room. The director, who was presiding at an impressive metal desk in the corner, motioned that we should join other petitioners seated along the whitewashed walls. We spotted Mr. Sayeed-Nejad near the windows, and hurried over to him.

"Bachaha, you are late."

Bachaha was a term of endearment, but Mr. Sayeed-Nejad looked very severe.

"You told us to be here at seven," Betsy said.

"And it's exactly seven-oh-two," I added.

"Mr. Manucher is the director of education. You must show respect."

Taking a chair beside Mr. Sayeed-Nejad, I accepted a glass of tea from Hassan-agha and stared through the window at the dusty courtyard. In two short weeks the caring man seated next to me, Ahmad Sayeed-Nejad, had become central to my life. Formal and proper in public, his reserve vanished when lounging on the floor of Fred and Tom's house in the copper bazaar. There he was playful, teasing Mr. Jones about crashing his bicycle, or ribbing me for eating too many pistachios. With a mischievous grin, he would recount a tale about a stubborn villager or an evil Arab. But the minute we entered a school setting or a formal parlor, his demeanor changed. He insisted that we behave differently there as well. Quoting a Persian saying, he half-joked, "I'm going to work very hard to turn you into human beings." It would take a lot of effort, he meant, for us to become proper Iranians. We understood that our actions, good or bad, reflected on him. Mr. Sayeed-Nejad was my touchstone; if he were pleased, other Iranians would be, too. But given how frequently I was corrected, I had a long way to go before I could become a human.

That day, waiting to speak with the director, correct conduct was crucial. We stood when he motioned to us. Elegant in a dark blue suit and starched white shirt, Mr. Manucher rose as we approached his desk. "Please sit down," he said in English.

The director settled into his chair, fingering a strand of light brown worry beads in his left hand. He turned to Mr. Sayeed-Nejad, and began to speak quickly in Farsi. Over the clack-clack of a typewriter nearby, I strained to understand what he was saying, but I could only make out a word or two. Betsy appeared baffled. Mr. Sayeed-Nejad, looking very somber, chimed in occasionally.

Abruptly, the director stopped speaking, and cocked his head towards us. Mr. Sayeed-Nejad took the cue. "Someone in the schools has complained that your American accent is inferior to a British one. That person doesn't want the students to sound like Americans."

"There's not much we can do about the way we talk," I said. "What did you tell him?"

"I told him that we all speak like our mothers speak."

"So what's going to happen?" asked Betsy.

"I proposed that he call a meeting of the high school English teachers to discuss how you can help them with their classes and any other issues they may have. Mr. Manucher agreed."

The director interrupted with a long commentary. Mr. Sayeed-Nejad gave a shorter response, then turned to us.

"Mr. Manucher suggests that you postpone your evening classes for women. He thinks you are very young to be teaching adults."

I was flabbergasted. This had to be the work of the principal. "Tell him that the students will be very disappointed," I said. "I'm sure they like coming to our classes as much as we like teaching them."

Mr. Sayeed-Nejad translated my comments. The director paused, a benevolent smile crossing his face. "They can keep teaching the women for now," I understood him to say.

"Thank you very much," I said in my best Persian, as we got up from our chairs.

"Goodbye," Mr. Manucher said in English.

"*Khodahafez*" ("goodbye"), Betsy and I replied.

I walked quickly out of the room, passing Hassan-agha at the door without a word. Mr. Sayeed-Nejad and Betsy hurried to catch up.

"What's the rush, Mary?" asked Betsy.

"I need some fresh air."

I, who seldom felt angry, was ready to do battle. What were we doing here? The Iranians certainly weren't enthusiastic about our presence. Even Mr. Tavana, the English-speaking principal, was having second thoughts welcoming two young, modern American "girls" to his school.

"So now what do we do?" I asked Mr. Sayeed-Nejad. "I don't understand the problem. It can't be about our American accents, which, by the way, they'd be lucky to have. Kermani English has a very Persian lilt to me. There's not a hint of the Brit anywhere."

"Be patient. We'll have the meeting with the teachers, and then we'll see."

"We might as well go to the bazaar and shop for lunch," I said, as Mr. Sayeed-Nejad turned back to his office. "We don't have anything to do until this evening."

Betsy and I headed down the street toward the center of town. My watch read 7:30 a.m.

I didn't know how to spend my time. It was incomprehensible that here, where everything was different from my total world experience, I was at such loose ends. I would have given most anything for news of the greater world. What calumny was the Soviet Union perpetrating these days? Who was playing in the World Series? The English language papers from Tehran reported everything but news, and no one seemed to care. Sitting cross-legged on my bed in our room, I'd devoured all the books I brought with me, all of Betsy's, and I was starting one about Genghis Khan borrowed from Fred.

When I wasn't reading, I was writing. In recent days, missives on thin blue air letters had sailed out to my parents, my brother, an ex-boyfriend, my college roommate, my grandmother, even an aunt. When the daneshsera's assistant principal showed up at our door, Dickens in one hand, tape recorder in the other, I was happy to put down my pen and spend an hour reading the first chapter of A Tale of Two Cities into his machine.

"It was the best of times, it was the worst of times ... it was the spring of hope, it was the winter of despair, we had everything before us, we had nothing before us...." Charles Dickens was speaking directly to me. Iran was positive, it was negative. It was good, it was bad. It was compelling, it was boring.

"You know it's going to get better, Mary," Betsy said, setting down her volume of Elizabeth Barrett Browning poems. "We'll get into a good routine when we start visiting classes." Betsy, my senior by a year, was of staunch New England stock. A couple of weeks in an unfamiliar routine didn't bother her. "It's an adventure being here," she said.

"I feel so superfluous."

"Relax. We've got our adult class—it's all ours, remember—and the ones at the nursing school will start soon."

"What's that principal called again?" I asked Betsy after the assistant principal had retrieved the recorder.

"I don't know," she said. "It's so hard to remember people's names here."

"Well, I know you need something to do," I said, "so I told Mr. Tape Recorder you'd be happy to read the next chapter for him." Our private naming system was born.

The Kermanis were making their own adaptations. Betsy and I were stripped of our surnames, becoming a casual Miss Mary or Betsy-khanum, while Fred and Tom retained the dignity of their family names—Mr. Jones or Agha-ye Sisul. Out of earshot, the good people of Kerman had another way of identifying Betsy and me. Although we could both look over the heads of most Iranians, Betsy was taller and wider. She became the "big" American girl while I, for the only time in my life, was the "little" one.

At last, on a warm Wednesday in late September, word came we were to meet with Kerman's English teachers in the principal's office at Bahmanyar High School. This announcement brought an unexpected complication. I'd dropped by Parvin Etesami High School for tea when Mrs. Nahidi asked, "Does Mrs. Mesbah have to attend this evening? She will be very uncomfortable."

Lowering her shrill voice to a whisper, she confided that when her colleague was a student at the University of Tehran, she had fallen in love with a fellow Kermani who was also studying English. As his family had less status and money than hers, her parents wouldn't allow them to marry. Instead, they chose an older man from a good Kerman family to be her husband. Unfortunately, the man she had wanted to marry was now an English teacher at Bahmanyar Girls' High School. It would be awkward if they met.

Perhaps we'd be the cause of their embarrassment, but I had no power to intervene. The director of education had requested that all English teachers attend.

That evening, Bahmanyar High School's principal, the chief of the pronunciation police, rose from his desk when we crossed the threshold of his office. "Please, sit down. We await His Excellency, the director of education."

Betsy and I joined three women teachers seated along the far wall of the office. Mrs. Mesbah, shrinking into the corner, was swathed in one of the darkest chadors I had seen, only her eyes peeking out. Mrs. Nahidi was also wrapped in a chador, but she appeared more relaxed. I could see her entire face. The third woman, a Zoroastrian, I was told, wore a blue suit, her hair hidden under a printed silk scarf. Mr. Sayeed-Nejad, Fred, and Tom sat down with the men at the opposite side of the room. The shah, his wife Farah, and their two children, Reza and Farahnaz, watched closely from their picture on the wall.

I nudged Mrs. Nahidi. "Which one is Mrs. Mesbah's former boyfriend?"

"Shhh. Mr. Heydarshahi's over there, the young man in the navy blue suit sitting next to Mr. Jones." Trying to be discreet, I checked out the losing lover. Was he looking at Mrs. Mesbah?

"Listen," Mrs. Nahidi said. "I hear the director's voice in the hallway."

Everyone stood when Mr. Manucher entered. The principal, with a flourish of compliments to His Excellency, relinquished the chair of honor and the meeting began. In flowery, formal Farsi, Mr. Manucher emphasized how fortunate the teachers were to have the assistance of such capable people as these young Americans. At least, that's what I think he said. Mrs. Nahidi couldn't translate as fast as he was speaking. The question was, the director continued, how best to take advantage of this opportunity.

Mr. Sayeed-Nejad, who had been well prepped for this discussion by his protégés, leaned on his crutches, standing to speak. These volunteers could be most helpful, he suggested, if the teachers used them in their classes for conversation and pronunciation. Before he could utter another word, Bahmanyar High School's principal jumped up, grabbing a hefty volume from the corner of his desk.

"They don't speak proper English," he said. "I can find a hundred examples here, in the Oxford English Dictionary, where their American pronunciation doesn't conform to British English."

A murmur of protest in English and Farsi buzzed around the room. Rising from his chair, Mrs. Mesbah's ex-boyfriend came to our defense.

"Many of us are familiar with American accents. An American wrote our textbooks. In fact, I studied with their author, Dr. Dorry, in Tehran."

"Dr. Dorry now works for the Peace Corps," Mr. Sayeed-Nejad said. "It's possible she'll visit the volunteers in Kerman."

The other teachers assured us our help was welcome. There was one request, however. Could we use British terms for grammar and punctuation? From that point on, periods no longer concluded my sentences. They ended instead with full stops or, to use predictable Persian pronunciation, full-es-stops.

"Then it is settled," the director said in conversational Persian that I easily understood. "Our guests can begin visiting your classrooms next week." The teachers nodded in approval. Smiling graciously, the director said his goodbyes. Mrs. Mesbah followed him out the door, releasing her chador only a little to invite Betsy and me to visit her classes. It was the first time she had spoken all evening.

As we milled around getting ready to leave, Mr. Oxford English Dictionary approached to tell us how welcome we would be at Bahmanyar High School where, he said, gesturing towards Mrs. Mesbah's ex-boyfriend, there was an excellent English teacher. The ex-boyfriend nodded at us. As she was leaving, Mrs. Nahidi assured me she was looking forward to my visits. With a hint of a smile, Mr. Sayeed-Nejad said, "See? I told you to be patient."

Days later, Betsy and I, loaded with purchases, were leaving the bazaar when she caught sight of Mrs. Mesbah's ex-boyfriend standing at the entrance, fingering a strand of dark-hued worry beads.

"Look, Mary, there's that English teacher who stood up for us the other night."

I gave him a wave and a friendly smile. We ambled over to say hello.

Our new colleague stared at the dirt floor of the bazaar, shuffling his feet as we approached. Greeting us awkwardly, his face a rosy red, he barely listened as I prattled on about our purchases—lamb, tomatoes, a melon.

"How do you find Kerman?" he asked, struggling to gain his composure.

"We like it a lot," Betsy said, "but we're having a huge problem with flies in our room. Do you have any suggestions?"

"You should buy a flyswatter. But don't let the merchant cheat you. You shouldn't pay more than two tomans."

We said our goodbyes and burst out laughing. A flyswatter! Really? How original. Mrs. Mesbah's ex-boyfriend now had a name: Mr. Flyswatter.

News traveled fast. "I understand you met Mr. Heydarshahi in the bazaar yesterday." Mr. Sayeed-Nejad was frowning.

"Who?" I asked.

"Mr. Heydarshahi. The English teacher at Bahmanyar High School."

"Oh, Mr. Flyswatter," I said before I could stop myself.

"What?"

"Never mind. Yes, we saw him in the bazaar."

"You mustn't smile and stop to chat when you meet a man in public," he said. "It's very forward. People are talking."

I rolled my eyes. What an overreaction!

"Mary-khanum, I need to speak with you," said Mrs. Nahidi as we left class a day or two later. "Our students tell me you were talking with Mr. Heydarshahi in the bazaar the other day. I know you mean well, but our customs are very different. We don't linger with men when we are out in public, especially in the bazaar. And if Mrs. Mesbah hears about this, she will be very unhappy."

Walking back to our room, it was hard to fathom that such a small act was causing such a big reaction; standards for behavior had an unfamiliar filter here. On the dusty roads of

Kerman, the ground felt unstable beneath my feet. I couldn't wait to get to the sheltering walls of the daneshsera.

It's Not All About the Chador

Journal entry

> Will I be able to communicate the experience
> of Iran to a person who's never been in the
> Middle East? A *National Geographic* knowledge
> of quaint customs doesn't cut it when you
> have to live with them—and Iranians take their
> customs very seriously.

When we finally broke the barrier to Kerman's classes, with Betsy visiting one school and me another, the reward was not as wonderful as I had expected; sitting and listening were our main activities. Several days into this new routine, seated on a folding chair in the front of the class, I watched Mrs. Nahidi introduce the English alphabet to a class of sixty-five seventh graders. Holding a piece of chalk in her slender hand, she stood at the blackboard, giving instructions in high-pitched Persian as she drew each letter. Struggling not to yawn, I focused on a spot in back of the room, past the rows of narrow tables and benches where the young girls in drab gray uniforms were attempting to form the ABCs on sheets of wide-lined paper. My mind wandered to the conversation Betsy and I had the day before at the home of Mrs. Mesbah and her husband, an older man who had a different last name, Moaveni. Iranian women often do not assume their husband's last name.

That discussion started with the chador. Betsy and I had spent Friday, the day of rest, in Mahan, a small town southeast of Kerman. Guests of Mr. Sayeed-Nejad's aunt and uncle, we lunched under a bower of branches in their garden on *albaloo polo*, a delicious combination of rice, cherries, and chicken, lounging on a shaded wooden platform covered by an elaborate Kerman carpet.

Everything—the setting, the company, the food—was new to us, but the most memorable part of the afternoon came when the aunt insisted Betsy and I wear chadors to visit the shrine of Shah Ne'matollah Vali, an honored Sufi dervish.

"The chadors were way too short for us, and we had such a hard time keeping them on our heads," Betsy said, relating the incident to Mrs. Mesbah and her husband.

"Yes, mine kept slipping down my back," I said. "I was so worried about the chador I hardly saw anything of the shrine. But everyone felt Betsy and I should put them on to show respect."

"Please excuse me while I translate," Mrs. Mesbah said, helping herself to a glass of tea and sitting down heavily on a straight-backed chair next to her husband. Her expanding pregnant belly seemed to throw her off balance.

Mr. Moaveni listened carefully to his wife. Then he spoke quietly to her. "My husband believes one should always be respectful of others," Mrs. Mesbah said. "He would like to know your opinion about Kerman's customs, like the chador."

Kerman's customs—Betsy and I talked about them all the time. Why do they…? How could they…? And chadors topped our list. Only a handful of women appeared in public without them; only foreigners braved the bazaar unveiled. Yet they seemed so restrictive, so diminishing, so anonymous.

Betsy threw me a look, as if to ask if I wanted to answer this. When I shrugged my shoulders, she turned to our hosts: "Kerman's customs certainly are different from ours. It doesn't even occur to western women to cover themselves like you do here."

"In many Iranian cities there are lots of women who don't wear chadors," Mrs. Mesbah said. "Their families are accustomed to it. But Kerman is conservative. It's taking longer for many here to accept unveiled women. They want to protect their wives and daughters from unseemly stares and comments. And they don't want them to appear flirtatious."

"But you didn't wear a chador in Tehran," I said. "Didn't you feel freer that way?"

"I did. Although sometimes it would have been easier to throw on a chador instead of worrying about my appearance."

Mr. Moaveni, when his wife translated the conversation, emphasized that Kermanis thought it natural that Betsy and I would appear in public unveiled. "We want Iran to be part of the modern world," he said through his wife. "Living in Kerman, teaching in our schools, dressing the way you do, you're showing our girls their future."

Mrs. Mesbah bit her lower lip, her brow furrowing. "The chador doesn't say everything about Iranian women. True, I wear one; we all wear them here. But I have a university degree and a career as an English teacher. Iranian women are respected in many walks of life. What we have on our backs is not so important."

I had glanced at Betsy. Both of our mothers were college-educated; neither of them worked outside the home. None of the mothers I knew in Illinois had jobs. My high school did not employ married women as teachers. "They might get pregnant," the principal said.

Mrs. Mesbah was not finished. "Speaking of customs, I believe some of ours are best. Take arranged marriages. You know that I met a man, Mr. Heydarshahi, while I was studying English at university. We were from the same town; we had so much in common."

I glanced sideways at her husband to see if he understood what his wife was saying. He seemed to listen a little more closely when she mentioned Mr. Heydarshahi.

"We fell in love," Mrs. Mesbah continued, "but my parents would not agree to our marriage."

"Why not?" Betsy asked.

"His family is from a different social class. My parents believed he would not be able to care properly for a wife and children. I was very disappointed. My family insisted I meet Mahmood, who holds a prominent position at Bank-e Melli, our national bank."

"How often did you see each other before you were engaged?" I asked.

"At our second meeting, I agreed we could marry, and we got together with our families at least three times before the official engagement."

"Did you love him then?" Betsy asked.

"Of course not. We hadn't had the opportunity to get to know each other well. It took time for me to understand what a caring, good man I'd married. Falling in love is not difficult. Recognizing the right person to be with for the rest of your life is very hard. My parents were wiser than I was."

"But what about Mr. Heydarshahi?" Betsy said.

"My heart is healed. I'm uncomfortable when I see him only because he has suffered."

Uncomfortable was an understatement. I remembered how she'd vanished behind her chador at the meeting with the director of education. Still, her voice was warm when she spoke to her husband.

Whispers in the back of the class brought me back to seventh graders and the alphabet. Mrs. Nahidi glared at the offenders, reprimanding them sharply. "If they don't practice," she said to me, "they'll never learn." I tried to look stern and pay attention as she returned to the blackboard, but was soon distracted again.

Mrs. Mesbah was an enigma—intelligent, pretty, educated, and yet her parents decided whom she was to marry. Back in our room, Betsy and I had dissected our afternoon.

"Well, Mr. Moaveni seems like a nice man," I said.

"Mary, he's at least ten years older than she is. It's almost like marrying your father. And Mr. Heydarshahi is much handsomer. But here she is, claiming that arranged marriages are better than picking your own partner."

Betsy and I couldn't figure it out. Mrs. Mesbah was about our age, but her assumptions about her life were so different from ours. We were halfway around the world from home in a place we had only recently heard of, while she was married to a man she barely knew, and living a mile from where she grew up. Our differences went way beyond veils and styles of marriage.

The ABCs were clear on the blackboard, but straggling across the copybook pages of the seventh graders when I snapped back to the present. Mrs. Nahidi was correcting a girl who had written her letters in the wrong direction. "English is written backwards," she reminded the class, "from left to right." In this land where everything seemed upside down, I felt like one of the students. We were all struggling with the unfamiliar: they with an alphabet that went the wrong way, me with a culture that defied my ingrained beliefs.

"Won't you do something with the students, Miss Mary?" asked Mrs. Nahidi. With just minutes until class ended, I glanced at yesterday's lesson, and stood up to face the rows of seventh graders. "Repeat after me. What is my name?" "What is my name?" said the class. "Good. Now answer with your name." Mrs. Nahidi threw in a quick translation. "My name is Parvin, Masumeh, Zorah, Maryam, Afsineh..." they answered, a bouquet of girls' names filling the air.

Aash Reshteh

"**M**iss Mary, today the teachers come to my house for *aash reshteh*. You and Miss Betsy come, too," said the home economics teacher, Miss Aghassi, as we stood in the teachers' room at Parvin Etesami High School. I liked her. Her English was limited, but she was open and friendly, not shy with me, the foreigner.

"*Aash reshteh chee-eh?*" ("What's aash reshteh?") I asked, attempting to switch the conversation to Persian.

"It is...aash chee-eh? ("What's 'aash?") she asked, turning to Mrs. Nahidi.

"Soup."

"It is soup," said Miss Aghassi.

Later that afternoon, Betsy and I stood bareheaded above the covey of chadored teachers winding its way through a warren of narrow, dirt roads. "I wonder how they know where they are," I murmured to Betsy. To me, these tight, walled alleys that snaked through the neighborhood looked exactly alike. I was certain I could never find my way out alone.

The teachers, heads down, hurried silently along the lane leading to Miss Aghassi's walled home. Mrs. Nahidi stayed close to Betsy and me, ready to help, should we need her. She grasped her chador firmly across her face so only her eyes were visible.

"Hello, meeses," sang out a young boy as we passed. Mrs. Nahidi turned and reprimanded him severely.

"He shouldn't be so rude," she said, "but he's just a small boy and doesn't see many foreign women."

"It's not important," I said. I wondered what she would do walking with us through Shah Square in front of the bazaar, where we attracted a good deal more attention. I had expected the novelty of two American women on the streets of Kerman to wear off, but so far it had not.

Our party halted in front of a high adobe wall, punctuated by a worn green wooden door with a large metal keyhole. To me, it looked like all the other doorways we had passed—no numbers, nothing to distinguish this one as the right one. Yet the women had no hesitation; they recognized a signpost that was invisible to me. The history teacher, holding her chador in place with one hand, rapped firmly with the other, and soon Miss Aghassi appeared, opening the gate onto one of the miracles of this parched country—a jewel of a garden, its verdant trees and bright flowers hidden from the curious eyes of the outside world. We followed her down a broad walkway towards a splash of bright red roses surrounding the bubbling fountain in front of the house. On either side, stately green cedars rose to meet the sky, and in a far corner, the branches of several fuller trees formed a bower over a low wooden platform, a *takhte* Mrs. Nahidi told me, where the family could relax in the cool shade. The dusty brown of the streets and walls vanished, taking my worries along.

In a small anteroom, Betsy and I, dressed in light cotton skirts and blouses, waited while the teachers removed their chadors and folded them carefully, revealing the European-style suits they had worn in class that day. The pile of white, grey, blue, and black flowered garments mounted on a nearby table. Mehri-khanum, Miss Aghassi's sloe-eyed young sister-in-law, invited us to sit down in the parlor.

Glasses rattled on the tray as Miss Aghassi made her way around the room, flip flops on her stocking feet, offering steaming hot tea to her guests. I sat on one of the many straight-back chairs that lined the walls of this formal reception area. A large Kerman carpet, its central floral medallion nesting in a solid royal blue background, covered the floor.

Miss Aghassi stood in front of me, tray in hand. "Befarmayeed." ("Be my guest.") All eyes were on me.

"Thank you. I couldn't," I demurred in my shaky Persian.

"Please," she said, offering the tea a second time.

"Oh no, you're too kind."

"I insist," she said, proffering the tray yet again.

"Thank you. I appreciate it," I answered, taking a glass of tea in a filigreed silver holder.

"Have some sugar," the hostess said. I picked several lumps from the bowl, and dropped them into the glass.

Mrs. Nahidi was smiling. Whew! I must have done the ta'arof correctly. I was such a novice with this elaborate system of politeness. Refuse twice, then accept. We repeated this ritual as Miss Aghassi and Mehri-khanum passed plates of cookies, then fruit, but it was a game to me. Why bother? How did one really say no?

Conversation continued, Persian on one side of the room, halting English on my side.

"Where is your mother?" asked the slender mathematics teacher, Mrs. Hemati, who was seated next to me.

"She's in Chicago."

"Oh, Chee-cah-go. Boom, boom!" I grimaced. I couldn't escape the scourge of Al Capone even in the desert. "Do you not miss your mother?" she asked.

"Oh, yes," I said, knowing my mom would get a big kick out of her prominent role in this tortured conversation. From my vast experience of nearly one month, I knew we would now proceed to the size of my family. Confessing to only one brother elicited great sympathy in this town where the brother and sister count often reached twelve or more. Be patient, I thought. Mrs. Hemati is trying her hardest. You should, too.

"How many sisters do you have?" I asked in my best Farsi.

"Oh," Mrs. Hemati said to the room at large. "She speaks such good Persian!" Luckily, Miss Aghassi reappeared before I had to say more. It was time for aash reshteh.

The guests rose from their chairs, retrieved their chadors from the table, and shed their shoes at the door. Betsy and I kicked off our dusty loafers, exposing our bare feet, the only ones at the party. A host of "befarmayeeds" caused a temporary roadblock at the doorway.

"You first."

"Oh, I couldn't."

"Please go ahead."

"Only after you."

The Americans lost the ta'arof battle. We led the way into the dining room, where a red printed plastic *sofreh*, or tablecloth, spanned the floor. Two large copper cauldrons of noodle soup were at either end; warm flat bread, bowls of thick yogurt, and plates of fresh tarragon, chives, and parsley filled in the area between. Betsy surveyed the situation, and lowered herself cross-legged to the floor at one end; I followed her lead, pulling my pleated skirt over my knees. Our colleagues wrapped their chadors loosely around their bodies, and filled in the places around us. Mehri-khanum ladled aash into each bowl, tiptoeing on the tablecloth to reach those in far corners. The teachers teased her as she hopped from place to place.

"What are they saying?" I asked Mrs. Nahidi.

"They tell Mehri-khanum that she is adding—how do you say—flavor to the aash."

"Oh, spice," I said, wishing I could join in the merriment. The women were having so much fun, while I sat there like a lump, incomprehensible banter flowing around me. As it was, I was anything but gleeful. My legs were cramping in this unfamiliar position, my skirt refused to conceal my knees, and from the smell of the main course, it was unlikely aash would become a favorite food.

I bent over my bowl and filled my spoon. Aash had noodles like chicken noodle soup, but that was where the resemblance ended. Sweet and sour with dull undertones, it tasted like nothing I had ever eaten. In my few weeks in Kerman, I had dealt with some very unfamiliar flavors—oily lamb, rosewater-scented ice cream, and cardamom-laced cakes—but I could not place the peculiar herb that seasoned this broth.

"What is in aash?" I asked.

"Noodles, made by hand. It is a lot of work. And red beans and spinach," Mrs. Nahidi answered, helping herself to another bowlful.

"But what gives it this unique taste?" I persisted, anxious to know so I could avoid it another time.

"Chesre. It's a special Kerman herb. I don't know its name in English. Please, have some more."

"Oh, I couldn't. I'm eating so much these days, I'm getting fat."

"Ooh, Miss Mary is getting fat," said Miss Aghassi. "Persian food is good for her."

"You know," said Mrs. Nahidi, who was anything but plump, "Iranians like to be fat."

"Americans don't think fat is good," I said. "I can't eat any more."

The conversation shifted away from me, laughter and camaraderie filling the room. My Iranian colleagues were so much more comfortable here than I was. This was not how I had imagined it would be. Envisioning my role in the Peace Corps, I had seen myself as a leader, my strong, competent actions guiding the local population towards a better life. But instead I was ignorant, uncomprehending, and dependent on the very people whose lives I was supposed to improve. And here were these women, reveling in each other's company, confident in their familiar environment, with little sense, as far as I could tell, that anything was lacking. If I were going to have any impact in Kerman, first and foremost I would have to be a very good follower. To use Mr. Sayeed-Nejad's adage, I needed to learn to be a human being—an Iranian.

"Miss Mary, I am sorry I have not the good English." Mehri-khanum sat down beside me.

"We'll talk in Persian. Uh... how old are you?" I asked in Farsi, grasping for something to start the conversation.

"I have eighteen years," she answered in hesitant English.

"Isn't she beautiful?" said Miss Aghassi, stroking Mehri's cheek. I stared down at my bowl. The open affection Iranians showed to members of the same sex was disconcerting. "When my brother saw her," Miss Aghassi continued in Farsi, "he just had to marry her."

"Where did your husband first see you?" I asked Mehri. This was Persian I could handle.

"My class marched in the stadium for the shah's birthday celebration. We were wearing our school uniforms. They wouldn't let us wear chadors. Hooshang, my husband, noticed me there, and sent a go-between to my parents to ask for my hand in marriage. After they decided he was suitable, I was allowed to meet him. I was a little shy at first; he's older than I am."

"How old is he?" I asked.

"Thirty-eight," Mehri answered.

Thirty-eight. More than twice Mehri's age.

"Did you want to get married?" asked Betsy.

"I wanted to go to school to be a teacher. My parents told me 'your husband's house will be your university.'"

"And now she's pregnant," said Miss Aghassi, caressing her sister-in-law's stomach. "Her baby will come in five months."

The party began to wind down. My feet were half asleep but I managed to stand up without falling into the soup. We put on our shoes, the teachers adjusted their chadors, and after many thank you's to our hostesses, Betsy and I joined the group bustling through the maze of alleyways to the main thoroughfare.

The moon was rising when we hailed a taxi and headed down Zarisse Street, back to the teachers' training school. In the early evening light, Kerman's domed roofs and tall minarets were stark silhouettes against the darkening sky, with nothing between them and the stars that were slowly carpeting the heavens. The quiet beauty of the scene made my heart stop.

"It's just awful that Mehri's parents wouldn't let her continue her education," Betsy said. "And she didn't even seem upset about it. How these women can put up with this kind of treatment is beyond me. Why don't they stand up for themselves?"

"I don't know, Betsy. Why should they miss what they never knew? From their standpoint, the life you and I have here is pretty unpleasant. We scrape by from one day to the next with no one to do the cooking and shopping, and we're alone without our families in a place where those connections are really important. Why would they want to be like us? The women at that party are a lot better at living their lives here than I am. I wonder if I'll ever figure it out."

"Not much to figure out," Betsy said as Kobra-khanum unlocked the gate to let us in. "They're repressed. If parents like Mehri's encouraged their daughters to go to college instead of marrying right out of high school, these girls would discover they are competent human beings."

"Really? What about Mrs. Mesbah? She went to college."

"And she's a teacher. That's some progress."

We strolled past the pistachio grove that separated our room from the gate. The nuts had been harvested only a week before; in the evening's shadows, the trees were a delicate fall pink. Students, still in their gray school uniforms, paced the courtyard beneath dim lights, memorizing the next day's lessons.

"I don't think it's simple, Betsy," I said, as I slid the key into the padlock to the door of our room. "Why should we have all the answers? I'm not even sure I know the right questions to ask."

I grabbed the blue curtains so they wouldn't catch in the doorway. Betsy pulled the door shut, and drew the inside bolt. The foreigners were in for the night.

A Day Trip

Musing

> The significance of place deepens when you've
> always been there: when the gods your ances-
> tors worshipped inhabited the very mountains
> and vast plains that form your world; when the
> birdsongs that that interrupt your sleep every
> morning awakened your grandparents and your
> great-grandparents; and when the miracles and
> calamities your community faced centuries
> earlier are so real to you they could have hap-
> pened yesterday.

It was Friday, the Muslim day of rest. After a week of sitting in Kerman's classrooms, Betsy, Fred, Tom, and I were off to the mountains with Mr. Sayeed-Nejad and his friend, Mr. Sanaati, headed for Baba Kamal, a place special to the Zoroastrians of Kerman. Before the Muslim conquest, Iranians all over the country followed this faith, perhaps the earliest monotheistic religion. Now only Kerman and Yazd had signif-icant Zoroastrian populations.

Mr. Sanaati's jeep sped into the square in front of the bazaar, which was eerily quiet, with none of the bustle of the other days of the week. He hopped out to greet us with a hearty "salaam alaikum."

"Please!" he continued in English, gesturing towards his vehicle. Mr. Sanaati, a burly fellow who owned an auto repair shop, spoke the little English he knew with a great deal of verve. We climbed into the jeep, ducking under its low roof—a shield from Iran's merciless sun.

"*Hahzereed?*" ("Ready?") asked Mr. Sanaati. With Mr. Sayeed-Nejad by his side, Mr. Sanaati was ready for anything. Minutes later, we were off the pavement and onto a dirt road, leaving the silent bazaar with its shuttered shops far behind. The lurching of the jeep and the billows of dust it churned up made front to back seat conversations difficult.

Just a few kilometers from town, the landscape was stark, like I imagined a moonscape to be: mountains of rock formations jutted out of the ground, flood beds streaking in front of them, an indication of severe winter rains; the only vegetation in sight was a tufty kind of briar that tumbled along the brown desert surface. "That's camel food," Mr. Sayeed-Nejad shouted over the noise.

"Look," Betsy said. "There're some camels over there." She pointed to a group of fifteen or twenty grungy-looking beasts grazing off the side of the road. Their young herder hunkered on a rock nearby.

"Stop," Mr. Sayeed-Nejad said. Mr. Sanaati jammed on the brakes. The scene before me had none of the romance these animals had evoked in my former life. Brave, gallant Lawrence of Arabia no longer galloped across sandy dunes in the desert of my daydreams. Drivers in rags, whipping tired trains of bedraggled beasts were my new reality. But I had never been so close to camels. As they nuzzled the ground near the road for any kind of sustenance, I was stunned at how large they were.

"Would you like to ride one?" asked Mr. Sayeed-Nejad. Of course we would.

Mr. Sanaati jogged over to the herder and, after a brief conversation, money changed hands. The rest of us unfolded ourselves out of the jeep. I was brushing the dust out of my hair when I caught Mr. Sanaati mimicking me, swiping his palm back and forth over his short black crew cut, a big grin on his face. I smiled back. Here, in the privacy of the vast desert, it was okay, it seemed, for men and women to be friendly.

The herder shoved the newfound cash in a worn pocket, selected the proper beast for boarding, strapped on a saddle, and checked the reins. He growled something at our camel, and walloped its raggedy shins with a hefty stick. The camel, yielding to his small master, knelt. Fred, mumbling something about bravery, hopped up on its hump, aided by a boost from Mr. Sanaati. The herder grumbled again, pulled at the bit, and the camel started to move. Fred, jaw set, knuckles white, swayed from side to side, an unwanted burden for this beast. Soon he was back on the ground, and it was Tom's turn. Around in a circle they went, the herder, the camel and Tom, his lanky legs dangling. In a minute he was ready to dismount, and Betsy was on the hump—and off again in no time.

Finally, it was me and the camel. With a boost from Tom, I was astride, jerking my skirt down over my knees. It was really high up on that hump, and unsteady, too—like perching on a flagpole. If I could have looked, the view would have been great. The camel, however, had had it. No going in circles for me. He would not budge, no matter what his master said. With a disgusted snort, he wheeled his head around to look me straight in the eye, drool slobbering down his long neck. I started to back up, but stopped just in time to avoid sliding off his rear end. Lowering his head towards my feet, he opened his mouth, baring big camel teeth. I jerked my feet back, shouting, "Get me off this thing!" My audience broke out in great guffaws while the herder walloped the camel on the neck to distract him from making a meal of my toes, hitting him again on the shins so he would kneel. I staggered off and backed away fast, putting as much ground as possible between me and the carnivorous camel. Hurrying back to the jeep my legs were

unsteady, as if I had been on a boat. "Hey, I thought we were
going to Baba Kamal," I said, my voice shaking.

Mr. Sanaati turned the jeep onto a narrow dirt road heading
up along a mountain that looked like it was constructed from
a jumble of huge building blocks—all brown angles, shadows
providing the only relief. As we twisted and turned up the
incline, I closed my eyes, wishing I were a religious person so I
could say a prayer about staying on the chosen path. It would
be so easy to fall off, so far to the bottom. The jeep slowed,
made an abrupt turn, went about twenty yards and stopped.
I opened my eyes to another of Iran's wonders—pine trees,
green grass, a brook gurgling its way through the scene. Grass!
Someone really cared about this place. "This is Baba Kamal,"
said Mr. Sayeed-Nejad.

Scrambling out of the jeep, I inhaled cool, almost moist
air. With a crutch for a pointer, Mr. Sayeed-Nejad picked a
spot for our picnic, and we settled down on the ground to eat.
Fred chatted away in Persian with the two Kermani men, while
Betsy, Tom, and I stuck to English. Mr. Sayeed-Nejad, who
seldom missed an opportunity to praise Fred, was effusive:
"Mr. Jones speaks Persian as well as I do. If I wasn't sitting
here looking at him, I'd think he was a Kermani." Fred tried
to put an "aw, shucks" expression on his face, but I could tell
he was pleased. Enough accolades for Mr. Perfect Volunteer. I
changed the subject.

"Mr. Sayeed-Nejad, tell us about Baba Kamal." I leaned
back on an elbow and took a swig of Canada Dry.

"Baba Kamal has always been holy for Zoroastrians," said
Mr. Sayeed-Nejad, arranging himself comfortably on the picnic
cloth. I could tell a story was coming. "One of their leaders is
buried here, but it is most famous as a place of refuge. More
than three hundred years ago, when the great Shah Abbas

reigned from Esfahan in the north, a judge in Kerman ordered that all the Zoroastrians in the area be killed in retribution for the death of one Muslim. Desperate, they came here to pray. They say that as they prayed, Shah Abbas had a dream that the south was on fire. He jumped out of bed in the middle of the night, called for his horse, and sped off to Kerman, several days' ride away. When he neared the city, he learned of the judge's decree, and sent an emissary to forbid the slaughter. The Zoroastrians of Kerman are sure that their prayers from this very place saved their lives."

How the importance of place deepens when you, your family, your ancestors were part of its history. It had been hundreds of years since Shah Abbas rushed to save Kerman's Zoroastrians. But the centuries of continuity in Kerman imbued the community with a shared experience, a living history. The Iranians sitting on the cloth with me were Muslim, yet Baba Kamal was a part of their remembered past.

"How did the Zoroastrians end up in Kerman?" Betsy asked. We had visited a school in their section on the edge of town with Mr. Sayeed-Nejad a couple of weeks earlier. He had emphasized how clean the Zoroastrian quarter was, compared to other parts of Kerman.

"They've always been here," said Mr. Sayeed-Nejad. "At the time Shah Abbas heard the prayers from Baba Kamal, Zoroastrians still lived in other parts of the country. But they were considered fire worshippers, not 'people of the book' like Jews and Christians. Eventually the mullahs forced most to convert to Islam. In Iran, only Kerman and Yazd tolerated Zoroastrians. But there's something else, something you shouldn't forget. People in Kerman are kind to others. We have big hearts here."

We kept on talking about the Zoroastrians—how in Yazd, where Iran's largest group lived, Muslims had not permitted them to wear clothes made from whole cloth until the twentieth century. I thought of Kerman's bazaar—the Baluchis, the villagers, the soldiers, Betsy and me—all in identifying attire. But for Betsy and me, at least, it was a choice.

Mr. Sanaati, who had been following the conversation in Fred's translation, emphasized their honesty.

"You can always trust a Zoroastrian," Fred interpreted.

"Yessss!" Mr. Sanaati said in English. "You don't even have to bargain with Zoroastrian merchants. They'll always give you a fair price," he added in Farsi. I doubted the not bargaining part. Everyone in Kerman bargained.

The shadows were lengthening and a fall chill filled the air. We climbed back into the jeep, and Mr. Sanaati navigated down the winding road that traced its way along the sheer mountainside toward the city. I clamped my eyes closed until we reached level ground.

OH, SO FOREIGN

We are all tattooed in our cradles with the beliefs of our tribe; the record may seem superficial, but it is indelible. —*Oliver Wendell Holmes, Sr.*

The Beggar

Ricocheting off the buildings, bouncing from the pavement, the hot air blasted me as I trudged toward the bazaar after a morning observing classes at Bahmanyar High School. At 6500 feet above sea level, October's breezes cooled the city in the evenings, but the midday heat was still oppressive. The bazaar's high domed roof provided refuge from the sun; shopping for dinner among the hundreds of vendors sequestered in its cool shade would be a relief.

I didn't notice her at first. She was just one of the pitiful creatures who surrounded me, pulling on my arm, my skirt, pleading, "Khanum, in the name of God, help me," when I stopped to buy some raisins inside the bazaar's entrance.

"*Boro, boro.*" ("Go, go.") The shopkeeper waved his hand dismissively at the group of beggars. Most obeyed him, fading into the shadows of the dimly lit marketplace. But the woman stayed, convinced I would relent and offer her a couple of cents, a rial or two.

We both watched the vendor as he put a weight on the scale, opened a small paper sack on the other side, and carefully measured out ten grams of raisins. Two tomans—a little more than a quarter—was the price we had agreed on. I handed him the money and took the small package, grinning when I noticed it was made from a sheet of notebook paper. Rather than "A & P" or "Raisins" emblazoned on its front, this package read "Parviz is a boy" over and over again. In its first life, my paper sack was English penmanship practice for some young student. Little was wasted in Kerman in 1964.

I put the raisins in my blue shopping bag, and bore deeper into the bazaar, the beggar whining at my heels. "Khanum, khanum, please, please..."

The two of us were not alone for long. "Hello meeses. Ver are you going?" I heard as two teenage boys caught up to me.

"In Kerman, men and women don't stop and chat together in public places," Mr. Sayeed-Nejad had reprimanded me just days before, his voice full of consternation.

These boys were strangers. What liberties they were taking! "May we help you?" asked one. "You are very beautiful."

"I vant to go to America," said the other.

"Thank you. I must go. I am busy." Seeing that the foreigner was not in a chatty mood, they dropped off as I continued along the worn walkways of the bazaar.

But the beggar was still with me as I paused to buy yogurt from a villager. Handing him my plastic jar, I asked for a kilo, hoping it wouldn't immediately spoil in the un-refrigerated heat of my room. He ladled the white curds into the container, and fastened its red lid tightly. The woman watched as I put the change from the purchase in my pocket. "Khanum, remember me."

On we went. "Khanum, please, help me. I have two children," she said as I examined full, ripe tomatoes at a vegetable stand.

"Go, go," said the vendor, shooing the woman. Cocking his head toward her as she backed away, he asked, "Don't you give money to beggars?" and handed me the two tomatoes I had chosen. I added them to the blue bag.

"I can't," I answered, my Persian inadequate to explain that I was too obvious a target. "Give to one beggar, and you'll never get them off your back," our Peace Corps field officer had warned. But something else held me back. I didn't want to acknowledge that this poor creature existed. How could she be so needy? How could I be so healthy? I was supposed to feel guilty, but I felt victimized.

"The Koran says good Muslims must aid the poor," the vendor said. "But perhaps you gave to another helpless one."

"Thank you," I said, feeling helpless myself. My beggar and I continued our shopping.

"Coming through, coming through," warned a stooped man wearing a beige felt cap, a mound of heavy carpets piled high on his back. As I halted to let him pass, a shaft of sun poured through a light well in the bazaar's high ceiling, illuminating the woman who had become my shadow. She, too, was hunched over, her torn light chador parting to show a shapeless, worn dress and gaunt collarbones. Milky white trachoma clouded one of her eyes. She caught me looking at her, and immediately resumed pleading. "Khanum, khanum, I am hungry."

My heart snapped shut. This was too much. Would I ever be able to simply shop for dinner? Anyway, I was finished here. Picking up my pace, I hurried toward the outdoor part of the market to buy meat. The beggar woman felt me close the door. She did not follow.

Kumbaya

Letter home

> The Iranians are masters in the art of tact. How
> something is said is much more important than what
> is said. My blundering directness is almost crude.
> No one could have convinced me that understanding
> another culture would be so difficult.

S imply put, I didn't feel like sitting in a classroom for yet another morning. It was 7:30; I would have to rush to get to Bahmanyar High School on time. Still fussing, I pulled on yesterday's blue plaid skirt and blouse, shoved my feet into dusty black loafers, and made my entrance into the daneshsera's courtyard. Immediately, teenage girls in gray school uniforms surrounded me, ready to practice their English: "Good morning, Miss Mary." "How are you?" "Are you tired?" "You are very beautiful."

"Good morning. Thank you, I am fine. No, I am not tired. I am late," I said, hurrying to the school's gate.

Waiting for a taxi going my way, I glanced up at *Qaleh Dokhtar* on the hillside across from the school. The rich brown of these crumbling third-century ruins, the Girl's Fortress, stood in sharp contrast to the vivid blue of Kerman's cloudless sky. Two months ago, I had never seen an adobe ruin or witnessed sheep being herded down a main street of town. I had never bargained in a bazaar, seen a woman in a chador, or been startled by a donkey's bray. But long weeks into my Kerman stay, they were part of my everyday landscape. Even the muezzin's tape-recorded calls to prayer did not evoke the

mysterious Middle East. Kerman's realities were becoming
mine. It was turning into home.

I climbed out of the taxi and hurried to the teachers' room.
Apologizing to Mr. Heydarshahi for my tardiness, I followed
him to his second-year English class, settling onto the uncomfortable chair near his desk at the front of the room, just as I
had been doing in English classes all over the city for weeks.

Reflecting on Peace Corps training, I had a lot of questions.
The theories seemed sound in Ann Arbor. To maximize our
effectiveness, volunteers would teach teachers, not individual
high school classes. Our job was to convince our colleagues
of the superiority of the aural-oral method of teaching, where
students reproduce language patterns verbally, acquiring flu-
ency much like a small child does. Iranian English teachers,
under our influence, would use this approach with hundreds
of teenagers, resulting in a veritable revolution. In Ann Arbor,
this concept had a ring of authenticity. I could speak more
Persian after three months of intensive verbal practice than
I could speak French after three years of studying it conven-
tionally. Iranian children studied English for six years. Surely,
with this new method, they should be fluent speakers when
they graduated.

But I hadn't counted on the power of custom or the confidence of experience. Kerman's English teachers were not
interested in taking lessons from newly trained Americans.
After that brief flurry of opposition led by the pronunciation
policeman, Mr. Oxford English Dictionary, they welcomed us
into their classes, even encouraged the occasional discreet
suggestion. But it was the teachers' responsibility to ensure
the students passed the standardized examination at the end
of the year.

My exchange with Mrs. Nahidi was typical.

"I've taught them three alphabets," she said proudly.

"Three?" I asked, thinking English had only one.

"Yes. Small letters, capital letters, and cursive writing." Put that way, the number of English alphabets had expanded.

"They must know these and the rules of grammar for their examinations," she added.

"But don't you think they will remember the grammar better if they use it in speech?" I asked, silently admitting I had not learned much about grammar and writing in Ann Arbor.

Mrs. Nahidi shrugged, a petulant look flitting across her face: *Just who is this American girl to be telling me how to teach English?* I imagined her thinking. *She's even younger than my daughter. I've been in the classroom for almost thirty years.*

What she actually said was: "You can practice with them at the end of the lesson." With those simple words, a routine was born.

Assuming my welcome, each morning I descended upon one of Kerman's five English teachers in four girls' high schools. Seated in a place of honor facing the students, I was silent, an ornament struggling to remain alert should the teacher send an inquiry in my direction. I sat and smiled, stifling yawns, smothering sighs as the teacher droned on, in Farsi, of course. I learned a lot of Persian in those English classes. As the days and weeks crept by, the highlight of these long hours was being called on to "do something" with the class, more of a side show than a revolution in language learning. To illustrate the lessons underway, I invented dialogs.

"Who did I see?"

"You saw the shah."

"Who was he with?"

"He was with Haile Selassie."

"Where did they go?"

"They went to the bank."

I was running out of events to enact, although this particular one was unforgettable: sleek limousines, crowds, flags, and my thrill in glimpsing two emperors. But in front of the class, I had distilled the experience to a call and response. The details that had made it so meaningful were not part of the transmitted memory.

These simple sentences were so routine I was desperate to try something new, something uniquely American. And what is more American than gospel music? My musical career to this point was undistinguished. Even my sixth grade music instructor thought I could best contribute by humming the melody of a song quietly in the background while my classmates sang the words in three-part harmony. But I was never in the background in Kerman. I had forgotten to be afraid.

So on this crisp fall day, sitting in the front of Mr. Heydarshahi's class in yesterday's rumpled clothes, I was ready when he asked, "Will you not do something with the students, Miss Mary?" Standing to face the class, I saw sixty pairs of dark eyes brighten at his suggestion. No more dull English. It was time for fun.

"Would you like to learn a song?" I asked.

"Yes, yes," the eighth graders chorused, leaning forward on their tabletop desks.

"The name of this song is 'Kumbaya.'" The chalk screeched as I wrote *Kumbaya* on the blackboard, guessing at its spelling.

"What does it mean?" asked Mr. Heydarshahi. I had no idea, but that did not stop me.

"Come by here," I answered. "It's a song the Negroes in our country sang when they were slaves," I added, hoping this was true.*

Mr. Heydarshahi translated. *Bandeh siyah*. Black slaves. I heard the Persian words buzzing around the room.

"Of course, we don't have slaves now," I continued, "but people still sing the song. Listen to the first verse."

"Kum-by-ya, my Lord, kum-by-ya," I sang, only a little off-key. The class started to stir. As Mr. Heydarshahi translated, I could feel the laughter he was trying to suppress. I ignored him.

"Repeat after me," I said firmly. "Kum-by-ya, my Lord, kum-by-ya." Still tittering, the class began to sing the line. Mr. Heydarshahi looked away, his shoulders shaking. Resolutely, I sang the second line, which, of course, is exactly like the first. My voice began to shake as well. Could I really be that off-tune? Maybe it was cultural—like Americans snickering at Chinese opera.

The girls couldn't suppress their giggles. Tears coursed down Mr. Heydarshahi's face, he was laughing so hard.

"Perhaps your teacher would like to lead this song," I said.

"I think I must leave the room." Choking back guffaws, he fled through the door.

"Let's do it again, without the laughter," I said, facing the amazed, somewhat abashed eighth graders. And we did. "Someone's laughing, Lord," was particularly apt. We followed that with "Someone's crying, Lord," and for our finale, "Someone's singing, Lord." Off-tune, just like me, Persian-accented American gospel music resounded through the halls of Bahmanyar High School.

---

* It may not be true. Scholars agree that Kumbaya, an older song, sprang to prominence in the U.S. during the civil rights movement.

Mr. Heydarshahi apologized profusely after the students spilled out of the room at the end of class. My anger dissolved. In the heart of the mysterious Middle East, I was the exotic one, rippling through the lives of the Kermanis while they provide the texture for mine.

Foreigners—Yea or Nay?

Journal entry

> I've lost control of my life, ceded it to Mr. Sayeed-Nejad and the Kermanis. I go where I'm told to go, visit who I'm told to visit, stay in when I'd rather be out. I'm pinned into my little corner of the daneshsera and can't do a thing about it.

Fortunately, there were not a lot of westerners in Kerman. It would have been tempting to glide into a group where English was the lingua franca, men and women were expected to get together, and the focus was on events outside the province of Kerman. Still, our Peace Corps contingent had grown. It now included Tom Taaffe, a dark-haired, blue-eyed southern Californian in a vocational training group; he lived at the agriculture school several kilometers outside of town. His job there was unclear to me, but I knew he looked forward to spending Thursday nights and Fridays partying with the guys, doubling the number of Toms in the bazaar. But there were not enough of us to be exclusive.

Mr. Sayeed-Nejad was our gatekeeper. Slowly, he intro-duced Betsy and me to the upstanding members of the city's tiny foreign community. My favorite was Mr. Levandowski, who headed the U.S. Agency for Development (AID) pro-gram in Kerman, known locally as Point Four. We met at a reception he hosted for the elite of the province to meet the U.S. consul from Esfahan.

That evening, Betsy and I followed a manservant into a wide hallway. As I wiped Kerman's dust off my shoes, the low hum of dignified party sounds escaped into the foyer. We hesi-tated at the door, searching the groups of elegantly attired men and women for familiar faces. We had done it again—under-dressed for the occasion. How plain our wool skirts looked amidst all that taffeta. But wait a minute. The leading attrac-tion of Kerman's classrooms is not intimidated by a few glam-orous strangers. Taking a resolute breath, I crossed the room to greet the consul, the other obvious American in the room.

"Why do Iranians call it Point Four?" I asked him after we had exchanged pleasantries.

"It was a Marshall Plan program where the United States sent food assistance to countries in need after World War II," he said, taking a bourbon and water from a tray proffered by a white-coated waiter. "Iran was one of the recipients. Point Four was subsumed by U.S. AID several years ago, but it's still known in Kerman by its original name. Our host directs the very small program we have here." His eyes flickered over to an older man with a shock of white hair who was engaged in ani-mated conversation with my roommate. "That's the director, Mr. Levandowski," he said. "I'll introduce you when he's free."

Of all the people Betsy and I met that evening, including the governor general of Kerman and his wife, the head of the department of agriculture, and the director of city planning,

Mr. Levandowski was the one who stood out. Looking directly at me, he spoke of his desire to improve the lives of the villagers, the stumbling blocks erected by age-old traditions, his concern for his employees, and his interest in us, the young Americans newly arrived in the community. His home would become a retreat, a safe place where I could be myself.

"I feel comfortable with him," I told Betsy. "He knows what's going on in the world; he talks about real things. I don't feel like he's judging me."

"Mr. Sayeed-Nejad says he's one of the good foreigners. Kermanis respect the work he's doing with the villagers," Betsy said. I wondered where I would measure on the good-bad foreigner scale.

After a day of "My name is Parvin. What is your name?" at one school or another, Betsy and I would sit in comfortable easy chairs in Mr. Levandowski's living room, sipping Scotch and soda, while his children—a boy, two, and a girl, four—played with blocks on the floor or chattered to their mother in French and Vietnamese. His petite wife, Suzanne, young enough to be his daughter, talked faster than anyone I had ever met, speaking to Betsy and me in a mystifying mixture of English and French. An excellent cook, she developed recipes with her husband to lure rural Iranians into supplementing their diets—with avocados, for example. These unfamiliar fruits, according to Mr. Levandowski, were rich in minerals and vitamins most village diets lacked, and easy to grow in Kerman's high, arid climate. "Really, I mean it," I wrote to my mother. "Try slicing avocado into chicken soup. It's delicious!"

Mrs. Ardabili, the English wife of the Iranian Episcopalian preacher, was almost the opposite of the outgoing Mr. Levandowski. A nervous type with washed out blond hair, she spent her days chasing after her two young boys while her husband ministered to Kerman's tiny Christian community. As we chatted in the parsonage over tea, I wondered if she had known what she was in for when she married this Christian convert from Azerbaijan.

"I think unmarried girls come to places like Iran because they are in trouble at home," Mr. Ardabili said, munching on a dry biscuit imported from his wife's motherland. "I will be your protector here."

I didn't think protection was what he had in mind. Reluctantly, Betsy and I agreed to attend his Thursday evening English services, the equivalent back home of spending Saturday night on our knees, praying.

"Tell me again why we have to hear that creep preach," I said to Betsy when we were alone. "He makes me feel slimy."

"I can't stand him, either, but we should respect his position. After all, he's a minister."

"Oh, great," I said, tossing my pillow at her.

Decked out in our Sunday finest, we showed up at church the next week. Our presence brought the total number of congregants to five—the minister's wife, an Armenian couple from Azerbaijan, and the two Peace Corps volunteers who didn't know how to say no. As we sat through an interminable sermon on being a Christian in an un-Christian land, I vowed never to spend another Thursday night like that again.

"He's such a creep," Betsy said to Mr. Levandowski, when we were in his study a few days later.

"That charlatan! I wouldn't set foot in his church. Actually, I think Islam is a better religion for developing countries."

"Why?" Betsy asked. "It seems so restrictive."

"Maybe to you," said Mr. Levandowski. "But I've spent a lot of time working in Africa where Islam is spreading rapidly. It teaches people to be proud, to strive for change in this lifetime. Christianity preaches humility: put up with suffering now and be rewarded in heaven. People in developing countries need to be empowered."

How I missed the world of ideas. What little I understood about Islam. It was difficult to perceive how Mr. Levandowski's theories were playing out in Kerman. The cultural norms seemed so set, so unreceptive to change.

Mr. Vicos, a "good" foreigner from Smyrna who had lived in Kerman since 1922, was an enchanting host when we joined him for tea. "He's looking for a new wife," Mr. Sayeed-Nejad teased. As he had already buried two, that didn't bode well for number three. A gold fob dangling from the watch pocket of his three-piece suit, our host regaled us with stories of the Kerman of yore. It was a walled city when he established his carpet export business, and the women wore pure white chadors. Those early years, when the British consulate in Kerman was the center of activity, were the heyday for its foreign population. "Why we even played golf," he recalled. When I looked at Kerman through Mr. Vicos' eyes, it was a dynamic city, evolving to accommodate the vagaries introduced by a foreign population that came, then went.

But there were other foreigners in Kerman, dangerous ones, in Mr. Sayeed-Nejad's opinion. Worried about our virtue and our reputations, he did not want Betsy and me to meet the American mapping crew, who were in Kerman on a joint U.S./Iran project. Nor were we introduced to the European and Canadian men who worked for CENTO, the Central Treaty Organization, which was installing a telephone system to link Karachi to Tehran. These men, in town on short-term contracts without their families, were off-limits, but not out of anyone's mind, especially the Kermanis, who shooed their daughters to the safety of their walled homes the minute one of these frisky foreigners appeared. And Mr. Sayeed-Nejad didn't even mention the Army.

I hadn't known the Army was in town until I caught sight of an empty dung-colored jeep parked on the main street just outside the bazaar, "U.S. Army," in somber green letters, scrolling across its door. Fred was the expert on Kerman, so I asked him about it.

"They're a typical bunch of Army jerks," he said. "They're here in the center of Iran advising the shah on border security. Go figure. I got invited to dinner once. They hate it here. Why do you want to have anything to do with them? If you wanted to hang out with Americans, you should have stayed in the Midwest. It's full of bozos just like these guys."

"Who said I wanted to hang out? I'm just asking."

But he was right. I hadn't even caught a glimpse of the Army guys, but I was pretty sure they were young, male, spoke English, and weren't Peace Corps volunteers. It was a tantalizing thought—American men in the vicinity of Kerman.

Days later, a U.S. Army jeep zipped around the square at the entrance to the bazaar, a cloud of dust billowing in its wake. A young, blond driver lounged behind the wheel, one arm slung over the back of the seat—so relaxed, so casual, so American. As the vehicle sped in our direction, his dark-haired partner yanked off his sunglasses and pointed them straight at us. Betsy threw me a glance.

"Why not?" I said. And without another word, we both raised an arm, and waved at the strangers in crew cuts.

The jeep screeched to a stop and zoomed back to the square full of noonday shoppers, where we stood out, tall and available. Minutes later, we had an invitation to see the movie *Hud* at Army headquarters.

"Can you believe we did that?" Betsy said, watching the jeep speed off down the street. "I'd never be so brazen at home."

"We're not at home. All the rules are different here. Why not this one?" I said. "It's not that I want to be surrounded by Americans, but I know how to behave around them. With Iranian men I keep getting in trouble over nothing. I just want to feel normal."

"Well, we're not Iranians," Betsy said. "We shouldn't be expected to act like them all the time."

"I doubt Mr. Sayeed-Nejad would agree."

The next night, flanked by our dates, Phil and Chris, Betsy and I sank back into the middle of a soft brown couch at Army headquarters, a large, new house with posters of Greece and Turkey on the walls. Ten men, peach fuzz on most of their cheeks, relaxed around the room. The lights dimmed, and the film began to roll. Paul Newman's character was behaving despicably when the couch cushions shifted and Phil's long arm crept around Betsy's shoulders. I must have tensed because Chris, who was bookending my side, whispered, "Don't worry. I'm safe. I've got a girlfriend back home in Missoula. We're going to get married when I get out of this hellhole."

Betsy edged toward me, and Phil's arm returned to the back of the sofa. *Hud* played on, Paul Newman's intense eyes capturing mine. Passion was on the screen, not in this room. Yet there I was, sitting shoulder to shoulder with this stranger who loved a girl in Missoula. What was I trying to prove?

Of course Mr. Sayeed-Nejad found out; this was Kerman. "If you behave like this, Kermanis will refuse to let you teach their daughters," he said, giving each of us a hard look. He pulled himself up out of his chair. "I'm late." Betsy and I stood rooted to the floor of his office, the clomp-clomp of his crutches reverberating on the hard floor as he disappeared down the hall.

Mr. Levandowski was not sympathetic when we related our story. "You knew you were violating Iranian customs when you went out with these men."

"But people don't care when we see the Peace Corps fellows," I said.

"That's different. They're family."

"But I think Iranians expect us to act like Americans, to see other foreigners," Betsy said.

"That's just the trouble," said Mr. Levandowski, his fingers rumpling his white hair. "They don't know what to expect from you."

Malicious Microbes

Visions of flying down an Illinois highway on a Harley-Davidson, my bare arms wrapped around my date's waist, were flickering through my head when I fell asleep several nights after our Army rendezvous. I woke suddenly, those images all but gone. Boy, did my throat hurt. Not a normal sore throat, like at the onset of a cold, but a pain that flamed into my ears and plunged down into my chest. My head throbbed, and my sacrum answered with an ache of its own. The silky dark of the room surrounded me when I unpeeled my eyelids and tried to focus. As I rolled over to flip on the light, a wave of nausea hit.

Betsy stirred in the cot next to me, slung her arm over her head, and curled up even tighter under the load of blankets piled on her bed. I wasn't worried about waking her. We had shared this room for three months. She could sleep through anything. Maybe aspirin would help. I sat up. Somehow, I had to pour a glass of water from the earthenware jug on the floor and retrieve the aspirin bottle from the grey cabinet next to the wall. I put my feet on the floor, grabbed the metal frame of my cot, and stood up, my head spinning. Eying my objectives, I began the long journey, first to the water, then to the aspirin, and finally back to my bed.

This cot was uncomfortable during the best of times. This night, the thin, lumpy mattress and weave of metal springs provided all the relief of a medieval torture machine. I tossed. I turned. I threw off stifling covers, then pulled them back up because I was freezing. Finally, a glimmer of dawn crept across the room. When Betsy woke up, I was seated at our metal table, a cup of weak tea in hand, trying to read Hans Zinsser's *Rats, Lice, and History*. Maybe it was lice. I certainly felt like I had the plague. "I'm sick," I said.

Being sick in Kerman was nothing new to me. In just ten weeks, I had suffered through three awful colds. The "common cold," our friend Fatimeh from the nursing school called it, her precise language striking an unnatural note in my ear. During these common colds I had learned it was extremely rude to blow one's nose in public. Mop-up actions were permissible, but blowing, honking, and snarfing, if they were done at all, were private activities.

My most common ailment was diarrhea. A surfeit of melon and pistachios was somewhat to blame for this malady that struck at least once a week. But unfriendly microbes lurked on hands and handles, skins of poorly peeled fruit, plates and glasses, and the exteriors of pastries and sandwiches—microbes that knew pale foreigners couldn't resist them.

If only my bouts with diarrhea had been a private affair, like blowing my nose was supposed to be. But our room at the dane-shsera was sixty yards from the bathroom. Sixty yards across a courtyard teeming with groups of young girls, who wanted to practice their English when there was not a moment to spare. Sixty yards past classrooms full of daydreaming students—a gauntlet of "How vare you?" and "I vant to speak English" between our room and the seclusion of a private bathroom stall.

This day, my cheeks flushed and my palms sweaty with fever, would be no different. I pulled my blue trench coat on over my nightgown, shoved my feet into flip-flops, and readied myself for the courtyard dash.

"Hello, Mees Mary. How vare you?" accosted me as I stepped into the glaring sun.

"I have a sore throat," I said, not breaking my pace. As I hurried toward the bathroom building, comments in Persian followed me.

"What's the matter with her?"

"She has a temperature. I know she does. Look at her cheeks."

My face freshly washed, I had just crawled back under the covers, when the first knock at the door sounded. "I understand you are unwell." Mr. Golzadeh, the assistant principal of the school, stood in the doorway. "What seems to be the matter?" he asked, a hint of British flavoring his English.

"My throat hurts, and I ache all over," I said, lying back on the pillow.

"She should eat 'cold,'" advised a voice in Persian from beyond, one of the students hovering outside the door. "She should eat yogurt."

"No, no," said another. "With a fever, she mustn't eat anything. Though, if she's hungry, 'hot' foods, you know, lamb and nuts, would be really bad for her."

"Cold food, hot food—all wives' tales," said Mr. Golzadeh. "Let her rest. She'll get better. I am here in the office all day, if you need me," he said in English as he left.

Mr. Golzadeh's knock was the first in a long line of raps. "You're sick. You mustn't be alone," said Kobra-khanum, who had left her cottage at the gate to perch on the edge of my cot. "I've got to fix lunch. I'll send Ali to sit with you." Ali was her eight-year-old son.

"Please don't worry. Betsy-khanum is here with me. I'm not alone."

Kobra-khanum, with her sons Ali and Reza.

But Betsy, it turned out, wasn't feeling so hot either. We were joined at the hip; I couldn't even get sick by myself. We were both in bed by the time Mr. Sayeed-Nejad swung in, ker-thunk, ker-thunk on his crutches. A tall, portly man in a charcoal overcoat and gray fedora followed him inside. "This is Dr. Moghadam," said Mr. Sayeed-Nejad.

The doctor's nose elevated as he surveyed our room. Looking at our abode through his eyes, I could understand why. Books were piled high on our only table and beneath the folding chairs. Glasses holding the dregs of the morning's tea shared the remaining few inches of the tabletop with crusts from last night's sandwiches. Yesterday's clothes were draped over the open door to our metal closet. A scorched aluminum kettle simmered on the kerosene heater. This was hardly the residence of elegant western women.

"Do you want to go to hospital?" the doctor asked, before so much as casting a glance at our throats. Trained by the Brits— no "the" before hospital, the English teacher in me noticed.

"No one goes to the hospital for a cold. I just want something to make my sore throat go away." Reluctantly, the doctor peered down our throats and took our temperatures.

"Your throats are very red, and you have fever," he said.

The doctor and Mr. Sayeed-Nejad conferred. Was that it? Was he going to leave? Instead, he sent Ali to direct his driver and jeep around to our room. We were going to hospital.

This was ridiculous. People didn't go to the hospital for a sore throat. I hadn't stayed in one since birth. But Mr. Sayeed-Nejad was not taking any chances. While the men waited outside, I stumbled into a skirt and blouse, and shoved my toothbrush, a comb, nightgown, and a change of clothes into the plastic carry-all I used for shopping. Betsy tied her tangled brown hair up with a bandanna and slipped her feet into Dr.

Scholl's wooden clogs. Struggling into my coat, I followed her into the back seat of the jeep. A group of daneshsera students gathered around the vehicle as Mr. Sayeed-Nejad swung into the front seat next to the doctor and his driver.

"*Koja meereed?*" ("Where are you going?") the girls called in Persian and English.

"Children, be quiet," Mr. Sayeed-Nejad answered them in Persian. "The teachers are sick. The doctor is taking them to the hospital."

The driver steered the jeep through the courtyard, out onto Zarisse Street, and headed down the road to Arjomand Hospital, a private facility built by Kerman's king of carpets. Mercifully, the trip was short.

We followed the doctor into a large, light room, unique because its dresser, table, and chairs were made from wood—a rarity in Kerman. I crawled between cool, white sheets, grateful that someone else was in charge. Female nurses in bright white uniforms greeted us with needles—one penicillin, one vitamin C, and one unknown. Sinking down into the bed, my eyes drifted shut. At last I could rest.

Or so I thought. Sleep would not come, but company did. In the other bed, Betsy closed her eyes, ignoring the parade of female patients and their relatives the nurses brought in so the poor, sick foreigners wouldn't be alone. It felt rude to ignore them, so I attempted to make polite conversation, my Persian doing as poorly as I was:

"Yes, I'm an American..." "I teach English..." "I like Kerman. The people are very kind and the skies are beautiful..." "I'm from Chicago. Where are you from?" "No, I'm not married..." "I have one brother. He lives in Chicago. How many brothers and sisters do you have?" "Of course I miss my mother, but she understands…" "Why am I in the hospital? I have a fever and my throat is very sore."

As they came and went, their comments to each other drifted my way.

"I don't understand why the foreigners are in the hospital," said one.

"They are alone. They don't have any family to take care of them," said another.

Unfortunately, she was right. We were in the hospital because we were incapable of caring for ourselves.

And if this wasn't embarrassing enough, Mr. Sayeed-Nejad showed up again, this time herding Tom and Fred. Why couldn't Mr. Sayeed-Nejad understand that constant companionship for the ill was not an American custom?

Tom Sisul was quiet. Fred, fractious and rarely silent, took one look and said, "You don't look all that sick to me." Mr. Sayeed-Nejad shushed him. Betsy pulled the covers up and shut her eyes. I looked around for something to talk about.

"Don't we have a nice room?" I said.

"Yeah, it's too bad sick Kermanis can't afford to stay here," Fred said.

Not to be deterred, I continued. "I didn't realize how much I miss wood furniture. I wish there were more tables and chairs like these around. They're so much warmer than all those metal things."

This was too much for Fred. "Tell me, you flew down here. You've driven to villages around Kerman. Did you ever, even once, see a tree big enough to use for furniture?"

I closed my eyes and lay back on my pillow. Fred and I agreed on one thing. Neither of us wanted him here. I didn't want to think about being a privileged foreigner, or about Kermanis who couldn't afford health care. I didn't want to think about why all office furniture in Kerman was made of metal. I didn't want to think, period.

Our stay lasted only two days. Just when I was getting accustomed to well-balanced meals appearing regularly without any effort on my part, it was time to go home. Dr. Moghadam pronounced us cured the morning after I woke up shivering in the middle of the night, my nightgown and sheets soaked. My fever had broken. Betsy, still in lock-step, was feeling better, too.

I felt uneasy as we hailed a cab outside the hospital. Our stay there had brought the differences between the Kermanis and us into high relief. They knew only scared foreigners, lacking families to care for them, would go to a hospital for a fever and a sore throat. It was assumed that we had the resources to stay in a private room in Kerman's best facility for the flimsiest of reasons. But money was never mentioned. Not a toman changed hands at the hospital.

Within minutes we were back where we had started, in our room on the courtyard, students milling around outside, a mile away from the john, wondering what creative concoction we could cook for dinner. Except for the inevitable questions about our health, we might not have been "in hospital." I never found out if the doctor sent the bill to Uncle Sam.

An Embarrassment of Nuts

The full, rich aroma of lamb burgers lingered in the bare living room of the guys' house in the copper bazaar. Betsy and I had been thrashing feverishly in a hospital room only days earlier, yet here we were on a cool November evening, relaxing after Peace Corps Kerman's weekly communal meal. It was Thursday evening, *shab-e jomeh*, the beginning of the Muslim Sabbath.

Tom Taaffe, the new addition to our group, placed a bowlful of pistachios between Betsy and me and handed us each a beer—our third of the evening. I really shouldn't, I thought. But I took a swig of beer and reached for a nut, glanced at the one I'd selected, then flicked it aside. It was a reject, one of those pistachios whose shell is impossibly closed. My third try was the lucky one. Absentmindedly, I pried the halves apart, and tossed the nut into my mouth, barely chewing before I swallowed.

Stretching out on the red kilim covering the long living room floor, I relaxed against a big bolster. Apart from the kerosene heater whose tin exhaust pipe bisected the room, the kilim and bolsters were the only furnishings. Mr. Sayeed-Nejad and Fred were playing backgammon, letting out victorious whoops whenever one bettered the other. The two Toms watched the game, and I noticed everyone sneaking an occasional peek at Betsy and me as we leafed through Fred's collection of *New Yorkers*, sipped Shams beer from green glass bottles, and munched on pistachio nuts—one for me, two for the pile of rejects on the floor.

I looked forward to these weekly get-togethers where I did not have to speak special English or explain my American behavior. One would think the male volunteers would appreciate some female company, but often they didn't seem to. Fred, the alpha male, set the tone. Touting his working-class California roots, with barely a glimmer of humor he dismissed Betsy and me as "privileged East Coast snobs," lumping us together like the Kermanis did. Indistinguishable, we became the pain-in-the-neck younger sister he was forced to entertain. Scathing criticisms careened off his tongue. "All you do is complain. You knew before you got here you couldn't ride a bicycle," he told me. But it was Betsy who resented the lack of wheels; I hated the early curfew. If I hadn't needed a respite from the confines of the daneshsera, I would have ignored him.

The Toms followed Fred's lead, although I doubted their hearts were in it. Tom Sisul wouldn't confront Fred unless absolutely necessary; Tom Taaffe was a polite, conciliatory fellow who wanted everyone to get along. Neither would ever be rude, so why the sly glances from the male quartet at the other end of the room? I dug down in the bowl for more nuts, the pile of shells and rejects mounting.

Pistachios were a major food group for me. Sometimes they were my dinner, other times a side dish to accompany a sandwich, perhaps a teacake, or if I was lucky, rice. In any other setting, my meals would have been unrecognizable: melon for supper; left-over stale bread at breakfast; and for lunch, the main meal of the day, some barely chewable concoction of lamb and tomatoes that either Betsy or I boiled up on our two-burner stove. Foraging for food was a hassle. The bazaar had an unending supply of pistachios, no preparation was required, and tossing them down was effortless. Pistachios were easy.

I unfastened the button on my snug waistband, and helped myself to a nut. Damn, another reject. Something was weird. I inspected the pile of shells. There were always some nuts that had not split open, but that many? I must have looked confused because a howl of laughter broke out at the back-gammon end of the room.

"Having trouble getting at those nuts, Mary?" Fred asked.

"There do seem to be a lot of rejects," I said.

Mr. Sayeed-Nejad could not contain himself. "We've been saving unopened pistachios for weeks. We added a few regular ones so you wouldn't suspect. Isn't it a good joke? Here, these are okay." He shoved another bowl of pistachios across the floor towards Betsy and me.

"No thanks, we've had plenty." I pushed the bowl back to the tricksters. A red flush crept across my face. I'd been caught pigging out, a *por khor*, one who eats to overflowing.

Betsy's pile of shells was as big as mine, but she was laughing. Fuming, I put my head down and studied my *New Yorker*. It was the pistachios' fault. They were such wimpy nuts, so cooperative, opening themselves up for the taking. Not at all like the nuts where I grew up. Nuts were big and bold in West Virginia, and knew how to put up a struggle.

Black walnuts didn't come by the kilo in Huntington's grocery stores when I was a child. Instead, wrapped in oozing, brownish green hulls, they plopped to the ground from two trees in our front yard. Should you pick up one of these squishy things with your bare hands, it wouldn't be a secret. Their brown stain marked you for weeks.

Each year, when the air was heavy with the smell of burning leaves and our lawn was carpeted with leaking hulls, my dad would announce the walnut harvest. Wearing our oldest clothes and grimy gloves, my little brother Don and I scampered around the yard, picking up gooey walnuts and tossing them into a gunny sack. Daddy, dressed for the occasion in gardening pants stained beyond an identifiable color, kneaded the sack, separated the hulls from the hard black shells, and put the nuts in a pail. Trying not to touch anything with his walnut-inked gloves, he headed for our cool basement to spread the bucketful of moist walnuts out on newspapers. My brother and I were forbidden to go near them while they dried.

A week or two later, it was time to crack some open. To get at the dark, sweet meat, my father hunkered on the concrete basement floor, put a dried nut on his heavy anvil, and struck it with a big hammer. My job was to take a nut pick, extract the nutmeat, and put it into a small bowl. When the bowl was full, we were finished. There was no absent-minded munching of this hard earned treat, though my father, who loved all things nutty, probably sampled a few with his evening Martini, leaving the rest for Mother's black walnut cookies.

Then there were hickory nuts. Pail in hand, we climbed into the woods behind our house to gather nuts under the wild hickory trees that dotted the hillside. If we timed our harvest correctly, they had already shed their brown hulls. Only cracking the shell remained, which again involved Daddy, the anvil, and his hammer. Mother's hickory nut cake was the end result. Nuts played only a minor role in my West Virginia childhood, a thin strand in the protective fabric of home and family, but in Kerman they were a barometer of my well-being.

Hiding behind the *New Yorker* in Fred and Tom's living room, I was still smarting. In this city, every action had the potential to expose me. Bare legs, even when the temperature reached 100, elicited whispers and stares. A sheet of flat bread sticking out of my blue tote bag was either a courageous act or one of defiance; to be caught carrying bread embarrassed Kermanis. While I knew my intentions weren't licentious, I didn't like being seen as shameless. This incident with the pistachios, half joke, half taunt, proved that it wasn't safe to let down my guard, even among Americans.

Betsy jolted me out of my thoughts. "It's eight o'clock, we're going to be late. Tom Taaffe's going with us to catch a cab." Pulling myself up from the floor, I smoothed my skirt, and refastened its waistband. As I peered down at the offending mound of pistachio shells I imagined them transforming into oozing black walnut hulls and hard hickory shells. There it was—my life in nuts.

"How'd you like our joke, Mary? You seemed kind of quiet," Tom said during our walk through the deserted marketplace.

"Funny, funny. I'll think of some way to get even." And I'll be damned if you guys will catch me gorging on pistachios again, I added silently.

When Betsy rang the daneshsera's bell, Kobra-khanum opened the school's imposing metal gate, stifling a yawn and complaining we were keeping her awake. It was almost 8:30. Hoping she would not detect the smell of beer, I apologized. Betsy and I hurried along the school's walkways, past the volleyball court with the sleeping donkey tethered to a light post, past row after row of pistachio trees, their nuts long gone, their fallen leaves blowing across our path.

Thankful for Esfahan

Letter home

> Can you believe it? Esfahan has Kool-Aid,
> Kellogg's Rice Krispies, Quaker Oats, Instant
> Maxwell House coffee, Knorr soups, Nestlé cocoa,
> even toilet paper, all arranged neatly in a store that
> caters to foreigners.

We were heading into the American holiday season—cold weather, mitigated by a cornucopia of food, parties, and celebrations. When Peace Corps Tehran declared that Thanksgiving was an official holiday even in Iran, Carol, Doris, and Dottie, English teachers in Esfahan's universities, issued a general invitation to Iran 4 volunteers to enjoy it with them. Betsy and I dashed to the telegraph office to accept.

How hungry I was for contact with familiar faces. And Esfahan, a twelve-hour bus ride northwest from Kerman, was a great destination, famous for its elaborately tiled mosques, wide tree-lined avenues, and long covered bazaar—all visions of Shah Abbas, the noted late-sixteenth-century ruler who made it his capital.

Honking horns and humming crowds woke me up. It took a moment or two to register that I was in a hotel near Esfahan's bus station, having arrived in the middle of the night. Shivering, I pulled on my coat and climbed over our suitcases to peer out the window. Four floors below, Iranian Peykan automobiles jockeyed for space with sleek Mercedes Benzes on the broad, tree-lined thoroughfare. Women in high heels and business suits brushed by others clasping somber chadors across their faces, bright plastic shopping bags edging out from the garments' folds. Well-dressed men, worry beads dangling from their pockets, shared the sidewalks with grizzled vendors and shopkeepers raising their store shutters. Groups of tow-headed tourists, bulky packs slung over their shoulders, meandered along the streets. From my perch above the action I could feel the city pulsing. This was definitely not Kerman.

The minute my feet hit Chehar Bagh, Esfahan's main avenue, I knew I would not regret those long hours spent on a cramped bus. Betsy and I lugged our suitcases along the street, gaping at the souvenirs gleaming from every store window. Touristy knick-knacks had never looked so good: decorated ceramic tiles, colorful enameled tea sets, engraved brass trays, flowery tablecloths—all tastefully arranged so someone just like me would want to buy them. I thought I was in Paris.

Just like a European city, Esfahan was in the midst of a strike. The cab and bus drivers were refusing to work, but we caught a ride with a private entrepreneur, arriving at the volunteers' apartment in Julfa, the Armenian Christian section of town in time to help with Thanksgiving preparations. This was a cooperative affair, orchestrated by Carol, whose slow Mississippi drawl belied her efficiency. Betsy parboiled small onions while Dottie sectioned oranges. Doris punctuated the proceedings with hilarious commentary, delivered in broad New York City tones. The whole process, fun from beginning to end, took less than an hour.

Later that evening, the welcoming aroma of an American feast filled the small living room. Twelve volunteers, men and women from sites as distant as Tehran and Kerman, sat cross-legged on the floor, devouring turkey. Those birds had roasted in pots in a restaurant two miles away. With requests like "Please pass the cranberry sauce" and "May I have some more squash?" we could have been in the United States. Soon, bits of orange segments from ambrosia, the finale to the holiday in Dottie's Georgia home, were all that remained.

"This was wonderful," said Ken, swiping his mouth with a coarse paper towel. "I haven't had a dinner like this since I left the States." The sole volunteer in a small town, he ate his meals in the local teahouse.

"Can't you get a servant?" asked Carol. "Ours doesn't cost very much. She shops, cleans, does the laundry, and cooks the main meal. At first I felt guilty about hiring someone, but all the Iranians at the university have help."

"I live in one room with no running water," Ken said. "It just won't work."

I poured another glass of rosy Armenian wine, listening to the conversation floating around me. "My freshman class at the university is studying Shakespeare," Carol said. "We'll read Scott and Byron next semester."

"Boy, you really do have everything in Esfahan," Ken said, a note of envy creeping into his voice. "My classes are struggling with 'Where are you going?'"

It was a long night, nine of us tossing about on pads and blankets strewn around the living room floor. Finally, rays of sunshine began to creep in around the curtains. I got up when I heard pans banging in the kitchen.

"I have to take these pots back to the restaurant," said Doris, pulling on a bright red jacket. "Want to come along? I could use some help. There won't be any taxis."

Chatting easily, we plodded the two miles down Friday-empty streets, shifting the heavy copper pots from hand to hand.

"Are you having problems making your money last from month to month?" asked Doris. "It seems like I'm always broke."

"I don't have anything to spend money on. No parties, can't buy wine, no pricey western foods to tempt me. Our Peace Corps allotment is just fine in Kerman."

We were split on whether the Peace Corps belonged in Iran. Doris insisted that the Iranian government could afford to hire teachers. Why should the American government pay for them? If Doris was right, that meant I had no justification for being here. That I spent most of my time in Kerman's class-rooms sitting silently, not doing much of anything, strength-ened her argument. But there had to be a reason I was in Iran struggling with a new culture, dealing with the social restric-tions imposed on Betsy and me. The shah would never spend oil dollars on foreign teachers for provincial high schools, I argued. Maybe my work would improve some Kermani girl's chance to get into Doris's university. But when I took myself out of the equation, Doris was right. Iran was wealthy. Why was the Peace Corps in such an affluent country? Politics, we were sure, played a role in determining which nations wel-comed volunteers. Even teachers were part of America's Cold War arsenal.

The pots felt even heavier by the time we turned into a narrow alley and entered a small restaurant. A stooped man, broom in hand, asked us what we wanted. The conversation in Farsi, about whose pots they were and why we wanted to leave them, went back and forth. Finally we convinced him to take them.

"I don't get to speak a lot of Farsi," Doris said after we left the restaurant and the pots behind.

"Well, that's one thing I have plenty of," I said. "After 'how are you,' or 'where is your mother,' the conversation switches to Farsi, leaving me in the dark most of the time."

I was immersed in the Persian language in Kerman. Without realizing it, I was absorbing its rhythm and flow, and my vocabulary was growing. In Esfahan's cosmopolitan milieu, it was difficult, even for volunteers who had excelled in Farsi during training, to hone their language skills.

Betsy and I spent the next two days doing things we could not do in Kerman. I played the international sophisticate at a party thrown by CENTO, declaring to a British journalist that only by visiting the distant provinces would he discover the real Iran. From my vast experience of almost three months, I was certain Esfahan was far too cosmopolitan to qualify as truly Iranian. I lived in the real Iran, with donkeys, chadors, dusty roads, and eight p.m. curfews for American women.

We left paradise Saturday night, our long legs scrunched into bus seats built for smaller frames. Twelve hours later, waiting in the women's section of a restaurant in Rafsanjan for bus repairs, images of that other world and the warm community of Peace Corps volunteers swirled about. Perhaps I lived in the "real Iran," but I had found a refuge. I was very thankful for Esfahan.

Christmas

Kerman seemed different when Betsy and I got back after our Thanksgiving respite. A struggling stranger when I left, I returned to a familiar, welcoming place. It was starting to feel like the holidays, something unexpected so far from home.

Thanksgiving in Illinois signaled the beginning of a frenetic, happy few weeks that raced by until the second day of January, when time jerked to a stop, snared in winter's long, cold nights. The signposts were much subtler in Kerman. The days, although cold, seldom were freezing; there were no Christmas decorations, piped in Santa Claus music, or sheets of wrapping paper stacked in the bazaar's corners.

The season, however, started with a gift. The day after we returned to Kerman, Betsy and I met with our after-school conversation class of high school seniors. On the blackboard was a large chalk drawing of both of us, "Miss Betsy and Miss Mary, we missed you," printed in block letters below. The images were flattering; even the punctuation was correct. With a present like this, no wonder we felt festive.

Betsy got into the spirit right away, deciding to decorate our room. "Go right ahead," I said. "You're the creative one." So she did, fashioning ornaments with cardboard and brightly colored yarn; making silver trumpets from tin foil; and stringing strands of the popcorn we had cadged from Mr. Levandowski who had U.S. Commissary privileges. (The Peace Corps strictures against using the commissary were a dim memory in Kerman where we seldom faced the temptation.) When a workman hauling a long cedar branch showed up at our door, explaining the daneshsera's vice-principal had sent it "for your holiday," Betsy really flew into action.

"A Christmas tree. Perfect! I can make snow from Tide and water." As soon as our tree was in place she mixed up a very odoriferous, soapy concoction in our only bowl, and dabbed it on the tree fronds.

It looked so gay in our little hideaway, we invited our colleagues to a party. I shopped for oranges, end of the season grapes, four kinds of cookies, and three types of candy. We added a dozen tea glasses to our cupboard, as well as another set of the rose-covered china plates found in every housewares store in the bazaar. Remembering that Mrs. Nahidi had bragged about Kerman's "good Gulabi tea," I bought a package, Gulabi printed in both Farsi and English on its label, imported straight from India, its seller claimed. In lieu of a real samovar, it would steep in a small teapot perched on the inverted lid of the kettle simmering on the kerosene heater.

Like the Magi from the East, our guests came bearing gifts: the covers of Mrs. Farvahari's photo album were elaborately decorated with leaping gazelles and entwined vines; Mrs. Mesbah presented us with a box of *ghaz*, a sweet nougat candy her husband brought home from Esfahan; Miss Aghassi gave us a tin of baklava, a specialty of Yazd; from Mrs. Nahidi we received a book of Hafez's poetry, written in Persian, "for when you learn how to read," she said. I was touched and surprised. Kermanis did not usually bring presents to a tea party. I had not realized our friends knew anything about Christmas and the gift giving it entailed.

Oohing and aahing over my roommate's decorations, our guests took chairs around the table.

"Miss Betsy's very creative," Mrs. Farvahari said. "Kermani women are good with their hands, too. Our friend Miss Aghassi is an excellent seamstress."

Mrs. Nahidi translated for Miss Aghassi, who demurred, but looked pleased.

"You have a very big kilim," Mrs. Mesbah said, looking at the woven red rug covering much of our floor. "How much you pay for it?"

"One thousand tomans," about $130, I answered, automatically shaving off a third of the cost so I wouldn't be chided for overpaying.

"You bargained well," said Mrs. Nahidi. "Usually, they cost a little more." My lie lay heavy on my lips as she looked around the room. "Where do you prepare your meals?" she asked.

"Right here at the table," Betsy said. "We're getting better at it."

Teachers play tic-tac-toe at the daneshsera Christmas party.

"Befarmayeed" ("Please, help yourself"), I repeated to first one guest, then another as I offered glasses of tea from our plastic tray. "Oh no, I couldn't," each insisted several times before accepting. Betsy followed with plates, oranges, and small knives for peeling. In the 1950s and '60s, in the places where I lived, oranges were squeezed. The knife stymied me, but our guests were experts. "Don't be uncomfortable, Miss Mary," Mrs. Mesbah said. "It's easy. See, I can take the entire peel off in one piece. Let me help you."

So we peeled and ate and rinsed tea glasses out in a bucket before refilling them. The first rounds of food were over when Betsy suggested we play games. After she instructed our guests on the finer points of tic-tac-toe and hangman, they grabbed their pens and began some of the most cutthroat rounds I have ever witnessed.

"Let's tell fortunes," Miss Aghassi suggested when the games were over. "Where's the book of Hafez's poetry Mrs. Nahidi gave you? You know his verses can predict the future."

Betsy handed her the volume, which she opened to an arbitrary page. "Close your eyes, and point," Miss Aghassi said. Betsy obeyed, and Miss Aghassi read the verse where Betsy's finger had fallen, in sonorous formal Persian.

"I'm sorry, I don't understand what it says," Betsy said. Mrs. Nahidi translated:

One passion has quickened the heart and the soul,
The Beloved's presence alone they have sought—
Love at least exists; yet if Love were not,
Heart and soul would sink to the common lot—
All things are nought!*

---

* From *Hafiz: the Mystic Poets*, translated and with notes by Gertrude Bell. Woodstock, VT: Skylight Paths, 2004, p. 59.

"What a good fortune, Miss Betsy!" Mrs. Mesbah said. "It means you will be very happy in love."

None of the fortunes revealed that day were sad. Pregnant Mrs. Mesbah's was about children, childless Mrs. Farvahari's was about accepting one's fate, Miss Aghassi's spoke of finding a true love, and Mrs. Nahidi's predicted wisdom in the later stages of life. Mine was a little different; it extolled the virtues of an open mind:

Tempted by one poor grain of corn! Wherefore
Absolve and pardon him that turns away
Though the soft breath of Truth reaches his ears,
For two-and-seventy jangling creeds he hears,
And loud-voiced Fable calls him ceasefully.*

The party was winding down. The last of the candy lay ignored on the ladies' plates, and I was making a final round with glasses of tea, when I heard Mrs. Nahidi ask in Persian, "Shall I say something about the tea?" Her colleagues nodded.

"Miss Betsy, Miss Mary," she began. "Here in Kerman we have a really good tea…"

"But I bought the tea you told me about, the one in the red wrapper," I said. "It says 'Gulabi Tea.'"

"Let me see the package." Confused, I brought out the offending product.

"See! Miss Mary bought the package with the blue label."

"Ohhhh," they echoed. "The blue label."

"Miss Mary, how much did you pay for this tea?" Mrs. Nahidi asked.

"It was less than I thought it would be. Ten tomans."

---

* Hafiz, *op.cit.*, p. 94.

"The blue-labeled tea is the imitation," Mrs. Nahidi said. "You must buy the package with the brown label. It costs almost twice as much. It's a very good tea. It comes from India."

Soon our friends were donning coats, draping chadors over heads and shoulders, and saying goodbye.

"We had lots of fun," Mrs. Mesbah said as she stepped into the daneshsera's courtyard, her chador wrapped tightly around her bulging body. "I really liked the games. The tree is beautiful, too, but don't you get tired of the smell of soap? Maybe it's because I'm pregnant, but it made me feel a little sick."

"I wasn't expecting to have such a good time," I said to Betsy as we rinsed off dirty cups and dishes in the bucket of water. "You're the lucky one. Love will find you, while I have to keep searching for an open mind."

Christmas day, instead of sitting in front of a blazing fireplace opening packages with my family, I was going to church. Betsy, whose last piano lesson was in the fourth grade, had been commandeered to play the organ for the holiday service; I couldn't imagine staying at the daneshsera alone on Christmas.

My thoughts were in Homewood. Eleven a.m. here would still be the middle of the night in Illinois. While we were in a taxi on our way to church in the Muslim Middle East, back home Santa was sliding down chimneys, filling stockings, and stuffing down milk and cookies. The cab stopped at the gate to the church's chapel. As Betsy and I scooted out, the driver was extolling his city's kind inhabitants and glorious skies. "All Kermanis know," he added, accepting our fares, "that this is the best place in Iran to live."

A small congregation, ten of us to be exact, gathered in the chapel for the English language church service. It began with hymns. As the ancient organ wheezed and sputtered, Pastor

Ardabili stood erect at the altar, intent on singing every verse
of every song. But he hadn't reckoned on my roommate. After
the organ and congregants had clashed their way through four
hymns, Betsy rose and faced the congregation. "This is the
final hymn," she said, "and I'm only playing the first verse."

The pastor moved on to lessons from the scriptures. As he
read, my mind wandered to Illinois and the lush midnight services at the Flossmoor Community Church. I could smell the
fragrant balsam wreaths, each with a single red bow, adorning
every pew. Banks of red and white poinsettias filled the stairs
leading to the altar, and garlands of pine boughs swung from
the sanctuary's wooden arches. My mother, brother, and I sat
on the center aisle waiting for the processional, then winked
at my dad as he strode past in his scarlet robe, one of four
baritones in a choir of thirty. The service was awe-inspiring,
hushed and magic. As the lights dimmed, twenty candle-bear-
ers appeared at the nave. Shadows from their flickering tapers
danced on the ceiling, lending an air of mystery to the darkened church. When Evelyn Riggs rose to sing "Ave Maria," we
held our breaths, waiting for her clear tones to fill the sanctuary with the wonder and hope of Christmas.

Something in the pastor's voice brought me back to Kerman.
"Christmas is being buried in commercialism," he said. From
his pulpit in the heart of Iran, Mr. Ardabili demanded: "Put
Christ back into Christmas!"

Church over, a stunning Christmas fete was waiting for us
at the agriculture school. Tom Taaffe had crammed his trunk
from home with holiday decorations; his living room was more
festive than my mother's in Homewood. A cedar limb in the
corner was festooned with delicate glass ornaments and strands
of popcorn. From crepe paper, he had fashioned a fireplace,

and hung stockings for everyone along its mantel. Red and green paper chains ringed the room, and candles were stylishly grouped on the buffet table.

We had started out cheerfully, squeezed into Mr. Sanaati's jeep, bouncing along the five miles of dirt road leading from Kerman to the school where Tom lived and worked. I balanced a saucepan of runny red Jell-O on my lap, while Betsy clasped a bowl of smashed candied yams and pineapple on hers. "Fred and I brought the good stuff," Tom Sisul said, pointing to the back of the jeep where bottles of beer jostled jars of *arak*, Iran's fiery vodka. Fred, in the back with Betsy and me, stared out the window; in the front, Tom and Mr. Sayeed-Nejad taught Mr. Sanaati to say Merry Christmas in English.

Tom Taaffe was waiting at his door as the jeep pulled into the ag school grounds. "Befarmayeed," he said, with a mock bow to his guests.

"Merry Christmas," we said, following Mr. Sayeed-Nejad and Mr. Sanaati into Tom's living quarters.

Betsy and I headed for the kitchen where Fatimeh, who worked for Tom Taaffe as well as the guys in the bazaar, was putting the finishing touches on dinner. The golden brown turkey, formerly an ag school denizen, was on the table.

"We had a bit of a catastrophe here," Tom said. "Fatimeh deep-fried Tom Turkey."

"Oops," Betsy said. "But he looks fine."

Our host handed me a glass. "Eggnog. My mother sent me the recipe, but I had to use the local hooch instead of rum."

"Not bad," I said, sampling his experiment as I strolled into the living room. "The arak gives it sort of a flaming grapey flavor."

"Cheers," said Mr. Sanaati, hoisting his glass.

"*Besalamatee*" ("To your health"), Fred and Mr. Sayeed-Nejad added.

Thirsty, we drained our glasses quickly. It was time to carve the turkey.

Fred and Tom Sisul downed another drink while Betsy and I loaded the buffet table. What a feast! Besides traditional Thanksgiving fare, Fatimeh had made three kinds of *khoresh* (stew). The rice was delicious, the yogurt thick, the greens fresh, the turkey breast moist. I couldn't remember a meal as perfect as this.

I leaned back in the stiff parlor chair and took a sip of beer. The men had foregone eggnog for straight arak. Both Toms had happy smiles on their faces, Mr. Sayeed-Nejad's shoulders were dancing, and Mr. Sanaati kept practicing "Merry Christmas." Fred, however, was noticeably quiet; his eyebrows were knit together, his face immobile. Maybe turkey, khoresh, and arak were just too much. Tom Taaffe pulled a Santa Claus hat on over his wavy hair, switched on the tape recorder, and started passing around the Christmas stockings. Bing Crosby began crooning "Silent Night" in the living room of the ag school by the desert outside of Kerman.

"Shut that crap up!" Fred demanded. "I came all the way to Iran just to get away from this kind of sloppy sentimentality."

Tom Taaffe looked stunned. Wiggling the peak of his Santa hat, he handed Fred a sock bulging with nuts, candy, and oranges. "Come on, Fred, get in the holiday spirit. See what St. Nick's brought you." But he turned Bing down a little before he handed out the rest of the stockings.

Fred dropped the sock on the floor and sat back in his chair, glowering. The rest of us exclaimed over the contents of our stockings, pretending everything was fine.

"Look," Mr. Sayeed-Nejad said, unwrapping a piece of the white nougat candy, "I've got ghaz from Esfahan."

"And these oranges are finally the right color," I said. "Not that unripe green they've been for months."

But Fred's outburst had sent a cold chill through the room. Darts of disapproval shot out from his truculent corner.

Shrugging his shoulders, Tom pulled off the Santa hat and passed around the bottle of arak. Bing Crosby was caroling "O Come All Ye Faithful." Fred began to pace.

"If you're going to keep this up, if you're going insult our Iranian guests like this, I'll have to leave."

"I'm not insulted," said Mr. Sayeed-Nejad. "How can I be insulted when we've just had such a wonderful dinner? And Mr. Sanaati's not offended. Look at him." We all looked. Mr. Sanaati, whose lack of English left him clueless about the problem, appeared to be happy, if a bit confused.

"This is ridiculous," Fred said. "I'm going home. What did you do with my coat?"

Betsy was intent on diffusing the situation. "Come on, Fred," she said, "we're miles from town. It's too far to walk. Let's go into Tom's room. They can listen to carols if they want, but we don't have to."

"Be my guest," said Tom, holding open the door to his bedroom. To my surprise, Fred followed Betsy, banging the door closed behind him.

The rest of us looked at each other. Bing was singing "Away in a Manger," but the Christmas spell was broken. Tom Taaffe dropped into a chair at the buffet table, putting his head in his hands. Shaking his head in disbelief, Tom Sisul sipped a glass of arak.

"What's going on?" Mr. Sanaati asked Mr. Sayeed-Nejad in Persian.

"Mr. Jones is very uncomfortable," Mr. Sayeed-Nejad answered.

Something inside of me exploded. To think I'd been working hard to impress this fellow, presuming he possessed the solution to the riddle of Kerman. Well, that was over. I didn't give a damn about what Fred Jones thought.

"It's time to go home," Tom Sisul said, pulling his long body up out of his chair. He ambled over to the door of Tom Taaffe's bedroom and knocked. "Come on you guys," he called. "We're leaving." Minutes later, we were in Mr. Sanaati's jeep, headed toward the lights of the city.

The ride back to Kerman was quiet. I tried sending my own shock waves of disapproval in Fred's direction, but he remained oblivious, staring out the window. As Betsy and I climbed out of Mr. Sanaati's car at the daneshsera's gate, Fred spoke for the first time.

"You'll be coming to our house New Year's Eve, won't you?" he asked.

"Sure," Betsy answered. I rang the bell. Mr. Sanaati and the others drove off into the night.

Tweest!!

"Tweest!" commanded our Iranian hostess, grabbing my hand and the hand of the tall, rugged Canadian she had chosen as my dance partner. It was New Year's Eve, and Mr. Sayeed-Nejad's admonition to follow the lead of the governor general's wife, who at this moment was sedately sipping tea, was proving impossible.

Despite Fred's abominable Christmas Day outburst, Betsy and I had planned to celebrate with the Peace Corps fellows, our curfew extended to 9:30. Instead, we were at a gala event thrown by the head of the Iran Oil Company in Kerman, a man with more than enough influence to insist on our presence, overriding Mr. Sayeed-Nejad's objections.

It amazed me that in this city of 65,000, its staunch Muslim elite was paying such attention to the holidays of a handful of foreigners and a few Iranian Christians. After all, their New Year would not arrive until spring. But Mr. Sayeed-Nejad wasn't impressed. "They could have at least invited Mr. Jones and Mr. Sisul," he said as he handed me the ultimate prize— the key to the daneshsera's gate. For one night, Betsy and I could stay out as late as we pleased.

"Let's twist again like we did last summer..." blared across the formal receiving room where more than a hundred Iranian and foreign guests gathered to usher in the western New Year. Elegant ladies, attired in chic pinks, reds, and blues, their ink-black hair wound in sophisticated French twists, posed placidly next to their mustachioed spouses, watching a few couples gyrate on the plush Kerman carpet to the voice of Chubby Checker.

"I'm Bill. Would you like to dance?" asked the Canadian.

"Sure," I said, pushing the wife of the governor general out of my mind. And twist we did, to the delight of the other partygoers who edged in to get a better look. Skirt swirling, around and around I spun, following Bill's lead as if we had been dancing together all our lives. But a CENTO colleague tapped him on the shoulder, and soon I was shaking my hips with a ruddy-faced Englishman, while Betsy cut the rug with a portly member of the U.S. Mapping crew. The music went on and on, and the Peace Corps "girls," the only unattached women in sight, were the most popular partners in the room.

What a change this was for me. This wallflower from Homewood was flying around the ornate carpet with one partner, then another, my timing perfect, my movements fluid. On stage, as I had been so much of my time in Kerman, I was the real deal—a young Iranian's dream, the emblem of westernization. It made me bolder. I twisted and jitterbugged my way across the room, pausing for the audience's applause at the end of each dance. This is who I am, I thought. I like dancing, I like men, I especially like handsome partners like Bill.

Kerman's leading officials lined the edges of the room, their suits perfectly cut, their shoes gleaming. The wives whispered together, dark eyes dramatized by thick mascara, cheeks and lips brightly rouged. Did they wish they could change places with me? Officialdom sipped tea, Pepsi, even Scotch, watching the Christians frolic on the dance floor. There weren't more than fifty in all of Kerman, most of us transients, in the city for a year or two. Even the Iranian Christians, Armenian and Assyrian businessmen and their families, had come from somewhere else. Yet here we were, bringing the fun and frivolity of the west to a deeply religious Muslim town.

The clock struck twelve, and fractured strains of "Auld Lang Syne" broke out around the room. The party couldn't be over. I wanted the music to go on forever. If only I could hold on to this freedom, abandon, certainty, pride. If I could feel as desired tomorrow as I felt at that moment, dancing in the arms of a handsome stranger on a magic Kerman carpet.

JANUARY

You may say it's just the January blues
That colours my views
But it's much deeper than that —*Paul Curtis*

Dissent

Letter home

> Privacy? I got grilled a couple of days ago about
> my bank balance. A student's father thought I'd
> saved too much money for a teacher. Nope, he's
> not an employee of the bank. And that was the day
> after a mailman spied Betsy in the bazaar and hand
> delivered a letter from her mother he just happened
> to be carrying around.

I had been in Iran four months, and the shock of John F. Kennedy's death more than a year before was still with me. The assassination of this young, charismatic leader was a raw wound, painful evidence that there was evil in the world. The Iranians I knew did not need to be reminded. The presence of SAVAK, the shah's secret police, was a constant warning that danger lurked in unexpected places.

SAVAK was everywhere. Some of its employees in Kerman were official, known to everyone, working in the office that processed my foreign residence papers, for example. But a taxi driver, a bazaar shopkeeper, a teacher—any of these people could be on SAVAK's secret payroll, reporting a troublesome remark, an unsanctioned meeting, a hint of distrust of the government to their superiors. Drastic action against the offender, jail or worse, could result. Smothering opposition to the shah's regime was SAVAK's main objective. And in 1965 it was very good at it.

SAVAK was not foremost in my mind that cool January, when the walled-in world of the daneshsera seemed even more stifling than usual. Most evenings Betsy and I were inside our room, dining on sandwiches, writing letters, reading one book after another. Most days we were in Kerman's cold classrooms, listening to English classes taught primarily in Persian. Where were the "warm and richly rewarding experiences" that volunteers described in the international Peace Corps newsletters? "You'd think they'd find something original to say about life in another country," I said to Betsy.

It was on one of those long evenings when the year was still new, that Betsy rebelled. "I'm tired of reading, I don't owe anyone a letter. Let's get out of here," she said.

"Where can we go? It's dark outside."

"The streets are lighted. If we walk up Zarisse Street, away from town, maybe we'll see something new."

"Probably just more walls."

But I slipped my feet into my flats and pulled on my coat. Off we went, past the empty volleyball courts; past the grove of pistachio trees, its branches bare; and past the door to the gatekeeper's cottage.

"We won't be gone long. We're just going for a short walk," I told Kobra-khanum, who was fixing dinner for her family. Looking astonished at such purposeless activity at this hour, she clanged the gate closed behind us.

Night had darkened the distant mountains when we headed up the empty road; Betsy and I were the only people in sight. But no danger lurked in the deep shadows of a Kerman evening. Robbers, muggers, or worse did not ply the streets of this city. Betsy and I headed up the road without a thought about our safety.

There was not much to see at this hour. Here, a tree branch draped over a high wall; there, the color of the gate was green, not blue; the unique details about the occupants of the Zarisse Street compounds remained obscured. First one taxi, then another, pulled up, certain we needed a ride. My raised head and eyebrows told them "no," and off they sped, leaving us to continue our aimless stroll.

But the deserted sidewalk and the dark, flickering shadows began to get to us, reminders that back home just these circumstances could conceal an unknown prowler. "Let's start back," I said. "It feels weird out here this time of night."

Minutes later we were knocking on the gate of the danesh-sera. Kobra-khanum let us in, a disapproving look on her face.

"You were right, Mary," Betsy said, unlocking the padlock to our room. "All we saw were walls. But at least they were different walls."

"What were you doing at the mappers' house last night?" Mr. Sayeed-Nejad was seated at the desk in his office, his brow furrowed, his eyes angry.

"What mappers' house?" I asked. "I didn't even know they were in our neighborhood."

"We just went for a walk up Zarisse Street. It wasn't late," Betsy said.

Mr. Sayeed-Nejad lowered his voice. "A man from SAVAK paid a visit to the director of education this morning. He reported you two were seen by the compound where those American mappers live."

"Then the SAVAK guy drives a taxi. Those were the only people we saw," Betsy said.

"You must be careful." Mr. Sayeed-Nejad's tone was urgent. "People talk."

The month of January continued to crawl, short days with endless evenings, confirming that Betsy and I had little to do. I had about given up on anything of interest ever happening in

Iran when, after her second period English class, the Zoroastrian teacher Mrs. Farvahari and I entered the teachers' room at Mayel High School. The room was buzzing with excitement, the teachers talking so quickly I couldn't get the gist of what they were saying.

"The prime minister's been shot!" Mrs. Farvahari said.

"You're kidding! Where? Do they know who shot him?" I asked.

Mrs. Farvahari shrugged her shoulders. "He was right outside the Majlis (Senate) where he was going to make a speech. They've taken him to the hospital. Someone's been arrested, but the government hasn't released any more information. I'll bet they'll blame it on the Communists."

That made sense to me. Everyone knew that SAVAK hunted down members of the Tudeh Communist Party, determined to crush any opposition. Perhaps one of them had escaped SAVAK's notice. Communists were held culpable for everything bad in the 1960s, the heart of the Cold War.

News about the condition of Prime Minister Hassan-Ali Mansur was sketchy. Newspapers were optimistic. He was recovering, they reported, publishing photographs of the shah by his bedside. Rumors flew around Kerman's teachers' rooms: they had shot the prime minister's attacker.... No, they had arrested four accomplices... SAVAK was pulling out his assailant's fingernails, one by one, so he would reveal who was behind this act. But nobody would tell me why this progressive, forty-two-year-old, western-educated aristocrat had been a target.

The omnipresent SAVAK was so ruthless in rooting out opposition to the shah's government I was amazed that a cadre of detractors had escaped its notice. But even in this atmosphere many Iranians continued to voice dissatisfaction with the shah, his family, his government and its practices. The spring before our Peace Corps group arrived, the University of Tehran was temporarily shut down to quell a huge student demonstration that had spilled over to universities in Esfahan and Shiraz. Hundreds of protesters were arrested. According to people we knew in Tehran, smaller demonstrations continued to erupt, students braving tear gas and the threat of imprisonment to demand a more democratic, less oppressive government, actions that never appeared in the English language newspaper. I was not aware of this type of activity in Kerman, which had the usual trappings of a provincial capital—departments of agriculture, education, health, city planning—but did not have a university. Kermanis in post-secondary training schools like the daneshsera for teachers, the agriculture and nursing schools were not caught up, to my knowledge, in the fervor of protest.

The Communists and big-city students were not the only sectors of the Iranian populace rebelling against the shah and his government. Although they gave me no indication, my friends in conservative Kerman must have been aware that across the country pockets of dissent were building in mosques and *madressehs* (Islamic schools). There, where worshippers were permitted to assemble, SAVAK had little sway as the faithful gathered to hear audiotapes smuggled in from the exiled Ayatollah Khomeini, who railed against the shah's godless government.

Dissent for Peace Corps volunteers in Kerman was embodied in Mr. Sayeed-Nejad's best friend, Jafar Sanaati. Mr. Sanaati did not seem like a rebel as he played backgammon, drank beer, and told stories in the guys' living room. But they reported he went to secret meetings. Neither Mr. Sanaati nor Mr. Sayeed-Nejad would discuss this. "*Divar moush dareh, moush goosh dareh*" ("The walls have mice, the mice have ears"), Mr. Sayeed Nejad said. "We Iranians just don't talk about politics. If we don't say anything, we won't put anyone in danger." While I never discovered the specifics of Mr. Sanaati's activities, I gave a silent cheer each time he walked into the house in the bazaar, proud that he and his comrades were still outsmarting SAVAK.

Five days after he was shot, the prime minister died in Pars Hospital. His murderer, Mohammad Bokharaii, and his three accomplices were quickly tried, found guilty, and put to death, surprising no one in Kerman's teachers' rooms. With a collective shrug, the chatter there reverted to the price of rice and the weather. After all, he was the shah's man. The Kermanis had not voted the slain prime minister into office. They had not watched his assassin murdered on national television; Kerman had no television in 1965. Radio broadcasts followed the official line; newspapers published only what the government wanted the public to know about the incident, and that wasn't much.

What a contrast this was with my country where Americans could talk about nothing else when our duly elected president was killed. A national tragedy became a personal loss for most of us; many months later, rumors continued to fuel very vocal conspiracy theorists, and I, for one, was still in mourning.

Long after I left Iran I learned what many others knew: those responsible for Mansur's death were part of a conservative religious coalition whose goal was to carry out Ayatollah Ruhollah Khomeini's vision of an Islamic Iranian state. Killing Mansur, one of the shah's men, sent the king and his secret police a clear message.

If the Kermanis suspected conservative clerics were impli-
cated in Mansur's assassination, they kept quiet about it. No
one ventured an opinion to me in the early months of 1965.
Tehran, after all, was a long way away, and some things were
best kept to oneself.

Letter to a Friend Back Home

Dear Karen,
    Happy New Year! It was great to get your letter,
but I'm sorry to hear you're catching every bug your
third graders bring to school. I've had my share of
colds, too. Maybe we're sneezing at the same time,
just on different continents. I'm sure you're doing
more with your students than I'm doing here. I
spend my days huddled next to the kerosene heaters
in classrooms all over town, waiting for a chance to
spend five minutes practicing pronunciation. Believe
it or not, it's the most English these girls speak or
hear during the entire lesson.

    While not much is happening work-wise, my
social life is definitely improving. I've met a man!
Here in the desert, a zillion miles from home, in a
place where these kinds of things aren't allowed
to happen, Bill comes into my life. He's Canadian,
and some kind of American Indian—Cheyenne,
maybe—and works for CENTO (that's the Central
Treaty Organization for those not in the know).
My roommate Betsy and I got invited to a big Iran
Oil Company shindig on New Year's Eve, and he

was there. Like that song from My Fair Lady, I could
have danced all night! He's an older guy, handsome,
though he's missing a couple of eyeteeth. Even that
adds to the mystery of Bill. So sophisticated, so
adult. And he likes ME!

Dating here is really complicated. We're not
supposed to, you know. I've just learned that "the
powers that be" are keeping their eyes on me. (I'm
not mentioning names because I'm pretty sure my
letters are read before they leave the country.) I can't
even go for a walk without someone reporting on it.
Don't they have anything better to do?

But I'm tired of trying to behave like an Iranian
woman. No one believes it anyway. When Bill and
his roommate Mike sent a note to the teachers'
school where I live, asking my roommate Betsy and
me to their house for dinner, I knew we should
say no. We said yes. There'd be four of us so we'd
chaperone each other. Why should anyone complain?

We've been doing this chaperoned-dinner thing
once or twice a week for a couple of weeks, and
so far no one has said anything. Bill and I can't go
ANYWHERE in public together. Betsy and I take a taxi
to Bill and Mike's house just in time for drinks. Dinner,
fixed by Bibi, their servant, is always delicious—
they have U.S. Commissary privileges, lucky fellows.
Really beats sandwiches! After Salisbury steak, or
something like that, we dance cheek to cheek to tapes
Bill brought from Canada. We're back at the school,
knocking at its gate before 8:00.

Bill's great. He's smart, funny, and he's really lived
life. Sometimes I feel very young around him, like I've
got so much to learn. Other times, especially when
he puts down Iranians, I even feel a little superior.

But isn't that the way relationships balance out, each of us strong in some ways, weak in others? I forget—it seems ages since I've had one. Having a romantic interest gives me something to think about.

So, your friend in the Peace Corps is rebelling in her own small way. When the Kermanis find out, which they certainly will, they will not approve. I really should be worried about my reputation, but right now, I just want to have fun.

Sorry this letter's been all about me. Hope all's well. Think of me when you stroll hand in hand down the street with that handsome fiancé of yours.

Love,
Mary

Frustration

Letter home

> I'm becoming disillusioned with the Peace Corps,
> at least as it is in Iran. They're talking about bringing
> in 100 new volunteers this year but they don't
> even use the ones they have. This will add up to
> more volunteers sitting out two years, playing at
> working. The PC should not send people who cannot,
> by definition, fit into the social structure of the
> society—like unmarried women.

The rain beat down on the courtyard as I sloshed my way through the daneshsera's puddles, hoping some of the mud weighing down my loafers would dissolve. This torrent was another January surprise, the downpours transforming dirt roads into slippery mud seas. During the hot, dry fall months, I hadn't thought about what would happen when those unpaved roads and packed-dirt paths got wet.

"Mail call," I said to Betsy, opening our door and kicking off my caked shoes. "Looks like you got a letter from Christopher."

Betsy had a new admirer, a volunteer from Rezaiyeh in northwestern Iran. Somehow he'd learned that Betsy enjoyed sailing, so he was plying her with letters and promises. When she flew to Tehran in early January with a broken tooth, he managed to be there, too. She liked him so much, she dragged out her dental work for three extra days. Although Bill's CENTO roommate and a fellow from the U.S. mapping crew were vying for her attention, this Christopher from Rezaiyeh was more intriguing to her.

"Gimme," she said, bounding over to the door. I handed her Christopher's letter, along with a brown envelope from Peace Corps Tehran. I had one just like it, directed to the Office of Education where we stopped every day hoping for mail, for news from home, news from anywhere.

Shivering, I wrapped a blanket around my shoulders and ripped open the Peace Corps missive. What would it be this time? Nothing significant, I was sure. When the Peace Corps had something important to communicate, it sent telegrams. Fred had gotten one yesterday announcing that our field officer, Don Croll, was swinging up in his Land Rover from the Persian Gulf with the Peace Corps doctor and his wife for an overnight stay. It was about time someone visited. While the rest of the Kerman volunteers had seen the Peace Corps staff on trips to Tehran, I had been idling here in Kerman since September with no visible official support.

I examined the latest communiqué, a wide-reaching questionnaire: Had my luggage arrived? Had I packed the right things for life at my Peace Corps post? Did our book locker contain books I wanted to read? How often was I ill? What was the nature of my illness(es)? How was my mental health?

That last question stumped me. Betsy, my frame of reference, didn't seem as unsteady as I felt; at least her temper was more in check. Usually calm to the point of placid, these days a flush of anger would burn across my cheeks at the slightest provocation. I had stomped off in a pique the day before when Mr. Sayeed-Nejad reported a teacher was unhappy with me for missing a class. Not my fault, not my fault! She told me not to come, I wanted to scream. My mental health? If I tried to answer honestly, the three lines allotted on the questionnaire were not enough.

But more than a hot temper was bothering me. It was January, a new year. I had been in Kerman for four months, and my flourishing romance was the only bright spot. My presence in Iran was impacting only one person—me. I was doing all the learning; the Kermanis remained largely unaffected.

There had to be more to the Peace Corps than this. I needed some positive direction, some insight into making a difference; so far, all I had were lots of well-intentioned Kermanis pointing out what I was doing wrong—most of which had nothing to do with teaching English. No action went unobserved; my behavior was dissected like a biology class frog. My reputation wavered when I wasn't home by 8:00 p.m., slithered downward every time I overslept, and really plummeted if I was observed in male company. With Bill in my life it would soon be in the cellar. It didn't stop there. In the eyes of many Kermanis, Betsy and I were a matched set, indistinguishable from each other, doubling our opportunities to be found wanting. Living at the daneshsera magnified these situations.

I glanced over at Betsy. Engrossed in Christopher's letter, she had shifted her position on her cot, her back walling me out. *Wouldn't you like to close a door and read your letter in private?* I wanted to ask. But there was no point; there was no door to give us even a brief respite from each other. Iranians dreaded being alone; this American longed for solitude. What started as a small hum was fast becoming a loud chorus: we needed a gate of our own, rooms of our own, our own bathroom, our own kitchen. We needed a home. There was no space on the questionnaire about my mental health to explain this.

Finally, someone from Tehran was going to observe our work and living situation first hand. Surely Don Croll, a Kerman volunteer himself less than a year before, would take this stumbling effort in hand, suggest some concrete ways to make our classroom presence more meaningful. And any empathetic American would grasp that Betsy and I should have the keys to our own home. It was a lot to ask of a one-day visit, but perhaps this visit would put things in motion.

Don blew into town on a gusty January afternoon with the doctor and his wife. They stowed their gear at the Hotel Akavan, getting to the house in the bazaar just in time for dinner. As they followed Fatimeh across the courtyard, I could hear her laughing at something Don said. "I'd forgotten that Mr. Croll sounds just like a Kermani," Mr. Sayeed-Nejad said as our guests shed coats, scarves, and shoes in the warm living room.

Happy chatter and a hint of home filled the air. How simple it was to socialize when I knew what to expect. How wonderful to talk without a language barrier, without worrying about saying or doing something inappropriate. Don Croll was an inclusive type, bringing Dr. Drake and his wife into the conversation, and switching to Persian to tease Fatimeh about the menu. Soon even quiet Tom Sisul was chatting with Betty Drake, whose pronounced New England tones carried across the room.

When Fatimeh's feast was ready, the nine of us sat knee to knee on the floor around a sofreh. We began with bowls of chicken soup, delicately seasoned with lemon juice and turmeric. Dishes filled with thick yogurt made from goat's milk, plates of fresh greens, mounds of warm flat bread, and lightly pickled cauliflower and eggplant accompanied *fesenjan*, succulent chicken cooked to perfection in a sauce made from ground walnuts and pomegranate syrup. A heaping bed of steaming rice adorned with a few saffron-orange grains completed the array.

When it was impossible to eat one more bite, I leaned back against a bolster, and sipped a beer. Warmed by food, drink, and conviviality, my laundry list of issues receded. Tom Taaffe cocked a full bottle of vodka toward Don, who grinned broadly and nodded. The doctor's eyes lit up as Tom lined up five glasses; when Mr. Sayeed-Nejad began to snap his fingers to an unheard beat, I abandoned any thought of serious discussion.

Conversation grew louder as the level in the vodka bottle dropped. I opened another beer, and decided I needed to know Paul Drake better. "Just why did you come on this trip?" I asked.

"To check up on your health," he said, saluting me with his glass. "You aren't sick, are you?"

"Paul thinks it's a good idea to see volunteers at their sites," Betty said.

"Oh! Does that mean you're going to visit our room at the daneshsera?"

"If there's time. What's there to see?"

"Life in a fishbowl."

"Enough of this serious talk," said Tom Taaffe, pouring another shot of vodka into his glass. "I'm not going back to the ag school tonight. Let's teach the doc and Don some of our songs. Betsy and Mary already know most of them. Come on, Fred. Which one shall we start with?"

"How about Pretty Baby?" A warm flush had crept under Fred's glasses, staining his cheeks and beaked nose red. He broke into song: "I've got a rose between my toes from walking barefoot through the hothouse wid you, pretty baby," he crooned, giving us the first line of a ditty he and his California buddies had dreamed up. Soon Kerman volunteers and Tehran staff members were belting out limericks, along with that other northern California plaint, "San Rafael, oh San Rafael, where the hell is San Rafael?" sung to the tune of "O Christmas Tree."

The witching hour for the daneshsera had come. Don shepherded Betsy and me into the Peace Corps's Land Rover parked outside the deserted bazaar. We were wound up and the tunes kept coming. All thoughts of confronting him with the impossibility of living at the daneshsera had vanished.

"Shh," said Don, as we approached the daneshsera's gate, "let me do the talking." Kobra-khanum accepted his apologies for our tardiness. As Don drove off down the empty street, Betsy and I towed a straight line along the path to our room.

Things were a little dim the next day. Determined my lessons would be exceptional in spite of my wobbly head, I led the seventh graders of Parvin Etesami High School in an enthralling dialog about Parvin and Parviz, the girl and boy stars of the beginning English textbook. The students were all mine, as today I was standing in for Mrs. Mesbah, now the proud mother of a baby boy. Surely at least one class would be observed by a visiting Peace Corps staff member. In the middle of my third session of the morning, the door squeaked, opening slowly. It had to be Don Croll. Good. This was one of the best classes, and the girls were shining today. But no, it was the school's obsequious caretaker with a message for one of the students. I went back to the lesson. There were no more interruptions.

So where was Peace Corps/Tehran? They hadn't dropped in on Fred or Betsy's English classes that morning, Tom had not had a visitor, nor had Mr. Sayeed-Nejad. We finally found them eating lunch at the Hotel Akavan before heading out of town.

"You guys have had a nice, easy morning," Fred said.

"Had to see Kerman's head of city planning." Don scooped his spoon into a plate of rice topped with stewed beans and greens. "We hope he'll take a couple of volunteers in the fall."

"But you haven't even seen our room," I said. "You haven't seen any of us in the classroom. How do you know what we're doing?"

"I'm sure everything's fine, Mary. Dr. Dorry's the one to talk to about your English classes. Remember, she's in charge of the language program." Soon they were off, heading north to Yazd and the volunteers there.

"Pretty useless visit," said Fred, as the Kerman volunteers traipsed down the narrow dirt alleyway leading from the hotel to the main street. "As far as I'm concerned, they can stay in Tehran." With that, Kerman's volunteers fanned out over the city to observe afternoon English classes.

A Pilgrim's Tale

As long, bleak January drew to a close, Gertrude Dorry called a conference in Esfahan for English-teaching volunteers. At last someone was paying attention. Twenty-five of us assembled in Esfahan's Hotel Pars, excited to see each other and curious about what she had to offer. An American linguist who had married into Iran, this formidable head of our English-language program infused our group with her enthusiasm. The potential for introducing creativity and the concept of change into the lives of our students was at our fingertips. All we had to do was use it. Dr. Dorry maintained that English clubs, where members learned crafts, played games, and sang songs, were the path to new ideas in this conservative environment. If Dr. Dorry could still be

full of optimism after twelve years in Iran, maybe I shouldn't
feel so bogged down. But I wasn't a joiner. I hated the idea of
clubs—too organized, too trite.

Betsy, a natural at arts and crafts, was enthusiastic about
the idea. In the privacy of our hotel room I voiced my doubts.

"Why should the girls want even more school?"

"Mary, at least we should ask them."

"I'm the most un-crafty person I know."

"That's okay. I'll teach crafts and you can lead them in
songs. We'll figure out the games as we go along."

"You haven't heard me sing."

Still, songs beat construction paper and glue. I didn't capit-
ulate during the conference, but in the weeks that followed
we started clubs in all four girls' high schools, propelling the
English language and its exotic American teachers beyond the
classroom and into the realm of fun. At 7:00 a.m. three mornings a week, "Old MacDonald Had a Farm," or some other
simple song, echoed slightly off-key from one of Kerman's
classrooms. English Club was in session.

I had worried that we would spend all three days of the
conference cooped up in the hotel, but the Peace Corps staff
built in some time for us to see the wonder that is Esfahan.
"*Esfahan, nesva jahan*" ("Esfahan is half the world"), goes the
Persian saying. I believed every word of it.

Betsy and I pulled our heavy wool coats closer to our bodies
as we pushed into the cold January wind blowing up from the
Zayendeh Rud. Esfahan's river had been a trickle when I saw it
in November, but with the winter rains, water rushed along its
banks carrying the hope of an abundant spring through the city.

We hurried down Chahar Bagh, the city's grand tree-lined
boulevard, turning in at the madresseh just outside the great
square. Even in the winter this school for religious training

inspired contemplative thinking, with its bower of plane trees and reflecting pool. Turbaned students in long brown robes paced back and forth, reciting words from the texts they held in their hands.

"I think this is my favorite place in Esfahan," Betsy whispered as we left.

"It's so peaceful," I said. "The outside world is only steps away, yet it's quiet and secluded here."

Minutes later, we were in the great square, Maidan-e Shah, a regal spread with two celebrated mosques abutting one another toward one end. Blue tiles ornamented with tendrils of green and yellow vines roofed the dome of the Royal Mosque, while the intimate Sheikh Lutfallah Mosque was more muted, its cream colored tiles conveying breathtaking elegance. The Ali Qapu Palace faced them across the wide expanse of the square, and the entrance to Esfahan's grand bazaar opened at the other end of the square.

Betsy and I headed straight to the palace. From the outside, this seven-storey wooden structure was less imposing than the others, but I loved the first-floor balcony, with its pool and fountain. Closing my eyes, I envisioned Shah Abbas and his courtiers sitting cross-legged on one of Esfahan's tightly woven silk carpets, cheering on polo players in the square below. After the game, the group would mount the palace stairs for an intimate concert in the music room on the top floor. The space's countless small resonating chambers, recessed around the wall, turned the notes of even a single instrument into the sound of an orchestra…. Four hundred years later, surrounded by walls of intricate, bottle-shaped niches, whose sophisticated design stymied today's most accomplished architects, Gertrude Dorry's assertion that Iranians needed more creativity rang hollow.

Still thinking about this incredible example of Iranian invention, I followed Betsy into the windy square. Hawkers peddled their wares around the entrance to the bazaar, but the bounty of colorful items for sale lured me into its cold passages. An odd-shaped jacket hung in a shop full of old things, its stiff fabric covered with hand-painted vines of delicate pink and red flowers. Intrigued, I asked how much it cost. Only when I started to walk away did the merchant begin to negotiate in earnest, eventually accepting about $15 worth of tomans, less than half its original price. It was much easier to bargain when I didn't really need the item. A few stalls down I found a set of camel bells to bring back to Bill. Would he find the Ali Qapu Palace as wonderful as I did?

Searching for a familiar face when I entered the conference area for the evening's film, I found Fred perched on a step, literally above it all. Catching my eye, he patted the empty space next to him. There was a strange force operating on us in this unfamiliar setting. In Kerman, we had settled on mutual disregard; in Esfahan, we were seeking each other out.

We chatted comfortably, familiarly, while Don Croll fiddled with the movie projector. Finally, someone turned out the lights and the film about the Peace Corps in Iran began. As the film rolled on, showing volunteers working in Ghazvin, in Rasht, in Abadan, Fred and I whispered together, two friends joking about Peace Corps propaganda. I hoped this new dynamic would last. I needed an ally—someone I could talk to, even confide in, someone who could run interference for me with Mr. Sayeed-Nejad.

The conference was over but the return trip to Kerman was turning into a saga straight from the *Canterbury Tales* for the two Toms, Fred, and me. We were only halfway home, stranded in the TBT Bus Company's teahouse in Yazd with fifty other passengers. We had been there, balancing on rickety chairs, for seven hours. Betsy was missing the drama. Laid flat with the flu, she was still in Esfahan.

The issue was water, the driver explained, the water he suspected was flooding the dirt road that lay between Yazd and Kerman. It had been raining off and on for days, but now the sky was a dazzling blue.

"We can't go today," he finally announced in a thick Azeri accent. "We'll try again tomorrow morning."

"Loud-mouthed Turk," said a man standing nearby, casting aspersions on those from Azerbaijan, the country's northwestern-most province. Raising his voice he challenged the driver. "How do you know the roads are bad? It hasn't rained for more than a day. I have important business in Kerman."

"How do I know? I know," said the driver. "Only God can control the rain. Your business is in His hands now. I'll see everyone tomorrow at seven."

It was a good thing the Yazd volunteers had a big house. The four of us trudged across the muddy bus lot, hauling suitcases full of dirty laundry, souvenirs, and Quaker Oats. After my Esfahan splurges, I had twenty tomans ($3) in my pocketbook; the guys were no richer. Our Yazd cohorts were our closest Peace Corps neighbors. We knew we would be welcome.

That evening, I struggled to get comfortable on the lumpy mattress on the floor, events of the past few days running through my mind. I no longer felt wary around Fred; we were going to be friends. I pulled my blankets up over my shoulders, and fell asleep wondering if he and Bill would like each other.

I barely had time for one dream when it was six a.m., time to get up. Tom Taaffe, complaining of the same achy flu that had struck Betsy down, decided to stay in Yazd. Fred, Tom Sisul, and I ate some bread smeared with quince jam, gulped a glass of steaming tea, and hurried down the road toward the bus station for our seven o'clock departure. We weren't halfway there when we saw our bus lumbering toward us. No, we weren't late, the bus driver assured us as we stumbled up the steps. The loud guy, the one with the business meeting that could not be delayed, had spearheaded a passenger insurrection. Our driver had been forced, yes forced, to leave early. But he had saved seats for us—in the very last row. Grumbling, we took our places at the back of the bus. I squeezed in next to the window, my knees jackknifed into the seat in front. The driver stowed our suitcases under the bus and climbed in behind the steering wheel.

The first hour of the six-hour trip south to Kerman passed easily. Fred and Tom dozed as the bus sped along the well-maintained dirt road, the only one of consequence running north and south between Yazd and Kerman. It was too bumpy to read, so I stared out of the window, my thoughts flitting from Mrs. Dorry and her English clubs, to Bill and just how I could finesse a relationship in a city where dating was licentious behavior. As the flat brown land began to glisten and puddles appeared, the changing terrain commanded all my attention. A murmur rose as the puddles turned into ponds that encroached on the road. The driver braked and braked again, struggling to keep the unwieldy bus from drifting. Wanting someone to worry with me, I nudged Fred. "We're in a damn river," he said, peering across me out the window. The dirt road between Yazd and Kerman had become the Zayendeh Rud, a riverbed, but the bus was no ship.

No one was sleeping as the driver forded first one deep gulch, then another. "*Yah, Ali,*" intoned the passengers, imploring the revered Shi'a leader to save them. The bus sank up to the tops of its wheels, taking my stomach with it, but somehow it kept going. "Allah, help us," the passengers cried. "Mohammad, care for your children." "Jesus Christ," Fred muttered. White knuckled, my chest tight, I murmured my own pleas to the Almighty, hoping someone up there would listen.

The driver found a dry patch of road, and the bus picked up speed. The passengers' pleas for divine assistance subsided, and relieved chatter filled the air. I settled back in my seat. "That was close," said Tom Sisul. An instant later, the driver swerved, throwing all of us sideways, the front wheel of the bus plunging into a deep hole. As it ground to a stop, there was a loud ripping sound. For a split second, it was ghostly quiet. Then cries inveighing Allah's help broke out as the passengers stumbled back to their seats. The driver opened the door and jumped out to inspect the damage. I watched him stoop down near the suspended front tire, shaking his head. Still bent over, he paced from front to back inspecting the undercarriage of the vehicle. By the time he reached my window he was muttering angrily. A strong odor of gasoline filled the bus.

"*Chee showd?*" ("What happened?") the passengers demanded when the driver returned.

"*Kharobeh,*" announced the driver. The bus was broken; its fuel tank split from end to end, it could go no more. Moans went up from the passengers.

"We'd better get off," Fred said, standing up.

"Let's hurry. All that gasoline..."

Soon fifty disconsolate wayfarers were milling around outside the *kharob* or "broken" bus, marooned in a landscape of scree shaved from distant mountains by the winds. Bisected by our flooded road, not a tree, not a goat, not even a crow interrupted the monotonous brown of the countryside that stretched as far as I could see. No telephones, no telegraphs, nothing. Who would know we were in trouble?

I was not the only one who was worried. "Wolves!" cried a middle-aged woman. "We'll all be eaten by wolves!"

"There, there, Mama," said her daughter, enveloping her own small daughter into her chador. "Someone will come. We won't be here long. There won't be any wolves."

"Wolves! No one's seen a wolf around here for fifty years!" the man with business in Kerman said.

This raised Grandmother's ire. "Oh yes they have. A wolf ate one of my uncle's cousin's sheep just six months ago. Not far from here, either. Only its wooly coat was left. Everyone knows the wolves have returned. Everyone. Just ask this nice foreign girl. You know about wolves, don't you?" she asked, turning to me.

Surprised I even knew the Persian word for wolf, I had to halt the pack of hungry carnivores that was prowling through my imagination. "There are so many of us," I said, "I'm sure the wolves will stay away."

"And we can get on the bus and close the doors," said her daughter. "We'll be safe there."

The daughter and I were still attempting to banish wolves from her mother's thoughts when around a curve, speeding toward us, came a bright red Mihan Tour bus, the TBT bus line's competition. Our driver hurried to wave it down. We learned later that we'd been traveling in a loosely-formed caravan because of the uncertainty of the road. While the drivers conferred, mother, daughter, granddaughter, and I stood off to the side, chatting—three women and a little girl, getting to know each other.

We watched the driver's assistant transfer our luggage to the nearly empty Mihan Tour bus. I climbed up the steps and sank into a seat Fred had saved for me. The two women scooted into their places farther back, the little girl settling on her mother's lap. With a chant of "Yah, Ali" we set off to ford more rivers, navigate more streams, and avoid more craters.

Twelve and a half hours after we left Yazd, our bus, full of tired, dirty, hungry passengers, arrived in Kerman. Reluctant to part from this group that had gone through so much, Tom, Fred, and I mingled with the others until one by one the passengers slipped off into the dark city. Bidding my friends goodbye, I took a cab to the daneshsera and rang the bell at the outside gate. While I waited for Kobra-khanum to answer, a sharp howl pierced the night air. *It's a dog—it's got to be a dog,* I thought.

"It was a very difficult trip," I said when she let me in. The heck with the heater, I thought, undoing the padlock to our cold room. I closed the curtains, kicked off my shoes, pulled on my flannel nightgown, and crept under my bed covers. While the long month of January ticked to an end, I slept.

THE WINDS OF CHANGE

Real adventure – self-determined, self-moti-
vated, often risky – forces you to have firsthand
encounters with the world. The world the way
it is, not the way you imagine it. Your body will
collide with the earth and you will bear witness
—*Mark Jenkins*

Brrr!

I was late, and it was all because the damn mimeograph machine at the Office of Education kept jamming, I fumed as I dashed up the stairs two at a time. The second-level English students were waiting for their exam.

This was Betsy's class, the one she had inherited when Mrs. Mesbah gave birth to baby Mohammad. But Betsy's mystery boyfriend had shown up unexpectedly, a Valentine's Day surprise, AWOL from his post in Rezaiyeh almost a thousand miles away, ringing the bell at the daneshsera and throwing Kobra-khanum into a tizzy over the stranger at the gate.

The unknown foreigner was named Christopher, and he was asking for Betsy-khanum, Kobra's son Ali had informed me when I answered his knock. I pulled on multiple layers of clothing to ward against the frigid weather and followed Ali across the courtyard. At last I was going to meet the famous Christopher, whose name came up with a particular inflection in Betsy's voice each time we discussed men. Ali's flip-flops spanked the pavement as he skipped past the administration building to the gatehouse where a lanky blond fellow stared at his feet, trying to ignore the group of girls whispering nearby.

"*Mary-khanum meeyad,*" Ali informed the guest. Christopher smiled.

"Miss Mary is coming," translated one of the members of his audience. He thanked her. The girls edged in as I introduced myself to the stranger.

"I'm really glad to meet you," I said. "Betsy will be so surprised. She's teaching a class at Parvin Etesami. Why don't we catch a cab and meet her outside the high school? She should be finished soon."

"He's Betsy-khanum's friend." I heard murmurs in Farsi from the observers.

"He's a Peace Corps volunteer, like we are," I said in Farsi, hoping to stem the rumors that would soon be flying around the schoolyard. "He's a friend to us all."

"Ooh, he's very handsome, so white, so blond," echoed in my ears as Kobra-khanum closed the gate behind us.

A week later Christopher was still around, encamped on the red kilim in the guys' living room while he pursued the serious business of romance. The courting couple faced the familiar issue of privacy. The house in the bazaar, private only when its occupants were teaching, was their only option. This was where I came in. "Sure," I'd agreed, "I'll teach your classes." That involved writing a test for the second-level eighth-graders. I had spent the day before at our gray metal table, pecking away at a stencil. The more typos I made, the harder my questions became. Now, in front of a classroom full of expectant faces, I was feeling a little guilty.

"Good morning, Miss Mary," the girls greeted me as I pulled out the exams from my bag.

"Good morning, class. You know there's a test this morning." Ignoring the groan that spread across the room, I continued: "You have fifty minutes. You must work alone. You must not look at someone else's paper." Just to be sure, I repeated the whole thing in Farsi as I passed out the exams: six rows, ten girls in each row.

God it was cold—close to freezing outdoors, and barely warmer inside. My coat covered two sweaters, a half-slip, tee shirt, skirt, and stockings, and still I shivered. The students bowed their heads, puzzling over the multiple choice/fill in the blank test. They, too, were bulked up in the Kerman version of the layered look. Gray school uniforms were outerwear, covering sweaters, shirts, undershirts, even jackets. Thick stockings encased their legs, gloves warmed their hands, and scarves protected their heads and ears. I heard a moan or two as I rubbed my hands together over the sputtering stove. "This is very difficult," one girl said. I ignored her. Misty chains of breath mingled in the room's frosty air. The thick adobe walls that cooled this room in the warm months kept it frigid in the dead of winter.

Drip-drip-drip. The kerosene fueled the fire so slowly the flame would surely die. I'll bet Betsy's warm right now, I thought. Cut it out, Mary. Don't forget, she helps you.

She did, too. I'd been pushing the boundaries of respectability since New Year's when I had met Bill, not an acceptable member of the family like the men in the Peace Corps, but one of those wild, western men from CENTO, working in Kerman for fast money, and up to no good in the opinion of the local populace. But I was an American. Why should my life be so constricted? Stubbornly, I was trying to manipulate—or should I say rationalize—the situation. If I were never alone with Bill, my actions shouldn't be suspect. That was where Betsy came in, joining Bill and me at his house for surreptitious suppers, neglecting to mention our rendezvous to Mr. Sayeed-Nejad, agreeing that it was unthinkable to forego romance.

The Peace Corps had put us together—two calm, stable American women, unlikely to cause any problems in a conservative town like Kerman. We had marched in step for the first few months, determined to be a factor in changing Kermani lives. I had been dependent on her company, someone who knew exactly what it meant to be young, American, and female. But recently, my thoughts wound around Bill, how to outfox Mr. Sayeed-Nejad, fool Kerman, so I could see Bill. Betsy's musings, I imagined, were consumed with daydreams about Christopher in far-away Rezaiyeh, and now Christopher in the flesh.

I wished I liked Christopher. Friends' boyfriends were tricky. I couldn't see what on Earth had drawn her to this particular man. It was awkward.

But Betsy was enthralled. Wasn't he handsome and brilliant? He was full of ideas on how to make Iran a better place for Iranians, she told me; a little western ingenuity was all they needed. Local knowledge counted for little in Christopher's explications; he had a solution for everything. Look at all that effort wasted on sprinkling water on walkways and roads to keep down the dust. Why not use oil? It was dirt cheap in Iran, and oil sprinkling wouldn't need to be done so frequently.

If oil is so cheap, I thought, why don't they use a little more of it to heat these frigid classrooms? Glimpsing two girls in the third row copying answers from each other, I stood up and glared at them. Not appearing the least abashed, they went back to their own work. Pacing back and forth in front of the class, I could not feel my toes.

Why was sensible, rational Betsy falling for this fellow, the one with easy answers and a know-it-all attitude? I watched them, heads together, poring over one of Christopher's sketches of a building he was proposing for Rezaiyeh. As they examined it, Christopher explained each line. When Betsy made a suggestion, he pulled a pencil out of his pocket, erased a wall and drew it in another place. At that moment, they were a team building the future. But none of us had any future in Iran. We were plunked down for two years in a place we hoped we would like. We could plan for tomorrow, next week, even next year, but after that? When we left, would even a shadow of our time there remain? At least a building was tangible. Planning together was very seductive.

I still didn't like this man. If he was such a great planner, why wasn't he in Rezaiyeh doing what he was hired to do? Yesterday's telegram from the Peace Corps had been very terse: Return to your post or go back to the United States. Betsy said that his superiors didn't understand Christopher's creative genius.

The students were questioning my creation as well. "Miss Mary, this test is very hard," one of the younger ones complained in Persian. "Miss Betsy didn't teach us how to answer these questions. Even Zohrah doesn't know the answers, and she's the best student in the class." I looked at Zohrah, who nodded her head in agreement. Capitulating, I peered up and down the rows at sixty students, each with an imploring look in her eye and a chilled red nose. They needed to get outside in the sunshine.

"We'll practice the exercises on the test in class tomorrow," I said. "You can take it again on Thursday."

One by one the girls filed out of the classroom. "Thank you, Miss Mary." "Goodbye, Miss Mary." "We'll study hard, Miss Mary." Soon they were warming themselves on the sunny side of the schoolyard.

No Ruz

Winter left almost as quickly as it came. Kerman was absolutely glorious during the weeks leading up to the first days of spring. The sky was the unblemished turquoise of the Friday mosque. Winter snows lingered on the mountains, and the midday air was crisp and promising. The pistachio trees in the daneshsera's garden were about to burst into bloom, and a hint of green tinged anything that grew on the desert's edge.

But more than spring was in the air. In the classrooms, on the pathways of the bazaar, along the street leading to the Office of Education, there was an excitement, a sense of anticipation that something big was about to happen. The vernal equinox ushers in spring, but here, more importantly, it signifies the start of No Ruz, the Iranian New Year.

"Mary-khanum," Mr. Sayeed-Nejad said, "you must buy presents for the caretaker's children."

"What am I supposed to get them?" I asked.

"Shoes."

"Shoes? Why shoes?"

"Everyone gets new clothes for No Ruz. Ali and Reza will need new pairs of shoes."

"Mr. Sayeed-Nejad, I never bought a pair of shoes for another person in my life, and here a cobbler will have to make them. Can't I give them money?"

"Money's okay," Mr. Sayeed-Nejad said. "About 200 tomans ($30) should be enough for both of them. And don't forget their parents. The same amount for them. You must get new bills from the bank." My stipend from the Peace Corps was only 650 tomans a month. But this was a time to be generous.

It was also a time to celebrate. The teachers at Parvin
Etesami High School invited me to their party the day before
the two-week holiday.

"What are you serving?" I asked my friend Fereshteh. I was
finally on a first name basis with Miss Aghassi. Her homemaking classes would do the cooking.

"Aash reshteh," she said. "You remember; it's a special soup.
You had aash at my house when you first got here."

My heart sank. How could I forget my first aash party?
What I remembered most was how hard aash was to swallow.
"Sounds great," I said. "Too bad Betsy won't be here. I know
she'd love it." At that moment, Betsy was on her way to distant Tabriz for the wedding of two volunteers—and to meet up
with Christopher. I would face aash alone.

"Aash takes a lot of time to make. We only fix it on special
occasions," Mrs. Nahidi told me as we wound our way through
the halls to the celebration. "Miss Aghassi's senior class spent
yesterday rolling out dough for the noodles. They're very thin,
you know. Today, they made tiny meatballs. They'll season
the broth with lemon juice, and add kidney beans, then *chesre*—I still don't know what that is in English—and at the very
end, they'll throw in a little spinach for color." I didn't know
the English for chesre either, but at Fereshteh Aghassi's last
September, it had been an alien, unpalatable flavoring. I girded
myself for an unpleasant meal.

A pungent, surprisingly pleasing, lemony odor rose from
the steaming cauldrons of aash as we entered the teachers'
room. It looked appealing, the green spinach and red kidney
beans accenting the thin white noodles and yellow broth.

Men and women teachers, usually glued to chairs at opposite ends of the room, mingled around the table, slurping down
big bowls of soup with large spoons. A holiday atmosphere

filled the air. I absorbed the happy chatter, pleased with how much I understood.

"Befarmayeed." Fereshteh echoed that multi-functional word. After the customary refusals I accepted a bowl and took a small sip of the broth.

"Well, how do you like the aash? Is it as good as the first time you had it?" "It's delicious," I answered, spooning in a bigger mouthful. "Did you make this the same way?" I was sure she hadn't; this tasted too good.

"Exactly the same," she answered. "I teach my students to make it the way we do at home. I even brought the chesre I dried last summer to be sure of the seasoning."

Bowl of aash in hand, I chatted with one group of teachers, then another. The conversation was light, thank goodness. My Persian vocabulary still couldn't handle anything very serious. I scraped the last noodle from the bottom of my bowl, wondering what had happened to my taste buds.

The soup cauldrons were empty; the party was over. "Happy New Year!" I wished my colleagues. We'd be apart during the two-week holiday.

The caretaker and his family were waiting for me at the gate of the daneshsera. "*Aid-e shoma mobahrak*" ("Happy New Year"), I said, offering envelopes of crisp new bills to Mohammed, Kobra, and their children, Ali and Reza.

"What do you do for the New Year?" I asked Ali, the oldest.

"We wear new clothes."

"And our mother puts the seven '*seens*' on the table," Reza added. These are foods that begin with the letter *seen*, like *seer*, *seeb*, and *sabzee* (garlic, apples, and greens). Each carries symbolic meaning for the start of the new year.

"Don't forget we set a fresh egg on top of the mirror on the table," said Ali. "My daddy says that if I watch it very closely, it will turn exactly when the New Year arrives."

"Didn't you jump over a fire?" I asked.

"Yes, the Tuesday evening before No Ruz," Kobra-khanum said. "When we jump, we say 'the red of the fire to my cheeks, the yellow of my cheeks to the fire.' It's a new start for the new year."

Saying "have a good time," I headed back to my room on the deserted courtyard of the daneshsera, wishing someone had invited me to welcome the New Year.

The next morning, the first day of No Ruz, I didn't care what day it was. I was running a fever, running the sixty-yard dash to the bathroom, and barely able to hold up my aching head. Word quickly spread that the foreigner was ill, and my room filled with the caretaker's relatives who were visiting. They were anxious to help, thrilled to get a first-hand view of the sick American, and extremely polite. I submitted to a doctor's ministrations and a diet of tea and yogurt. No, I didn't know what had made me sick, I told all who asked. It wasn't the aash— none of the teachers were ill. Maybe it was the egg I had boiled for my dinner. Whatever the cause, it knocked me flat for four days. I missed my mother. It was lonesome having to straighten out my own bedclothes and get all my sympathy in Farsi.

Bill didn't know what had happened to me. Deep into a very unconventional romance, we were planning a surreptitious rendezvous in Shiraz, just the two of us, toward the end of the No Ruz holiday; my silence would be puzzling. Kobra-khanum reported that a driver from CENTO had asked after me at the daneshsera's gate. "He wanted to come see you," she said. "Like I would allow a strange man to come into the girls' school! But I did tell him you weren't feeling well."

"Well, if he comes again, give him this note," I said, grabbing pen and paper to let Bill know I was sick, but he shouldn't worry.

"*Chashm*" ("I'll do what you ask"), Kobra said, gathering up her chador as she got ready to leave. "You'll feel better soon. After all, you ate the soup I made."

I was beginning to perk up when Fred, just back from a trip to Tehran, came knocking. As he was a member of the Peace Corps family, Kobra let him in to see the patient. "I hear you've been sick," he said. "You do look a little pale. Listen, Mr. Sayeed-Nejad said we could take the Office of Education's jeep and driver. Let's go to Mahan. The weather's beautiful. It'll do you good to get out." We'd visited Mahan, Mr. Sayeed-Nejad's hometown, when we'd first arrived, wandering through the area's most famous site, the shrine of Shah Ne'matollah Vali, a famous Sufi poet and sage. The order of dervishes he founded more than 500 years earlier was still active.

The twin minarets of the mausoleum rose high above the town, their bright blue peaks beckoning us. I was surprised that Fred had sought me out for this excursion. We were friendly these days, but didn't usually spend time together, just us. It was probably Mr. Sayeed-Nejad's idea; he didn't want me to be alone.

"Remember when we visited here last fall?" I asked, as we climbed out of the Jeep and headed toward the shrine's compound. "It was the first time I ever wore a chador."

"Well, you don't have a chador this time. You'd better put on your scarf."

We ambled through the garden where hundreds of bold yellow pansies were planted around its long pool. Gazing into the water, I saw the reflections of tall cedars, their deep green contrasting with the blue of the shrine's dome, and the brown

of the mountains in the background. Gardens are the gems of
Persia. Why hadn't I been able to see how beautiful this one
was when I visited last fall?

It felt like a lifetime ago that Kerman's four new volunteers
had driven to Mahan with Mr. Sayyed-Nejad and Mr. Sanaati,
but it was only six months. Betsy and I had made our chador
debut on a hot fall afternoon. After Mr. Saanati parked the
jeep close to the Shah Ne'matollah Vali Shrine compound,
Tom and Fred had waited for Betsy and me to arrange our
unfamiliar attire. "You're never going to pass for proper Iranian
women," Fred had said as my chador slipped to the ground.

The afternoon sun was blazing as we hurried through the
shrine's garden, seeking shade in the mausoleum. But what
a mish-mash it had seemed inside: faded plastic flowers from
1960s Japan filled fifteenth-century niches of decorated ceramic
tiles; bare light bulbs hung by their cords from the high ceilings.
With their flowering tendrils wandering from one square to the
next, the tiles seemed too elaborate, too complicated. And
then there was that chador. An unwieldy distraction, it was
either slipping from my head or tripping me on the steps as we
made our way through the shrine's many passages.

Now, months of time and experience later, Fred and
I entered the mausoleum again, my scarf tied tightly at my
throat. The central domed burial vault had been completed
in 1437, a pamphlet in English informed me. As we explored,
one thing after another caught my attention: those tiles, that
woodwork, the dome's graceful arch. How had I missed their
beauty? As we were leaving, I noticed something I did remember from my first visit—a small vase of artificial flowers shoved
into one of the shrine's niches. Today, the pink and yellow
of Japan's plastic blended easily into the tendrils of vines and

abundance of flowers that adorned the five-hundred-year-old tiles surrounding that niche.

Fred and I strolled back through the garden toward the gate where our Jeep was parked, its driver waiting. The late afternoon light outlined the mausoleum's minarets in bold relief against mountains flushed by the setting sun. My eyes were shedding their western filters; I was finally seeing the jewel that is Iran.

Dreaming in Shiraz

Delicate pink roses blossomed along the roadway to the city of Shiraz, their heady aroma adding an ethereal layer to my escape into another world. Stolen time with Bill in a luxurious hotel far from Kerman seemed the perfect antidote to the cloistered daneshsera, but the closer the taxi got to the city, the more nervous I felt. My mother definitely would not approve. This assignation was almost as outrageous in Homewood, Illinois, in the mid-1960s as it was in Iran.

The trail of roses ended shortly before the cab driver turned into a walled hotel compound, its tree-lined driveway curving up to a pillared doorway. Entering a cool, dim lobby exuding old-world opulence, I did a double-take: a dozen dwarves were in attendance—standing at the door, waiting patiently beside the registration desk, or manning the minuscule elevator—all in maroon uniforms and black captain's caps. The hotel had selected every bellboy on its staff for his diminutive size. Remaining in the background while Bill registered at the desk, I tried to appear calm. No need to show my passport; everyone assumed I was his wife. But I had never spent all night with a man.

Minutes later, a porter was at the window of our large room, standing on a chair to pull open the curtains. Our narrow balcony overlooked a garden filled with the pinks and purples of spring, a screened-in area dominating one of its corners. "Shiraz is a city of gardens and nightingales," the porter said. "At this hotel, the nightingales are caged so in the evenings you can always hear their songs."

Then Bill and I were alone. "Come here, you," he said, holding out his arms.

Later, I lay next to my lover, watching his chest rise and fall as he slept. A cool evening breeze played across our bodies, and I heard the muezzin's call to evening prayer. As it darkened, the trill of nightingales filled the air. Time would slow on this No Ruz holiday while we squeezed all the rhythms of an intense romance into these few days together.

Poetry was everywhere in this land, but in no place more than Shiraz, where the mausoleums of the revered poets Hafez and Sa'adi nestled in gardens heavy with the sweet fragrances of the new year. These men were so central to contemporary Iranian life it was hard to believe Hafez had died in 1389, Sa'adi even earlier. At Hafez's shrine, Bill gave a couple of coins to an old man to discover our fortune in the bard's poems. Smoothing the gray stubble on his chin, he opened the book with a flourish, and asked me to point to a place on the page. In elegant Persian he read the verse I indicated, then translated:

When you sit by your love measuring wine,
Remember the lovers who measure the winds.

Except this, I can speak of no flaw in your beauty;
Fidelity and honesty are not the shape of your face.*

Neither of us wanted to interpret this. I liked the part about
"no flaw in your beauty;" Bill was sure we shouldn't keep track
of how much we were drinking. And what did the line about
fidelity and honesty have to do with us?

Lying side by side in the dark, we contemplated our future
together. Bill's job with CENTO would be over soon; the
Iranian trainees were almost ready to operate the new telephone system. Bill would go home to Canada to wait for the
next job. He wanted me to come with him.

"But if I did, could I go with you to places like Kerman?"

"Sometimes, I guess. But most wives want to stay at home
where they're comfortable. They get used to it, and the money's good." Wives. There was that word again. But this was
1965. For me, living together unmarried was impossible.

"I just can't imagine life without you, Mary," His passion
was contagious. No one had ever wanted me so much.

Clouds hung heavy in the sky the day we cruised along the
road to Persepolis. About an hour's drive from Shiraz, it is
Iran's most famous archaeological site. A few kilometers from
our destination, the driver braked to a slow crawl. Filling the
road, spilling out into the countryside, were flocks of bleating goats and sheep, their fat tails bouncing from side to side;
overflowing donkey carts filled with pots, pans, small children,
and tribal rugs; men and women either striding beside the
carts and flocks, or mounted on sturdy horses—the men in
high brown felt hats, the women wearing skirt on top of skirt

---

* "Hafez." *Anthology of Islamic Literature*, edited by James Kritzeck. Mid-
dlesex, England: Penguin Books, 1966, p. 284.

of vivid colors. "They're Qashqa'is," the driver said, blowing his horn as he edged his car into the mass of migrating tribal people. "They've been causing a lot of trouble these days," he told me in Persian. "Actually shot and killed a couple of Literacy Corps teachers a few weeks ago."

As our driver maneuvered the car through the flocks, a mother-aged woman, her voluminous skirts draping over the mare she was riding, shook her fist at us, shouting. Who could blame her? The taxi was pushing her off the road. I was stunned when Bill stuck his head out of the window and shouted, "Get out of the way, you old hag!"

"Please," said the driver, this time in English. "We must be quiet. There are very many of them."

"I'm not afraid of a few guys on dilapidated donkeys. This road was made for cars, not a bunch of sheep and goats," Bill said. But he pulled his head back in.

"Bill, the Qashqa'is have more right to be here than we do. They've always migrated to the mountains in the spring."

"You just have to take their side, don't you? No Iranian can do anything wrong. What about my opinions?"

"This isn't about you. It's about letting the Qashqa'is live like they've always lived. What right do you have to come over here and impose your choices on Iranians?"

"And you're so special? Tell me, Miss Goody Two-Shoes, just how are you changing anything? At least the people I'm training will be able to run the telephone system after I'm gone."

I turned away from him, the cacophony of the Qashqa'i migration fading into the distance, my eyes full of tears. More than anything, I wanted to push open the car door and flee. But on this remote road escape was not an option. We sat in silence until Persepolis was in sight.

Persepolis, *Takhte Jamshid* (Jamshid's throne) to Iranians, is an imposing site of leaning columns, expansive plazas, and demolished palaces spreading over more than a mile. Bill and I hired an English-speaking guide who filled our awkward silence with the site's early history. Persepolis had been a ceremonial city for royal and noble Iranians; they celebrated important holidays like No Ruz in this impressive setting, and courtiers from other lands came here to pay tribute. Dating back to 515 BC, it was the one of the most significant cities in the ancient world, only to be destroyed in a burst of flame set by Alexander the Great's drunken mercenaries 200 years later.

The guide stopped in front of the entrance to the metropolis, a grand staircase rising twenty meters to the terrace above. "Royalty arrived here on horseback," he said, "trotting up these shallow steps." Bill pointed to the bas-reliefs of courtiers and animals along the staircase, asking why their faces had been hacked away.

"Arabs!" The guide uttered the word like an expletive. He explained that a thousand years after Alexander conquered Iran, bands of Arabs intent on spreading Islam destroyed all facial images they encountered, believing their religion prohibited the depiction of humans or animals. "Many Muslims in Iran do not agree," he added. "It's not in the Koran."

"Looks like they missed some," Bill said, indicating some complete figures lower on the staircase walls.

"Those were buried in hundreds of years of sand. They were uncovered thirty years ago when the archaeologists began to dig."

I didn't absorb very much here. As we rambled around the ruins, I replayed the scene with Bill over and over in my head. Could I really love a man who was so callous, so superior, so resentful? The columns of Persepolis, still standing after two thousand years, faded quickly as we drove back to Shiraz.

It was hard to stay angry with Bill. "Come on, give me a smile," he said as he nodded to the porters holding open the hotel door. "You're not surrounded by uniformed midgets every day. This is special." He was funny and fun; such an engaging distraction in a place that offered so few. But that night Bill drank a lot of vodka. And I was more comfortable sleeping with my back to him.

Our last day in Shiraz, I couldn't wait to get outside. Bill and I got lost trying to find the bazaar, which was split by a modern thoroughfare, its domes extending for blocks on either side of the street. As we entered, the familiar aromas of cardamom and saffron, people and animals, fresh greens and winter-worn potatoes permeated the pathways.

We had started the morning uneasily, but by the time we found the bazaar, we were wrapped up in the adventure. He laughed when I declared the divided bazaar maimed; when he tried to bargain for some strawberries, I teased him, and finished the job. I bought a narrow, hand-woven band with geometric designs and roped tassels to hang on my wall. The merchant claimed Qashqa'i men wore these as belts around their waists at their weddings. A good story, but we noticed donkeys sporting similar, if larger, bands across their behinds. Bill couldn't stop ribbing me about donkey weddings. Things were back to normal for the fugitives from Kerman.

That night, lingering over dinner and a bottle of Shiraz's famed wine, we continued to talk of marriage. Perhaps I would stay in Kerman for the rest of my Peace Corps stint, but I would consider the possibility of wedlock. As I fell asleep on our last night in magical Shiraz, the caged nightingales were singing their hearts out.

A Visit to
Mr. Arjomand's Village

Letter home

> "Owning" a village seems so strange to me,
> but several of our friends' families are landlords.
> Our nurse friend Fatimeh invited Betsy and me to
> Kupahyeh, her family's retreat in the mountains. The
> night there was glorious—the stars so close I wanted
> to reach up and grab one. Fatimeh says Kupahyeh is
> fifteen degrees cooler than the city, a good place to
> escape the blistering summer heat.

The day began at the ungodly hour of 6:30 a.m. when five sleepy Peace Corps volunteers and Mr. Sayeed-Nejad crawled into Mr. Sanaati's jeep and headed into the hinterlands, bound for the mountain retreat of Kerman's most prominent carpet family, the Arjomands. We were late for our rendezvous at the intersection of two dirt roads west of Kerman, but Mr. Arjomand was even later. We had decided to head back to Kerman for breakfast when thick swirls of dust from Mr. Arjomand's large Land Rover appeared in the distance.

"So sorry to keep you waiting," our host said, his British English perfect. "We had trouble finding petrol this morning. Just follow me." After he introduced us to his other guests, a Bulgarian couple who imported carpets from Kerman, we took off toward the mountains.

Crossing dry riverbeds, our two-vehicle convoy climbed into the foothills, negotiating jagged mountain passes before descending into a valley dotted with villages. We turned onto a birch-lined road, halting in front of a house nestled in the midst of one of the loveliest settings I had ever seen. If gardens are the gems of Iran, this one was the Hope Diamond. Fragrant roses in opulent first bloom surrounded a large pool, its fountain spraying mist into the dry mountain air. A canopy of trees sheltering the compound's paths and streams lent an air of intimacy to the surroundings.

Kicking off our shoes, we followed our host into the residence, a home completely devoid of furniture, its floors covered with the intricately medallioned Kerman carpets made famous by the Arjomand family. Sitting cross-legged around a sofreh laden with piping hot bread, boiled eggs, creamy yogurt, cherry jam, fresh goat cheese, and a plate of garden greens, the conversation flowed easily, the banter switching back and forth from English to Farsi. What a change from the formality of the straight-back chair receptions of the city. It's hard to be proper sitting on the floor.

Breakfast finished, we toured the gardens, Mr. Arjomand pointing out the wide variety of fruit trees flowering in the orchards. "Over here," he said, "we've walled off a section to grow oranges and lemons. In the winter, the area is glassed in and heated with kerosene stoves." Turning to Mr. Sanaati, he repeated what he had said in Persian. I inhaled the delicate fragrance of sweet lemons blossoming where they didn't belong.

We left the compound and strolled toward the center of the village where houses made from stone, each with a cellar for animals, were built into the mountainside. Women in short, functional chadors squatted in the bright outdoors, chatting as they sorted dried beans or chopped vegetables; their children trailed after us as we passed by. "Hello, meeses. I love you," I heard in English. Then, in Farsi, "She must be from Tehran. See, she's not wearing a scarf on her head."

Villagers pose for a picture in Mr. Arjomand's village.

"*Nakhaer, Amreeka-ee-am*." ("No, I'm an American.") Perhaps Iran's capital was home to the most westernized women they could imagine, but I didn't want to be mistaken for a disdainful Tehrani. I pulled out my camera and asked one of the women if I could take her picture. She shifted her chador away from her face, and posed proudly in front of her house.

"Me, me next. Take my picture." Boys and girls surrounded me, backing up for solemn poses as I snapped a few more shots. Promising to give Mr. Arjomand copies for them, I hurried to catch up with my party.

"I'm confused," I said, when I reached Mr. Arjomand. "Do you actually own this village?"

"Yes. We own the land. Before the shah's reforms, my family owned all the villages in this valley. Since the land reforms, many are cooperatively owned, but this one is still in the family. The women in all these communities weave carpets for us."

"But what does it mean to own a village?"

"As landowners we receive a portion of the crops and animals the villagers raise. And we have an obligation to help them in times of need."

"Have the shah's land reforms made any difference?" asked Betsy.

"There have been a lot of changes in all these villages, the ones we own as well. See those fields over there? USAID taught the farmers how to contour plow the hillside to reduce erosion. A member of the Literacy Corps is working with the children in this village. The new health clinic in the village to the east serves the whole valley.

"Life in Iran is changing for all of us," Mr. Arjomand continued. "On the whole, I believe it will be a better place, but some things never change. Come, I want to show you something."

We followed him past house after house, chickens scratching in the dirt, children tossing balls back and forth, until the cultivated fields on the village edge spread out before us. "Look," he said, pointing. A lone tree, adorned with hundreds of bits of cloth and strands of beads, spread its branches wide; stubs of candles littered the ground beneath its boughs.

"The villagers take special care of this tree," Mr. Arjomand said. "It was just an ordinary tree, one of a few that hadn't been chopped down for fuel. Then, about ten years ago, a village woman dreamed that Imam Reza, one of Islam's earliest 'saints,' visited this very spot, touching the tree. The next day she sacrificed a goat to commemorate her holy vision. Now, the people consider the tree a sacred symbol. They lit those candles in its honor."

"But why is it covered with cloth and beads?" I asked.

"The village girls tie them on when they want something special to happen, like marriage or a child. Just superstitions. Like I said, some things never change. They call it 'the tree of hope.'"

On our walk back to the Arjomands' verdant compound, Fred and our host were deep in conversation, punctuating their comments with broad gesticulations and wide smiles. If they were laughing about the superstitious village girls, I was not. I was struck by how the people who lived here had transformed this arid landscape. Mr. Arjomand, with imagination and money, nurtured an oasis worthy of a sultan; the villagers, lavishing scarce water on a special tree, created their own symbol of faith, of hope.

Ali-agha, Mr. Arjomand's manservant, had spread a large red carpet in the garden on a platform next to a small stream. Slipping out of my shoes, I settled down against a bolster. The men pulled off their city trousers, relaxing in their *zir shalvari*, the long, soft cotton "under trousers" that served as loungewear for men all over Iran. Ali-agha placed platters of hot steaming rice and strips of broiled lamb in front of us. After mixing the yolk of a raw egg and fresh-churned butter into a plate full of rice, I helped myself to a sizzling piece of meat, sprinkling it with pungent sumac. *Chelo kebab*, Iran's national dish, is often overrated in my opinion, but this was delicious. When we finished, Ali proffered tea that had been brewing on top of a brass Russian samovar nearby. Leaning back against the bolster, I sipped the fragrant beverage, the weight of city life lifting like the morning mist.

As the afternoon passed, the Bulgarian couple, Mr. Arjomand, and Fred sat cross-legged on the carpet playing bridge. I watched Fred interact with the others. Brow smooth, eyes alert, his bids were decisive, as if he were the partner of a lord of the desert every day. Of the five Peace Corps volunteers here, Fred was the one who intuitively knew how to be a Kermani.

Ali-agha placed a backgammon board and a bottle of vodka on the carpet near Mr. Sanaati. The faces of the entire male contingent brightened.

"Time for that book I brought along," Betsy said. "Not much to do here." She was right. Neither of us played backgammon or bridge, and women could not drink in Mr. Arjomand's garden.

Reading proved impossible as the men's voices grew louder. Their bridge game abandoned, Mr. Arjomand and Fred faced each other at the backgammon board, slapping the pieces from line to line with great authority and much braggadocio. Mr. Sanaati broke into song: "*Mastam, mastam*" ("I'm drunk, I'm drunk"), he sang, bellowing the words to a Persian drinking tune, while Mr. Sayeed-Nejad snapped his fingers. Tom Taaffe, glass in hand, looked a little lost. Tom Sisul sat against a bolster, a happy grin on his face. Mr. Arjomand's English had lost its clipped tones.

The afternoon shadows lengthened and I started to fret. What had begun as such a perfect party was fast disintegrating. Our group's behavior embarrassed me, and I was worried about the winding dirt road that lay ahead.

"Shouldn't we leave now while it's still light?" I asked Mr. Sayeed-Nejad. "Mr. Sanaati has to drive."

"*Nahrahat nahbasheed*" ("Don't worry"), he said.

"Mary's right." Fred surprised me by agreeing. "Mr. Sanaati has had a lot to drink. We should go now. Maybe I should drive."

Mr. Sanaati, hearing his name, wanted to know what everyone was talking about. When Mr. Sayeed-Nejad translated, Sanaati's response was adamant. We would leave when he was ready, and he wasn't ready yet. He was perfectly capable of driving. He wasn't drunk, and he was insulted that Mr. Jones thought he was.

More vodka was consumed while angry tempers subsided. By the time we convinced Mr. Sanaati to leave, the mountains were the dark purple of dusk. Tom Sisul folded his long legs into the front seat of the jeep alongside Mr. Sanaati and Mr. Sayeed-Nejad. The rest of us slid into the back. Mr. Sanaati gunned the gas pedal, and we were off.

"Say your prayers, Mary," Fred muttered. "Rides with drunk drivers can be pretty scary."

The jeep zigzagged from one side of the road to the other, zooming up hills and around terrifying hairpin turns. Mr. Arjomand's garden, the villagers' tree of hope, my earlier contentment, vanished as I clung to the seat.

"Slowly, slowly," Mr. Sayeed-Nejad said in Persian as the jeep careened over ruts and rocks, crevasses, and gullies.

"Slow down!" said Tom Sisul.

"Yes, slow down! You're going to kill us," Betsy said, her voice shrill.

"*Yavash, yavash!*" ("Slow, slow!") Fred said.

"Mr. Sanaati, you're going too fast!" Tom Taaffe chimed in. But Mr. Sanaati ignored us all. The jeep swung from side to side as it sped along the road, tossing us first one way, then the other.

"Look, I can see Kerman's lights. We're almost home."

The words were barely out of my mouth when the jeep's front wheel slipped off the road. Mr. Sanaati jammed on the brakes, struggling to keep the vehicle from tumbling down the embankment. I banged into the roof, Tom Sisul's wide shoulders keeping me out of the front seat. We landed in disarray as Mr. Sanaati managed to get all four wheels back on the road. Fred grabbed me around the waist and pulled me toward him. "Are you okay?"

"I think so," I said, collapsing against his chest.

Mr. Sanaati swerved his jeep into the bazaar's square, jamming on the brakes in front of its entrance. "Get out," he said. We obeyed.

"Bachaha," Mr. Sayeed-Nejad's trembling voice echoed through the empty square, "we are very fortunate. God gave us all new lives tonight. *Alhamdulillah!*" ("God be praised!")

Bam

Fred and I were inseparable during the days following that wild ride. Strolling side by side through the bazaar, we shared our discoveries: the heavy wooden shop doors that fascinated Fred, their huge metal hinges and complex padlocks each different from the other; or my favorite oddity, the vendor who hawked chickens and flowers. We ignored the lone carpet seller in that maze of pathways, the one who had refused to speak to me just days before, rejecting my queries with a sharp upward jerk of his chin. No, that movement said, I won't deal with the likes of you.

Sitting side by side on the creaky cot in his room, the sun shining through glass doors, Fred revealed he was conflicted about his college degree, the first in the family. Wasn't working with one's hands more valuable, more tangible, than sitting behind a desk? I, on the other hand, was proud that my grandmother was a college graduate. Did this make me an elitist? Fred, often so scathing, so negative, could be a charming, sensitive confidant. We edged around new feelings for each other, calling them friendship.

Fred entertained me with stories about his family in California: his feisty Italian American mother who, he claimed, would tell anyone to go to hell whenever she felt like it; his ill-tempered father who had been a welterweight boxer in his youth; his sassy, sharp-tongued older sister who let him tag along with her friends until she wed at eighteen. And he told me about his high school sweetheart Maria, a brilliant Radcliffe junior, whom he planned to marry after the Peace Corps.

I could not imagine my mother being that blunt with anyone. Although my father could raise his voice in anger, he was most famous for incredibly boring lectures—on the virtues of one type of tea over another, or how Indo-European languages spread across Eurasia. And I certainly had not encouraged my little brother Don to hang out with me. Fred's family seemed refreshingly direct, and his girlfriend a long way away.

But my boyfriend Bill was in Kerman. "He wants to marry me," I said, "but I'm just not sure. There's no way I can tell if we'll get along when we leave Iran. We can't act like a couple here."

"Yeah. The Iranians treat the Peace Corps like we're one big family. It's fine for you to hang out with your brothers, but you'd better not be seen with Bill. Whether they deserve it or not, the men working here on short-term contracts have rough reputations. Kermanis shield their women; they want to protect you, too."

"I guess so. But it feels more like prison."

When it came to Bill, I was worried about more than couplehood. I didn't want to be left behind in Canada while my husband earned our living in far-away places. Then there was his unbridled jealousy. If I was reading a newspaper, he pouted; if I was laughing with his roommate, there could be an explosion. But I loved his sense of humor, his big heart, his conviviality. Maybe if Fred met Bill he could help me with this quandary. Fred was enthusiastic when I broached the subject, suggesting lunch together.

Days later, Tom Sisul, Fred, Betsy and I gathered around a table on the shady side of the Hotel Akavan courtyard, waiting. I plucked nervously at the napkin in my lap; my boyfriend was late. We were about to order when Bill appeared in the doorway. Tall, with broad features, one could tell he was a westerner by the way he moved. Betsy waved and he strode across to our table.

"Had a devil of a time finding this place," he said. "My driver had never heard of it."

Soon he was sipping a beer and soliciting Fred and Tom's advice on what to order. By the time lunch was over, they were joking like old pals. I would not have to ask Fred's opinion of Bill. I could tell he liked him.

"Hey, have you guys ever been to Bam?" Bill asked. "No? You really ought to see it. It's such a different town, with those huge ruins, and palm trees everywhere."

One of CENTO's contractors was going to Bam the next day. Bill couldn't come along—his supervisor was in town—but as we didn't have conflicting teaching commitments, the rest of us could drive down, stay at CENTO quarters, and hitch a ride back with an Iranian trainee a day later. Getting out of town was a great idea. We set out for Bam the next morning.

Squeezed in next to Fred in the back of the CENTO Land Rover, I peered out the window as the driver navigated through mountains eroded by wind, and rocks springing out of the desert in angled formations. Other than occasional flocks of goats scrounging the wasteland for nourishment, there was nothing but rocks and dirt and heat. Oh the heat! It was still April, yet we were baking at 350 degrees in a metal Land Rover oven.

"Stick a fork in me. I'm done," Betsy said, running her bandanna across her forehead.

Finally, rounding a curve along the rim of a hill, we saw Bam nestling in a sea of palm trees and orange groves below. Arg-e Bam, its famed abandoned town and citadel, rose like a specter in the background.

"I've never seen a palm tree before," I said, as the road cut through acres of tall trunks topped with bursts of green fronds.

"I've seen plenty of them in southern California," Fred said. "Here, most of Kerman's dates and oranges come from Bam."

The Land Rover pulled into CENTO headquarters. "You'll have to bunk in the tent outside," the director told us. "We're full up in here." That was no problem, we assured him; we had brought our sleeping bags.

The four of us spent the next hours exploring the streets of Bam, Fred sauntering next to me like he belonged by my side. Soon we were part of a familiar scene: a pack of young teens in somber suit jackets following our group down the road. "Ooh, you speak such good Persian. Welcome," one after another greeted us.

"Tell us about the old town," Fred encouraged a skinny teenager determined to practice his English.

"The Bam, she is very old," the boy said. "She has—how do you say *Zardoshti*? Oh, Zoroastrian. She has the Zoroastrian fireplaces. And the Bam, she has one mosque, of course. And church for foreigners. The Bam she was very famous."

"What happened?" Betsy asked. "Why did everyone leave?"

"My grandfather says about very bad Afghanis with horses. Then more bad men come from Shiraz. Soon, only army stay here. Now, the army, he is gone. Today, the Bam, she is for guests."

"We'll see it tomorrow," Fred said.

We dined that evening with the men from CENTO. As I toyed with mashed potatoes straight from the U.S. Commissary, I felt Fred watching me, his steady gaze an unasked question. I didn't know where to look; my appetite vanished.

It was just 8:30 when our host began to yawn. "We keep Iranian hours here. Early to bed, early to rise…." We said goodnight. Tom, carrying a kerosene lantern, led the way to the large tent where we unfurled our sleeping bags.

"Anyone feel like taking a walk?" Fred asked, looking at me.

"Sure, I'm not tired yet," I said.

"I'm heading for bed," "Me, too" said Tom and Betsy.

Shoulders touching, Fred and I strolled into the night, the lantern glow of the tent fading behind us.

"Brrr, it's cold," I said, hugging my arms. Dark, too. Only a ghostly sliver of the moon was visible in the night sky. We stumbled along the uneven path, barely able to see each other. Fred grabbed my elbow: "Come on, we're going to break our necks walking around here. The gate's next to the road. Let's stop there."

With Fred still holding my arm, we picked our way toward the edge of the compound. On one side of the gate was CENTO's headquarters; on the other side, the empty road that led either southeast to Pakistan, even to China, or northwest to Kerman, to Europe. If I could set off in any direction, which way would it be?

Resting against the wall, I stared out through the dark, feeling rather than seeing Fred by my side. I startled as he edged his arm around my waist.

"I don't think this is such a good idea," I said, moving away from him.

"I think it's a terrific idea."

Putting his arm back around my waist, he leaned back and surveyed the stars, their numbers endless, shimmering white specks on the black dome of night. "When I was a kid, I was always trying to find the constellations," he said. "Hey, there's Orion." As I tried to find the hunter chasing his prey across the heavens, he cupped my face in his hand, kissing me on the lips.

Dawn was breaking when I awoke, guilt gnawing in the pit of my stomach. Betsy was sound asleep against one wall; Tom snored gently against another. Fred lay flat on his back, glasses off, his blue eyes wide open, staring at the top of the tent. I avoided his gaze and headed for the shower at the back of the CENTO house.

The warm trickle of water provided no solace. Here I was, playing out the Hafez fortune Bill and I had heard in Shiraz, "Fidelity and honesty are not in the shape of your face." To top it all off, now there were two men to conceal from Iranians: the one who expected me to drop everything to marry him, and the one who was charming his way into my life.

"You were gone a long time last night, Mary," Betsy said as we walked together into the house for breakfast.

"Yeah, well it was nice out," I said, focusing on the path ahead.

A half an hour later, full of brewed coffee and commissary Corn Flakes, our group set off for Bam's old city.

Arg-e Bam, a walled city constructed from adobe bricks, the trunks of palms, straw and stones, spread over six kilometers, one of the largest city ruins in the world, according to our Iranian guide, a former English teacher. He led the four of us up the hill and into the site through its one remaining gate.

"This long, narrow stretch was the bazaar," he said in precise British tones. "More than fifty shops lined the area." Half listening, I looked over at Fred, who was never far from me.

"Bam was an important oasis," the guide continued, "a station along the Silk Road that stretched west from China. It was also known for cotton fabrics. In the 1500s, more than 10,000 people lived here."

We picked our way along the narrow alleyways: past the ruin of a *zurkhaneh* (gymnasium) where men had hefted heavy pins while chanting verses from the Koran, just as they do in modern times; past the *caravanserai*, where visitors rested from their arduous journeys.

Arg-e Bam, the old city. The Chahar Fasl tower rises above the site.

"The citadel," the guide said as we clambered higher and higher, "housed a large garrison of soldiers, with stables for two hundred horses. The prison is one of Bam's oldest structures. Its bricks were made before Mohammed's time, God be praised." I peered into the prison hole. God, it was dark in there.

By the time we reached the governor's quarters at the top, a frigid wind was howling through Chahar Fasl, the imposing square turret that rose sixty-five meters above the valley floor.

"This tower is called Four Seasons," the guide said, "because the wind changes direction with each new quarter of the year." I gazed out from the high summit of the old city—over the new Bam,* over the valley of palms and citrus trees, roads and villages, over the cluster of civilization that petered out into the nothingness of the desert. It was spring; the winds were changing.

In stark contrast to our blistering trip to Bam, it was freezing as we headed back to Kerman later that day. Next to Fred again in the Land Rover's back seat, I wrapped my jacket more tightly around me, playing the last two days over in my head. How did the people of Bam ever make the decision to abandon the only homes they knew, to leave the familiar behind for an unknown future? Could they have changed their minds if it didn't work out? I had never been good at decision-making, usually letting the options eliminate themselves until I ended up with only one. But here, sitting in this Land Rover, even my choices were unclear. Despite the kisses of the night before, Fred and I were supposed to be in love with other people. The only place I had any control was in deciding whether or not to leave Bill. I did not want to face that choice.

Fred reached between us, putting his warm hand over my icy one. "Hey," he called to the driver, "does this thing have any heat? It's cold back here." I stared out of the window and watched snowflakes fall on the desert.

---

* Bam suffered the worst earthquake in Iranian history on December 23, 2003. The town was decimated, and more than 26,000 people lost their lives. The extensive ruins of Arg-e Bam collapsed, including its high tower, Chahar Fasl.

Get a Move On

Letter home

> One thing I know is that I don't want to go home
> and get married. I'm still too young.

The rumors were everywhere, breezing through the bazaar, climbing over the walls of the daneshsera, and creeping into government offices all over town. The foreigners were leaving. The Army had gone, the U.S. Mapping crew was on its way, USAID would be out of Kerman by July. And in a matter of weeks, CENTO would turn over most of its operations to the Iranians it had trained. As far as I could tell, coincidence was the only reason for this mass exodus, but everyone had an opinion. By mid-summer, the only westerners left in town would be the Episcopal minister's British wife, the Greek rug merchant (in Kerman since the 1920s), and the Peace Corps. Bill was shaken by the news. I was more sanguine; my need to make a choice was vanishing. I was not ready to leave Iran.

We were lunching on the shady side of the Hotel Akavan courtyard with Betsy, Tom Sisul, and Fred when Bill broke the news.

"CENTO's leaving. We're on a hurry-up schedule, so we should be out of here in a couple of weeks." Silently, I thanked the powers that be for divine intervention. Then he added, "Guess that means you'll be going home sooner than you planned, Mary."

Before he could go further, I interrupted. "Bill, this is a conversation we should have alone. These people don't want to be involved in our personal decisions." I glanced over at Fred who was following this exchange intently. He knew about my recent meeting with the director of education, Mr. Manucher.

That conversation had started out on a surprising note. The daneshsera was renovating many of its buildings, he told Betsy, Mr. Sayeed-Nejad, and me. As our room would be expanded into a classroom, we would need to find a new place to live, a room with a family, perhaps. My heart sank. Even less privacy.

"Betsy and I would like a home of our own, someplace where we won't be a bother to anyone."

"I'm sure Mr. Sayeed-Nejad will help you find an appropriate place," Mr. Manucher said, nodding toward our mentor. We rose to leave.

"Miss Mary, there's one more thing," he said, addressing me in Farsi. "You know you are an example for our young girls. You must be careful of your actions. The foreign men working here are not to be trusted. You should stay away from them—especially the tall one with the missing teeth. He's got a very bad reputation."

Bill. This was all about Bill. Mr. Sayeed-Nejad looked smug. He had warned me. The shah and Queen Farah threw reproachful glances in my direction from their pictures behind the director's desk.

Although I didn't know why Bill was considered so disreputable, there was no justification for my behavior. I, who hated making choices, had made a lot of them. I knew my involvement with any man was beyond the pale here.

I hadn't gotten around to telling Bill about the director's pronouncement. For an instant at the Hotel Akavan, I thought CENTO had solved my problem. They were leaving, Bill would go with them, I would stay in Kerman. But Bill wasn't buying into my version of the new reality.

"You'll come home with me, that's all there is to it," he said over drinks in his dining room. "I can't leave you alone in this god-forsaken place for a whole year."

I leaned forward, determined to meet his eyes. "Bill, I don't think Kerman's a god-forsaken place; I like it here. And I'm not alone. There are five of us."

Around and around we went, evening after evening. Finally, I said it:

"Bill, I'm not going with you. That's it. You'll have to leave without me."

He was quiet for a moment. "All right, I'll go," he said at last. "If this is what you really want. Just remember, someone loved you and you broke his heart."

Fred, the two Toms, and I accompanied Bill to the airport. He's shrunk, I thought, watching him climb the airplane stairs. The days of uncertainty, my disloyal behavior, the alcohol had leeched the warrior out of this Cheyenne Indian. Looking into the bathroom mirror that night, a cold-hearted stranger returned my gaze.

The school semester was almost over when Bill left Kerman. The older students had stopped attending classes weeks before. They paced up and down, hewing to the shade during the sunny hours, taking advantage of the lamplight at dusk, their lips moving as they absorbed math, literature, and science, word for word. This was a trying time for everyone. The seniors' final examinations were prepared in Tehran, arriving in Kerman just days before they were given. It would be weeks before the results were known. Teachers had taught to the test all year long. I had no senior classes and no idea what was on these exams.

It was a good thing there was a lull in the English-teaching action. Betsy and I had to find another place to live, and we had to find it fast. When the director of education announced we'd be leaving the daneshsera, we didn't have a hasty departure in mind. Renovations at the school started with the bathroom building, which grew overnight to include more shower and toilet stalls. We were still debating where to live when a large crack developed in the dome of our roof. Dirt sifted in through the ceiling, and clumps of adobe cascaded to the floor. Almost immediately, piles of dirt, bricks, and mud appeared right outside our door, ready for urgent repairs and the planned renovation.

"Betsy, hurry up. If we don't get out of here we're going to be entombed in this room." I'd been up since dawn, sneaking peeks at two men, each with a rolled up pant leg, using their bare appendages to mix an adobe concoction for our roof. Dirt and dust streamed in under the doorsill, clouding the air. I felt like an unwelcome guest whose hosts were pretending she wasn't there. In a land where tomorrow was usually an unspecific time, it had arrived in our corner of the compound.

"You're right. Let's get out of here," Betsy said, holding her breath as she stepped into her shirtwaist dress. "We have to catch Mr. Sayeed-Nejad before he takes off for Tehran to get his passport."

Mr. Sayeed-Nejad was distracted these days. He'd been selected to go to the United States for the summer as a participant in the Experiment for International Living, a program not coincidentally administered in Iran by the Peace Corps' Gertrude Dorry.

We padlocked the door and hurried across the courtyard, greeting girl after girl with either "salaam alaikum" or "hello, how are you?" as we hurried to the gate. At seven-thirty a.m., the pavement was already collecting the heat of the day.

Mr. Sayeed-Nejad was not at his desk. We shoved the mail waiting for us into our bags and sat down. In a back office corner the secretary's fingers flew across her keyboard, the machine's roller moving in the direction opposite from the way my typewriter moved. Of course. She was typing in Farsi.

Finally, we heard Mr. Sayeed-Nejad's crutches in the hall. He had barely stowed them beneath his desk when Betsy blurted: "Mr. Sayeed-Nejad, we have to find a place to live right now. They're tearing down our room. The dust is awful."

"Bachaha, don't worry. They won't take off the roof while you're sleeping. Besides, I have some news for you. There's a building, just off the pavement, not too far from the bazaar, with two apartments, one upstairs, one down. If that married couple from CENTO would live in one of them, I think the director of education will give his consent."

Among our friends from CENTO was a married couple from India whose presence would provide a shield of respectability. Although most of their colleagues had departed, they were still in Kerman and would be thrilled with free housing. I doubted they would be around much longer, but there was no point in troubling Mr. Sayeed-Nejad with that bit of conjecture.

Hours later, Betsy and I followed Mr. Houshangi, the exuberant owner, into a modern brick structure in a part of town I hadn't visited before. If the daneshsera was in the posh part of the city, this apartment building edged a transitional neighborhood. Women and children gathered around a communal water pump directly across the street, washing clothes or filling water buckets for home. Very unusual—I hadn't seen women working in the open in Kerman before. Twisting, wall-lined alleyways wove into the neighborhood beyond; I could see no poles for electricity.

The two-storey building fronted a wide dirt street; its second floor balcony faced the throngs at the water pump, the mountains surrounding Kerman rising in the distance. A walled courtyard, devoid of anything growing, was in back of the small first floor apartment. The upstairs felt huge: four rooms, a big kitchen and, best of all, a shower and toilet—a private toilet, mind you. Both floors were empty—lots of nooks and crannies, but not a single shelf, cupboard, or counter. A lone light bulb dangled by a long cord from the ceiling of each room, rooms with doors. How wonderful it would be to close a door, to be alone for a change.

Betsy and I looked at each other. "We'll take it," we said. The water would be turned on in a week; we could move in then. Running water where we lived—a real luxury, even if we couldn't drink it. Mr. Houshangi handed each of us a key to the building, and danced down the stairs. He was renting to foreigners, a boon to his pocket and his prestige.

I stared at the key in my hand. No more knocking at the gate, no more keeping Kobra-khanum up at night. I could open the door whenever I wanted, let in anyone I chose, lock out the world. What a difference a key makes.

Betsy and I didn't look at our mail until we were back at the daneshsera that evening. Ignoring the layers of accumulated dust, we perched on our cots to read our letters. I was engrossed in an escapade of our family dog, Spike, when Betsy blurted, "I don't believe it!"

"Believe what?"

"Christopher's been transferred to Kerman. This letter is dated five days ago. He should be here any day."

"You're kidding! You mean the Peace Corps actually fell for it? Don't they know you're a couple?"

"They know," Betsy said. "Christopher told them when he applied for the transfer."

"Where will he live?"

"With Fred and Tom. They've got a room they're not using." I couldn't wait to see the reactions of Fred and Tom.

"Like hell he will! I'm not going to live with that obnoxious blowhole!" I watched the familiar sight of Fred's storm rising: angry words spilling out of his mouth in precise, cutting sentences; every corpuscle of his body tensed for action.

Betsy and I had gone separate ways to Tom and Fred's house. First stopping at a minuscule bakery for some date-filled treats to sweeten the news, I'd hurried through the clanging copper bazaar to the guys' place. Soon after I dropped the bombshell, Betsy was at the door, her eyes shining, her words rushed as she gave her version of Christopher's impending arrival. Although nothing in her tone or demeanor implied anything but the expectation of shared enthusiasm, she'd brought sweet red cherries as her offering.

Fred threw a knowing glance in my direction and heaved a sigh of surrender. This new roommate was a fait accompli; the Peace Corps was paying the rent. "Well, I guess he can stay here for awhile," he said, popping a fat cherry into his mouth. Christopher arrived that afternoon.

The next few days, I spent mornings teaching my final classes at the nursing school, and afternoons sorting through the piles of belongings Betsy and I had accumulated. The furniture—cots, table, and chairs, our two-burner camp stove and tin box oven, a twenty-gallon drum for drinking water, our Peace Corps book locker—was minimal; it wouldn't fill one of our new rooms. But did I really need that half-knitted scarf? The remaining artifacts of our lives—vacuum-packed tins of Quaker oatmeal, dishes and utensils, souvenirs from Esfahan— we tossed into plastic shopping bags. Cardboard boxes, those staples of American packing, were nonexistent here.

The morning we moved, the daneshsera's gray donkey pulled his cart up to our room. Christopher was a handy helper, moving most of our furniture into the courtyard. As I scurried around, checking out cracks and crevices for hidden treasures, Betsy worked with her boyfriend. I was almost envious. How wonderful to be in love. How amazing not to have doubts.

While Christopher and the donkey driver lifted beds and bags onto the cart, Betsy and I said our goodbyes to the girls milling about. "You're leaving us, Miss Mary, Miss Betsy? Oh please don't go," said one student after another. "We'll ask the principal to build you another room."

He wouldn't have done it. Betsy and I were resident curiosities at the daneshsera. English was not part of the curriculum, so I had never taught a single class to these high school graduates, Kerman's future elementary school teachers. Behind these walls, we had interacted with the students for almost nine months, yet I knew the names of only a few. I'd greeted their teachers as they hurried to class, but had only a few meaningful conversations. I'd been a guest at the daneshsera, not a part of it.

Taking one more look around the room, I tossed a fugitive package of mouse poison—no place is mouse-proof—into the last remaining bag and closed the door behind me.

The little gray donkey gave a final bray of protest as he began the journey to our new home. Christopher, Betsy, and I hailed a taxi. *"Khiabun-eh Cinema Nur"* ("the Light Movie Theater's street"), I told the driver, and we were off.

Hours later, I stood facing the last class of the semester at the nursing school. Thirty-six girls looked up at me, their expressions pleading *please, oh please, don't make us work hard today*. I relented, my mind spinning to invent something fun that could pass for an English lesson. I settled on the day's move, practicing all the items the donkey had carted to our new apartment on Cinema Nur Street. The students stumbled at book locker; we settled for shelves, which did not exactly match; and they began to giggle at mouse poison. They knew *mouse*. Had I really brought a mouse to my new home? Poison? What's poison? "Ohhh, Miss Mary, you need a cat. Poison is dangerous. A child might eat it." With that, class was over.

As I was packing up my belongings, Farideh, one of the shyer students, stayed behind. "Miss Mary, where on Cinema Nur Street do you live?" She had something for me; she'd pay me a visit at my new home the next morning at ten.

Back on Cinema Nur Street, Betsy and Christopher had unpacked our dishes, setting them on the floor in a corner. The stove took up half the table.

"The shower doesn't work, Mary," Betsy called from her room in the back of the apartment. "Mr. Sayeed-Nejad telephoned the landlord. Someone will be here to fix it tomorrow."

"Okay. One more grimy day won't make much difference."

I closed the door of my small room, the one I had chosen because of its wonderful view of the mountains, oblivious to the very dusty road ten feet away. As I stood at the tall window, the women and children at the water pump across the street pointed up at me. Time for curtains again. Maybe the ones from the daneshsera would fit. A breeze kicked up outside, and I could feel the grit from the street blowing in through the window. A thin film of dust covered my suitcase. Although I had mopped the floor just that morning, new footprints revealed my every move. We had left a garden and landed in a dustbin.

Sitting down on my cot, I grumbled as the mattress sagged under my weight. The heat, the dust, the noise were depressing. A minute later, I hopped back up. There was something I could do. No more creaky, droopy springs for me. Why not sleep on the floor, Iranian style? I yanked the lumpy mattress off the bed frame and shoved it against the wall, in a corner partially shielded from the window. Pleased with my decision, I dragged the empty frame into the hallway. Crawling along the dusty floor, I tucked in the cotton sheets. Still full of resolve, I retrieved Betty Friedan's *The Feminine Mystique* from the book locker, which was easy to find. Apart from the kilim on the floor, it was the only piece of furniture in the living room. I was abandoning James Bond thrillers. It was time for the serious stuff.

Hours later, I lounged on my pad, trying to read the seminal book on feminism by the light of a forty watt bulb dangling ten feet away. The door to Betsy's room was closed, an occasional laugh sneaking out through the cracks. It was almost 8:30; Christopher would go back to the bazaar soon. I turned out my light.

The doorbell rang promptly at ten the next morning. I skipped down the stairs, curious about Farideh's surprise. When I opened the door, she was there, holding something under her chador.

"Befarmayeed," I said, motioning to the stairway.

"No, I can't come in. I just wanted to give you this," she said, pulling a wiggling, young white cat from the chador's folds. "I know you like cats, and this one has already caught two mice at our house. Here, take him."

"Thank you, Farideh, but I couldn't. I travel a lot. Who will take care of him when I'm not here?"

"Don't worry. I'll come and feed him. You must take him. All the students agree." Reluctantly, I held out my hands to grasp the struggling animal.

"What's his name?" I asked.

"Veely."

"Veely?"

"Yes, I named him after Veely Brandt—you know, the German leader." And with that she was gone, leaving me in front of my new apartment with a feline Willy Brandt.

Even German chancellors get hungry, so after lunch at the Hotel Akavan, Betsy headed home and I went to the bazaar in search of ground beef—just enough for one Willy-meal; meat spoiled quickly in the desert heat.

It was naptime for all but Americans with a mission when I unlocked our door on Cinema Nur Street and climbed the stairs. Willy was nowhere to be seen. Sticking the meat in the box oven so he couldn't drag it all over the floor, I headed for the bathroom. The door was almost closed when Betsy called, "Mary, I meant to tell you…" That's all I heard. With my next step, I was falling, falling into a deep hole. Shrieking, I instinctively held out my arms, catching myself by the armpits, stopping my plummet to the well far beneath the building.

"Mary, Mary, are you okay?" Betsy rushed into the bathroom just as I was scrambling out of the two-foot square opening in the floor. "I tried to tell you the landlord's men have been working on the shower. They left the trapdoor to the plumbing open when they took their afternoon break."

I couldn't speak. My heart was thudding right where my vocal chords should be. I stumbled into my room and fell down on my mattress. God it was hot in here. Not a donkey was braying, not a sheep was bleating, not even a fly was buzzing. Only the ragged sound of my breath broke the silence. My body began to shake, tears smeared my cheeks. Then Willy was beside me. Kneading the pillow, purring loudly, he curled up next to my head.

A LONG, HOT SUMMER

"Who are you," said the Caterpillar... Alice
replied rather shyly, "I-I hardly know, Sir, just
at present—at least I know who I was when
I got up this morning, but I think I must have
been changed several times since then."
—*Lewis Carroll*

A Long, Hot Summer

"They're coming, they're coming!" I called to Fred. "Quick, bring the tea and lie down here by the door. We don't want them to see any movement." It was *Chehlum*, the last day of public grieving over the death of Hussein, the son of Ali, the grandson of Mohammad. A procession from the local mosque was passing right in front of my apartment.

The Peace Corps had inundated volunteers with memos, warning us to stay out of view during these public rites. And if they'd forgotten, Fred's neighbors in the bazaar and ours along Cinema Nur Street suggested in the most diplomatic of terms that we shouldn't be around when the mourners passed. The baker down the road told us to expect them sometime before noon.

The view from my second-floor apartment was perfect. It was almost ten when I heard the faint echo of sorrowful voices. As the sounds grew stronger, I crept closer to the balcony for a better view. Fred was next to me on his belly. Up the street the procession came, forty, maybe fifty men and boys clothed in black. A mourner holding a portrait of Hussein led the group, accompanied by two standard bearers flourishing elaborately embroidered black flags.

Chanting, the marchers struck their chests rhythmically with clenched fists, striding four paces, then halting. "*Yah, Hussein,*" resounded through the throng. Four paces, then halt, the dirge continued. Then they were gone, their mournful prayers fading in the distance.

The waves from Hussein's 680 AD martyrdom near Karbala, in what is now Iraq, surged through Shi'a Iran every year with the intensity of a recent tragedy. Mourning started on Ashura, the tenth day of the lunar month of Moharram, commemorating the day when Hussein and a small army of one hundred family and followers were overwhelmed by a thousand men directed by Yazid, a rival for the leadership of Islam. Hussein was beheaded, his followers slaughtered, his sons murdered, and the women and children taken into captivity. In modern Iran, public laments over Yazid's triumph culminated on Chehlum, forty days later.

The atmosphere during these weeks was almost festive; something special was happening. Black mourning flags hung in front of mosques and at the entrance to the bazaar. Lying in my bed at eleven p.m., I listened to a mullah's voice echo over a loudspeaker. For the only time I could remember, there was activity in Kerman after dusk. The coppersmiths were sponsoring their own set of dramatic reenactments of that devastating battle more than a thousand years ago. Fred and Tom's house in the bazaar was in back of the temporary stage, keeping them either in or out of their house during the *rosés* (performances). They had been guests of honor at the first rosé, sipping tea next to one of Kerman's leading mullahs.

I wasn't invited to a religious occasion, but the feeling pervading those weeks of mourning was one of inclusion. The Kermanis were concerned for my safety during displays of religious fervor. My colleagues, tears filling their eyes, wanted me to understand how they suffered, how Islam had suffered, how a good world had been vanquished when Hussein died on that Iraqi plain. Evil had won; the Sunni Muslims would eventually rule. These good Shi'as agonized over this defeat as if it had happened yesterday.

Almost as quickly as the procession of men beating their chests passed along our road on that blazing hot June day, mourning was over. The flags, the stage in the copper bazaar, the tears on the teachers' cheeks all disappeared. Betsy and I were out and about again, keeping to the shady side of the street on our way to the bazaar to buy construction paper, scissors, and glue for our summer camp.

Sitting at the breakfast table, ignoring the pile of art supplies we had amassed, I slathered quince jam on a piece of *sangyak*, watching its syrup seep into the flat bread's stone-shaped depressions. This camp idea was pure Gertrude Dorry. Heaven forbid that we laze around during the hot summer months. Instead, this was the time to instill creativity in our junior high school girls. I was not an artsy-craftsy person. No one disputed this. At the sleep-away camp of my childhood my clay pots were lopsided, my jewelry more glue than glitter. Betsy had jumped into the breach, volunteering to let me lead the girls in sports while she commanded the scissors and paste. Just great, I thought. I didn't shine there either.

"Why the glum look, Mary?" Betsy asked as she sat down at the table, breaking off a piece of warm sangyak. "Come on, I've got some news that will cheer you up. Christopher and I are getting married."

Married! Why hadn't I seen this coming? And why did she want to spend the rest of her life with him? An hour of Christopher was more than enough for me. I kept those thoughts to myself, hopping up to give her a big hug.

"You're kidding! Betsy, that's great! When? Where?"

The details were fuzzy. They still had to tell their parents, but they hoped to wed in Kerman's Episcopal Church in early September. I would be the maid of honor, and if Mr. Sayeed-Nejad was back from America in time, he could give the bride away.

"We'll live here, of course," she said. "And you can have the downstairs apartment when Firoozeh and Rasheed go to Canada."

That part was settled. They were leaving the following week. I had known the CENTO couple's stay would be temporary, but living alone in that apartment with Christopher and Betsy as my upstairs chaperones wasn't part of my plan.

But it was easy to get caught up in the excitement. Betsy was radiant; she had never been so sure of anything, she confided. Christopher, the proud man of the house, strutted his stuff everywhere: the bazaar, his office at Kerman's city planning bureau, our apartment. Fred and Tom couldn't conceal their enthusiasm. "Look at it this way, Mary," Fred said. "You'll have your own place, and with Christopher out of our house, Tom and I won't have to listen to his hair-brained schemes. Couldn't be better."

Betsy dove into domesticity. Instead of eating lunch at the Hotel Akavan, she began to hone her culinary skills, no easy task without cookbooks or refrigeration. Our first guests were Christopher's American-educated officemate and his wife who were homesick for cheeseburgers. With no yellow cheese or burger buns any place in town, I melted goat cheese on sang-yak bread while Betsy fried lamb patties. Sipping warm beer, Christopher's friends regaled us with stories of Texas, where they had never eaten cheeseburgers quite like these.

In the midst of all this homemaking, the first month-long session of camp began. Six days a week Betsy and I hailed a taxi for Bahmanyar High School, where even at seven a.m. exercising on the sunny side of the courtyard was impossible for our thirty junior high campers. We crowded into the shade for our warm-up drills, all of us decked out in skirts and blouses. Jogging in place and jumping jacks were so unpopular we soon switched to kids' games. "Ring Around the Rosy" could be followed by the popular "Mother May I," and everyone loved the "Hokey Pokey."

Exercises over, it was time for either English or arts and crafts. The youngest girls, studying another language for the first time, were thrilled to speak their first English sentences, and I loved hearing them. Cutouts and collages emerged from Betsy's art projects, some of our campers exhibiting real ingenuity. One morning, attracted by a gaggle of girls tittering in a corner, I went over to see what was going on. With one continuous cut, a creative fourteen-year-old had fashioned explicit figures of a couple having sex. Shocked, I grabbed the offending cutout. "How did you know about this?" I asked. "We all know," the girl said. "We sleep in one room at home."

Home in the heat by ten in the morning, I watched Betsy and Christopher feather their nest. Christopher dragged long wood planks up the stairs into our kitchen. Days later, a waist-high counter stretched along two walls with storage shelves above, convenient additions I had to admit. On a bazaar expedition for camp supplies, Betsy discovered pink and maroon fabrics, sewing them into a bedspread and curtains for her room. I wasn't sure why she bothered. She and Christopher planned to move into the vacant back bedroom after they married.

Thank god for the Peace Corps book locker. At night, I lay on my mattress, escaping into the world of James Bond espionage. I had given up on Betty Freidan's *Feminine Mystique*. Her frustrated housewives with their truncated careers, vacuum cleaners, and cans of Campbell's soup were irrelevant in my current situation.

It was hard to be comfortable in our new apartment. For one thing, I should never have chosen that front room for my bedroom. Its striking view of the mountains at sunset didn't compensate for the noise and dust of the street below. But most significantly, the betrothed couple had designated it their future dining room.

"You won't mind if we paint in here, will you, Mary?" Betsy asked. "We just have to get some of these things done before the wedding."

"Paint? Paint what?"

"The walls. Christopher and I think the dining room will be stunning in navy blue."

"You want to paint my walls blue? Where will I sleep?"

"Don't worry. We won't spill anything, and it's too dark to work at night."

Somehow, I agreed. "It feels like sleeping in a deep hole," I said to Fred, who was off to Shiraz for a six-week summer school session at Pahlavi University, leaving me alone to deal with the nesting couple and paint fumes. "They've painted as high as they can reach. Now they have to find a taller ladder to do the last couple of feet." Indeed, it was an odd looking space: exuberant strokes of dark blue reaching randomly into unpainted white near the ceiling, the small room imploding under the coat of heavy color.

Relaxing on the edge of Fred's bed, I watched him pack khaki pants and shirts with button-down collars. "I hate to leave you," he said, "but teaching college kids is a good gig for me. I just wish you could come to Shiraz. But we'll go some- place great on vacation when school's over." My stomach clinched. I knew Fred cared. But he would be gone until the end of the summer, Mr. Sayeed-Nejad had already left for the States, and my colleagues from the schools were just that— colleagues. I doubted I would see them until the fall.

Letter home

> Right now I'm alone and rather depressed,
> probably because of the early morning hours I've
> been keeping. But by seven, when our summer
> session begins, it's too hot to stay any longer than
> absolutely necessary in the sun. I've never drunk so
> much water in my life.

Betsy must have noticed I was dragging about. "I've got an idea," she said. "Let's go to the movies this afternoon. They say the theater's cool." Cool was enough for me. We'd tried the cinema once before—a sitting room drama dubbed into Persian—and had been totally baffled. But I was willing to be confused if I could be cool.

The movie was *The Searchers*. "Salaam alaikum," John Wayne said to the Indian. "Salaam," the Indian replied, holding up his right hand in greeting. So far, so good. As they galloped across Arizona's barren landscape, the plot was obvious, the words few, their meaning clear. And the theater? Blessedly cool.

I had never been interested in Westerns at home, but that summer I couldn't see enough of them. There was something familiar about interlopers in dry, mountainous settings. Nibbling on pumpkin seeds, Betsy, Christopher, and I sat in the cool theater during the afternoon, or in the family section outdoors at night, watching the action, unconsciously grasping the conversations, growing into the language of this country. When a man and his wife took seats in front of us one evening, he turned and apologized for having his back towards us. "*Gol pusht o ru nadareh*" ("A flower has no back or front"), I answered, delighting both of us with my fluid ta'arof.

Still the summer dragged. Fred's letters from Shiraz were full of parties and swimming pools. Summer meant swimming to me. As a seven year old in West Virginia, the minutes crawled after lunch at the pool at Dreamland, a haze of chlorine fumes surrounding me, until at last Mother let me plunge back into the water. In Homewood, I lay at the pool's edge, slathering my body with baby oil to tan even browner, hoping the lifeguard with the long eyelashes would notice me. Even Freddie Lanoue's "drownproofing" in Peace Corps training had held a certain appeal. Before our summer camp began, I tried to persuade the Kermanis to let me hold swimming classes in the pool rumored to be in the depths of the bazaar. "The mullahs will stone you if you put their girls in bathing suits," Mr. Sayeed-Nejad said, quashing this ambition. Why I thought these desert daughters should learn to swim was no mystery. I wanted to be in the water.

Willy the Cat was as bored as I was. We spent an hour together watching an army of tiny ants dismember a large fly. They were so efficient, so determined, so focused. Ants were fascinating, but was this how I should be spending my time? At twenty-two years old, I should be busy every instant. Dust, blazing sun, yammering teenage girls, and star struck lovers comprised my days. In the fall it would be worse. I would be alone in that dreary downstairs apartment. Fred would be back in town, but only until January, the final month of his Peace Corps service. And there was that fiancée waiting for him in California. Why should I hang around by myself to teach a crowd of kids "The Itsy Bitsy Spider," or to freeze or boil in Kerman's classrooms until I was asked to "do something with the students"? Bored and lonely during the sweltering days, it was even worse most nights as I tossed on my mattress in that navy blue hole, perspiration soaking into my sheets, wondering if Fred was writing his girlfriend back home as often as he wrote me.

Toward the end of July, dreaming uneasily in a dawn-lit room, something crawled across my chest and down my arm, startling me awake. Jumping up, I flicked on the light: a huge camel spider* with hairy legs was speeding across the floor. Yelping, I grabbed a shoe and chased it into the hallway. Betsy was out of her door in no time, watching the enormous arachnid glide down the stairs and disappear.

"Yikes, that thing was at least four inches long," she said.

"I've had it. I'm out of here." I gulped for air.

There was no going back to sleep. There was no going back. Waiting for the sun to rise I tried to read, but my eyes skimmed over the words, understanding nothing. The living room didn't feel right in the dawn light; neither did the kitchen. What was I doing here?

The day's heat had started to accumulate when I brushed away the crumbs of breakfast and sat down at the table, pen and paper in hand:

"Dear Dr. Dorry, I am requesting a transfer out of Kerman and out of teaching English."

I could think of little other than my precipitous request for a transfer. Terminating my service in Iran was one of Tehran's options. "If they send me home, I'm going to live in a leafy green tree in the middle of an island," I wrote my parents the next day. They would be supportive of my decision to leave Kerman, even the Peace Corps, but what about Fred?

---

*   Not truly a spider, this arachnid of the order Solifugae often inhabits dry climates. The largest can grow to a length of five to six inches.

Fred's response was immediate.

> Dear, Dear Mary, ...Please take no steps until I
> see you—(like getting yourself sent home before our
> vacation)—but send in that vacation request—tell
> them Trebzond, Istanbul, anything. We are going
> to need that month together, after this month's
> waste....

I read Fred's letter in the taxi going home. I read it again
in the kitchen, swatting flies and trying to ignore the raised
voices coming from Betsy's room. Suffocating in the coffin of
afternoon heat, I read his letter lying on the mattress in my
room, smearing the ink on its pages with my sweaty palms. I
had wanted a definitive letter from Mrs. Dorry, but this was
so much better. "If you leave Kerman, I definitely will," Fred
wrote. With these pages, he was casting his lot with me. Maybe
what I really needed was a vacation.

I was not the only one who needed a break. Something was
up with Betsy and Christopher. As soon as my key clicked in
the door, they would vanish into Betsy's room, shutting the
door behind them. It had been ten sizzling days since I had
written to Tehran requesting a transfer, a week of wondering
if this day was the last I would spend in Kerman, in Iran. My
roommate and her fiancé, oblivious to my tension, were no
longer nesting. No new curtains or culinary creations, just
whispers behind closed doors.

Lounging on my mattress one evening, *Dr. No* in my hand,
the front door banged shut. Willy bounded into my bedroom,
Betsy right behind him, tears welling in her eyes.

"What's going on?" I asked.

"Oh, Mary, it's so hard. I don't think we can get married—at least not in September. Both sets of parents are against it. They say we're rushing into things."

"Betsy, I'm so sorry. This must be awful for you. What are you going to do? Everyone here thinks there'll be a wedding in September."

"That's what I wanted to tell you. I've asked to be transferred. I mailed my letter to Tehran today. Christopher's going to send one, too."

"Why didn't you say something, Betsy? I had no idea what was going on."

"I don't want to be disloyal. Christopher and I still want to get married. But isn't it strange that you and I are both leaving Kerman? After all our hard work to get this apartment, neither of us is going to live in it."

Later, lying on my mattress, I stared at the paint-sodden walls. One day Betsy and I are delighted to be together in our new apartment; the next, we are fleeing the city. It was almost as random as those strokes of blue reaching towards my ceiling.

The next morning, July 31, I was on my own with the campers while Betsy and Christopher continued to sort things out. As my taxi sped toward Bahmanyar High School, I threw together an outline for the day's session. Still mulling over my impromptu lesson plan, I rang the school's doorbell.

"Classes are canceled for today," Javad, the caretaker, said. "In fact, classes are cancelled for the rest of the week. You should go home and stay indoors."

"What's going on?"

"The sickness is spreading. Be careful."

I hailed a taxi and headed home. Cholera. It had to be cholera. Two days earlier, dining with an adult student and her husband who was a doctor, Betsy and I had learned of the mysterious disease spreading into Kerman province from the east. "We think it's cholera," Dr. Azari said, "but that hasn't been confirmed. Still, you ought to get vaccinated; it takes six days to take effect." He promised to keep us posted.

The taxi pulled up in front of our building. I dashed up the stairs:

"Betsy, Betsy, you'll never guess…"

"We're in the living room, Mary," she called. "We already know," she added as I burst through the doorway. "Christopher just ran into Dr. Azari. The three of us are going to his office this afternoon for vaccinations."

Sitting side by side in the director's chairs Christopher had brought from Rezaiyeh, they were holding hands. "But there's something even more important," Betsy said. "They've blocked the roads into Kerman province. No one can come in or leave. Looks like none of us will be transferring any time soon."

The living room walls started to close in on me. "You're kidding! No one can come or go? How about airplanes?"

"Nope. Remember, it takes days for the vaccine to take effect, and no one's been vaccinated." Cholera immunizations were not effective for very long, so they were not part of a standard vaccine protocol for foreigners or Iranians.

I was too keyed up to stay barricaded in our apartment. Every inch of me wanted to witness the city under quarantine. I made excuses: Willy had to have food, I wanted to be sure Tom and Tom had heard the news.

It must be serious if the whole province is quarantined. I wasn't worried about catching cholera. Its bacteria are not airborne; one has to come in contact with something contaminated by feces, and even then soap and water are effective deterrents.

But cholera was on everyone's mind. "It's clean," the yogurt seller said as I waited in the cool shadows of the bazaar for him to weigh my container. "No one I know has the disease," said the butcher, wrapping Willy's chopped beef in yesterday's newspaper. "I picked these cucumbers myself, and I'm healthy," the vegetable man said. Purchases in my bag, I headed for the guys' house.

"They canceled our classes today, too," Tom Sisul said. "There are long lines in front of the health center, but no one's putting a name to the disease."

"Yeah, wouldn't you know the government would vaccinate people before it admits there's a problem," said Tom Taaffe, stooping down to hand me a glass of tea. No longer at the agriculture school, he was living with Fred, Tom Sisul, and Christopher in the bazaar.

"Why don't you come with us to Dr. Azari's this afternoon? He wouldn't mind giving an extra injection or two," I said.

"I'm going to wait it out," said Tom Sisul. "I don't think we're in any danger."

"Me, too," Tom Taaffe said. "I hate needles. We'll just wash everything."

Dr. Azari had more information that afternoon. A contagious disease had broken out in a village 160 miles away, killing twenty-eight people before cholera was identified as the culprit. "People waste away from extreme diarrhea," he said. "They can die from dehydration in just ten hours. The disease spreads to their caretakers." Similar outbreaks in two eastern provinces brought the death total to eighty; four hundred more had been treated. "Be sure to boil your water," Dr. Azari added as we left his office, Band-Aids on our biceps and stamps on our yellow health certificates.

"Boil the water, we've got to boil the water," was Betsy's mantra during the taxi ride back to our apartment. Here was something we could actually do. I had our teakettle in mind for the task; Christopher's plan was more grandiose. "Come on," he said, "we'll boil it all at once. We'll just set the water drum on the stove."

"Better put the stove on the floor," said Betsy. "That container's too heavy for the counter."

It was pretty heavy for us, too, but somehow the three of us managed to roll the partially full twenty-gallon drum onto our two-burner propane stove, which miraculously did not break. We fired up both burners and sat back to wait. Three hours later, the propane tank was empty, the water barely warm enough for a bath. Back to the teakettle.

The emergency messages from Tehran started that evening when an Iranian from the remaining CENTO staff rang our doorbell. A U.S. airplane was coming the next day to inoculate all foreign government employees, he reported, but the CENTO staff and the U.S. Mapping crew had been vaccinated. Who else besides the Peace Corps was around? They couldn't be flying in a doctor just for us. With the airport closed, how were they flying here at all?

The next morning, August 1, the bell rang at seven a.m. A messenger from the Office of Education was holding a telegram from Peace Corps/Tehran. "Meet the U.S. Air Force plane at the airport at 10 a.m. today to be vaccinated," it read.

"The director says you may use a department car and driver," the messenger added, confirming our suspicions that the contents of telegrams were anything but private.

"But we've already been vaccinated," Betsy said. The department factotum shrugged and got back on his bicycle.

He had scarcely left when there was another ring at the door. I followed Betsy down the stairs; a uniformed officer from the gendarmerie was waiting.

"You must go to the airport at ten a.m. to be vaccinated for cholera," he said.

It was my turn to protest. "We don't need an airplane; we've already had the shots."

"This is not in my control," said the gendarme, backing out of our doorway.

"This is ridiculous," I said to Betsy. "Can you imagine what it costs to send a plane to Kerman? Why didn't the Peace Corps ask if we wanted help? Dr. Azari would be happy to vaccinate the guys. We should telegraph back and tell them to keep their plane in Tehran."

"They seem pretty insistent on coming," Betsy said. "Besides, it's too late. It's a three-hour flight. They're already in the air if the plane's going to arrive at ten."

"I just wish I'd thought of sending a telegram earlier. We'd better go to the airport and prove we're okay."

It was bedlam at the Office of Education. While some government offices had inoculated their employees, this one had not. It was either stand in line for hours, even days, at the health department, or cast your lot with the foreigners. None of the messages to us had even hinted at vaccinating anyone but foreigners, but the more we tried to discourage these anxious men, the more determined they became. The two Toms, already seated in the department's largest Land Rover, scooted over to make room for Betsy and me. The driver climbed behind the steering wheel, and at least eight others piled in for the ride. Off we went, office personnel hanging out of doors and windows.

Word of an American rescue operation had spread; when our Land Rover pulled up near the runway, a dozen men were pacing back and forth outside the Iran Air building. "No, I don't know when the plane is coming," I explained and explained.

"No, I don't know the plans for vaccinating the public." "I don't know, I don't know…"

The rescue mission was three hours late. At last, a whir of propellers sounded overhead. "*Meeyand, meeyand!*" ("They're coming, they're coming!") bounced around the crowd. Within minutes, a small, Army-green plane, "U.S. Air Force" emblazoned on its side, skidded to a halt on the dirt runway fifty yards from the terminal. A door on the side of the plane opened, a set of steps slid to the ground, and two people emerged. Wearing white jumpsuits, one Air Force pilot and one military nurse comprised the team.

"Where are the consulate officials?" the young pilot asked when they reached the throng, now at least thirty men, milling about at the runway's edge.

"There's no consulate here. You'll have to settle for the Peace Corps," Tom Taaffe said, stepping forward. "We're the only Americans in Kerman right now."

"Identify yourselves," said the nurse. We did.

"Mary and I have had our shots," Betsy said. "The other two volunteers haven't."

"Who are all these other people?"

"Some are colleagues who hope you can vaccinate them."

"I'm only authorized to inoculate foreign nationals working for the government," the nurse said, brushing her short brown hair back off her face.

A murmur of "what did they say, what did they say?" spread through the waiting group. The translation brought a loud groan. The nurse continued: "Now where are the two who need vaccinations?" The Toms got their shots and stamps on their health certificates.

"Can I throw those away for you?" Tom Taaffe asked, cocking his head toward the spent syringes. Shaking her head vehemently, the nurse shoved them in one of her jumpsuit's many pockets. "Geez, she must think we're druggies," Tom said. "They sell syringes at the pharmacy, for Christ's sake. I was only trying to be helpful."

"I'm Dr. Homayoun from the Department of Health." A portly, white-haired Iranian stepped forward from the crowd. "Did you bring vaccine for us? No Iranian planes have been allowed to come in with a supply for the province."

"We received no such request from the Iranian government," the nurse said.

Their mission accomplished, the nurse and the pilot strode back to the small U.S. Air Force plane. My chest tightened as it disappeared into the clouds, heading back to the safety of Tehran, taking my chances for escape with it. If I had insisted on leaving this place with no exit, I would have been quarantined at the Tehran airport for six days, waiting to see if I had cholera. Here I was free to move about. But I wasn't free to leave.

A subdued group of Iranians and Americans got back in the Land Rover, the Iranians frustrated with their foreigners, their foreigners feeling foolish. A fifteen-hundred mile round trip and who knew how much money—for two people who had ready access to the vaccine. And worse, the Americans had been allowed to fly into Kerman while the Iranians had not.

Tempers were running high. At an emergency meeting of Iran's only political party that evening, Tom and Tom, unable to explain why the Americans did not bring badly needed vaccine for Kerman, were asked to leave, the subtleties of diplomatic protocol meaningless in this situation.

The quarantine continued, the Iranian government putting its own rescue plan into action, ferrying in vaccine to the health department. Cars with loudspeakers trolled the streets, warning people to avoid uncooked food, boil their water, get vaccinated. Restaurants and cinemas were shuttered. Officially, only two people in the city died, and fewer than twenty others were treated for cholera, but the word in the bazaar and among the women gathered at the neighborhood water pump told a different story. The servants and bakers, the kerosene and water carriers, the taxi drivers and their wives were certain the toll was much higher, that they and their families were fortunate survivors.

Eight days later, the quarantine was over. Relieved to get back to work, I pushed our campers into jumping jacks in the Bahmanyar High School courtyard. I had been sitting around for way too long.

But I'm forgetting the refrigerator. Left behind by the U.S. Mappers, it was a small victory during this time in limbo. Reasoning a refrigerator would be good for whoever replaced us, we were still under quarantine when a porter, doubled over under the weight of the large white appliance, struggled up our stairs.

"It runs on kerosene, just like your heater does," his supervisor said, "but here it cools by evaporation and condensation. We brought you the best one, but it looks like it needs a new wick."

That was not all it needed. Parts in hand, I searched the bazaar for matching pieces. Cloistered in Kerman, uncertain of my future, at least I could get this machine working. Finally, flopping on my belly on the kitchen floor, I pulled out the burner one more time, Willy at my head, Betsy and Christopher bending over to watch. At last, the cotton wick fit properly, its long tail dipping into the pool of kerosene. Minutes later, I lit the wick, turning it down until only a blue flame remained.

"You've got it!" Betsy said. Soon, a cool breeze wafted out when I opened the refrigerator door. If I could conquer this, I could conquer anything. What a shame to leave Kerman after such a triumph.

Ground beef for Willy's meals, yogurt and cucumbers for mine, had been chilling in our refrigerator for less than a week when planes began to fly in and out of the city, their passengers producing proof of cholera vaccinations. Betsy and I were wearing the pavement thin at the Office of Education looking for letters from Tehran, when a telegram arrived. Our field officer, Don Croll, was driving to Kerman, arriving the next day.

Don climbed the stairs to our apartment, joking about how we were prisoners of our fate. Slouched in one of the director's chairs in the living room, he accepted a Pepsi, and made small talk. Betsy twisted the hem of her skirt. Christopher's foot tapped on the rattan floor covering. Willy on my lap, I fiddled with his ears until he jumped away. Finally, Don set his near-empty bottle down on the floor and fished around in his briefcase. "I'll bet you've been waiting for these," he said, pulling out three envelopes. "Go ahead. Read them." Draining the last of the Pepsi, he lit a cigarette.

We tore open our letters. I scanned mine quickly, my heart thudding as I read: "Your request for a transfer is denied."

"I'm being moved to Tehran," Betsy said "effective as soon as camp is over."

"Tehran?" Christopher sounded shocked. "They're sending me to Kermanshah. That's not even close to Tehran."

"It's about four hundred miles away," Don said, picking up his empty bottle and carrying it into the kitchen. "Hey, I didn't know you had a refrigerator."

"How about you, Mary?" Betsy asked.

"Dr. Dorry says stay in Kerman or go home."

The conversation went on, but the facts didn't change. Peace Corps/Tehran's decisions seemed arbitrary and heartless. "What kind of choice is that, to stay or go?" I asked Don. "Betsy and Christopher are being transferred. Surely I can be, too." It was the principle of the thing. Maybe I didn't want to leave Kerman, but this wasn't fair.

"Mary, if you're unhappy with your work here, why do you think it will be different someplace else? I agree with Dr. Dorry," Don said. "Take a break. Go on vacation, and decide when you get back. Betsy and Christopher are a different case. Everyone here expects them to get married. If they don't, they can't stay in Kerman. It's too conservative."

"But why does Christopher have to go to Kermanshah? Can't he be stationed in Tehran with me?" Betsy asked.

"Kermanshah's got an opening for a city planner."

"Oh bull," said Christopher. "You'd find a place for me in Tehran if you wanted to."

None of our protests had any impact. Don climbed into his Land Rover and headed north to Yazd, leaving us to cope with Peace Corps' decisions.

All was still a muddle days later when Fred returned from Shiraz. The Toms and I met him at the airport. Fred and I were very proper, shaking hands, joking. Everything about him felt familiar—that reddish handlebar moustache, the blue eyes that made me feel so special. Sitting next to him over lunch at the Hotel Akavan, his knee grazed mine. "Okay if I drop by a little later?" he asked as we parted.

"So what did Dr. Dorry say?" Fred asked. The afternoon heat filled the hazy sun-lit living room as we circled around delicate topics.

"Just a minute. I'll get the letter." I pulled the long envelope from a pile of correspondence in my room and brought it to Fred. He tilted the chair back as he read.

"She's made the right decision as far as I'm concerned. You're not going to find a nicer town than Kerman—or a better guy than me." He reached for my hand. "You're going to stay, aren't you?"

"Maybe. I told Croll I'd decide after our vacation. It's been one strange summer."

Summer was not quite over. We were spending our last day of camp at the Kerman Orphanage for Girls. Although our campers encountered poor, sick children daily, and giving alms to the poor is a basic tenet of Islam, Betsy and I were determined to make these teenagers aware of children less fortunate than they, a very Protestant goal for two privileged young women from towns where poverty was invisible. So, a half a world away, in a town whose people had a firm, if different grasp on the responsibilities of one human for another, we were on our way to the orphanage.

We almost skipped down the street, Betsy, the girls, and I, this last day of camp. You wouldn't have missed us—a flock of adolescent girls, their broad smiles brightening somber gray school uniforms; the tall foreigners, practically girls ourselves, in light summer dresses—my long, light brown hair dangling down my back, Betsy's tied back in her ever-present bandanna. Those on the street must have noticed the cardboard box for the beanbag toss one of the girls held high—eyebrows, nose, and ears outlined in blue paint above a broad, cutout mouth.

The orphanage gate opened, and a matron led us into the dining room. Thirty young girls, attired in identical print dresses, their dark hair cropped short, sat on folding chairs waiting for our program to begin.

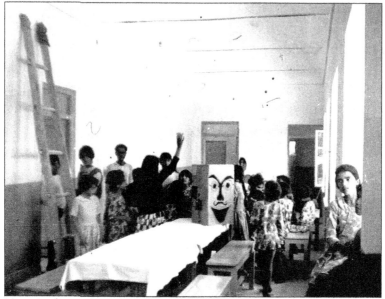

Visiting the orphanage in Kerman at the end of summer camp.

"*Beeya, baazee koneem*" ("Come, let's play"), said the oldest of our campers. Another placed the cardboard box with the wide mouth on a table. Each of our girls took a beanbag and the hand of a young audience member. Lining up, the beanbag toss began. Girl after girl tried to lob the bag between the gaping lips on the box. More often than not, the bag landed on the floor, the young girl reddening at her botched attempt. How awful to fail when everyone's looking. Why had I thought throwing these things would improve anyone's life?

"Enough of this," Betsy muttered. "Maybe they'll like the songs." She signaled the campers that it was time for their second act.

"We're going to sing 'My Hat It Has Three Corners,'" I announced from the end of the first row. One of the older girls translated; the children looked confused. Things did not seem any clearer when we followed that number with "Old Macdonald Had a Farm," although an "oink, oink here and an oink, oink there" was met with definite disapproval when I explained oink was American pig-speak. The young audience remained passive until encouraged to join in the "Hokey Pokey." Putting their right feet in, and their right feet out, everyone in the room began to giggle; shaking it all about had never been so much fun. Even the matron got into the act, hopping up to put her left arm in, and her left arm out.

"Let's make a circle and do it again," Leila, one of our boldest campers, suggested. I took the matron's hand, Betsy grabbed that of the assistant, while Leila and the other campers filled in the circle with their small charges. We put our heads in, our heads out; legs in, legs out; ear in ear out. On and on we went, singing between hoots of laughter. Finally we ran out of body parts, putting our whole selves in with a great deal of verve, and shaking it all about for the last time.

The presentation of rag dolls the campers had worked on diligently during the summer was the grand finale. One after another, each little girl put her hand in the bag to pull out her very own doll. "I made that one," Sorayah, one of the youngest campers, told the smallest of the girls. "I made her just for you." "Thank you," the girl said, holding her new toy in both hands. "She's very beautiful."

Lining up behind their matron, they thanked us and said goodbye. "Khodahafez," we echoed as we went out the door. "Khodahafez, everyone."

Betsy spent her last few days in Kerman saying goodbye to colleagues she would not see again. I followed her around, not really believing that the intense time we had shared over the past year was ending.

"You'll write, won't you?" I asked.

"Of course I will, wherever you are."

Betsy and Christopher were the first to leave. Kerman's volunteers stood on the tarmac in the smothering sun as they climbed up the steps of the plane to Tehran. Eleven months earlier, Betsy, Tom Sisul, and I had made the opposite journey. For a year that had felt stifling a good deal of the time, so much had changed.

Back in the apartment Betsy and I had shared for this long, hot summer, I wandered from room to room, hearing only the echo of my footsteps and Willy's claws skittering along the floors. Betsy's maroon and pink curtains and bedspread were still there. But those bandannas, the Dr. Scholl's sandals, the New England tweeds were gone. The vitality she had brought to my life—her spot-on sense of humor, her joy in everything from art projects to piano playing, her freewheeling thoughts on life and love—had flown off with her on that plane. Khodahafez, Betsy.

INTERLUDE

Out beyond ideas of wrongdoing and rightdoing, there is a field. I will meet you there.
—*Jalal al-Din Rumi*

Interlude

Letter home

> You can't imagine how it felt to walk down
> Tehran's crowded streets, weaving in and out
> of mobs that didn't even know I was alive. And
> skyscrapers. And friends. And steak. And no chadors.

Floating on my back in the Sea of Marmara, wispy clouds dotting the sky above, it was hard to believe that just weeks before I'd been in Kerman wiping the dust off my shoes and hewing to the shady side of the street. Vacationing in captivating Istanbul, a city defined by water, our visit was almost over before I dashed down the steep, sandy beach on one of the Princes Islands and threw myself into the sea. Buoyed by the deep salty water, I reached over to Fred and squeezed his hand. He looked so whimsical floating next to me, his feet sticking up out of the brine.

Fred and I had traveled through myth and history, desert and rainforest during this end-of-summer interlude. On our journey, Mount Ararat sprung up unexpectedly from the fields of black lava that dominated the terrain—a snow-capped summit reaching into the clouds. It seemed impossible that outside our bus window history was meeting legend: Noah, his ark, the animals two by two, the dove, the mountain. But a few hours later, Erzurum's cobblestone streets, horse-drawn carriages, and cold stone buildings reminded me of Europe. And Ankara, Turkey's capital, could have been anywhere, with its modern government buildings and wide streets. How close things are in this part of the world.

Rasht, which we visited before our trip to Turkey, seemed more Russian than Iranian to me, located as it is in the north of the country. Brass samovars crowded tiny antique shops in the bazaar, bakers sold thick loaves of hearty bread, and the jabber of caged ducks filled the air. Traveling through rice paddies to the coast at Bandar Pahlavi, a twenty-minute bus ride away, the Caspian Sea stretched west to Baku in Soviet Azerbaijan, and beyond to more of the USSR. We lunched on fish kebabs and strolled along the shore, fending off men trying to rent scuffed rowboats. Children chased each other while their mothers rinsed tribal rugs in the sea. I found a shell-encrusted rock and tossed it into the still waters. "For luck," I said.

Tabriz, the capital of Iranian Azerbaijan, was the first stop on our bus trip northwest to Erzurum in Turkey. With a few hours to explore, Fred and I paused in front of the bazaar, one of the world's largest. Despite the cheerful tiles that framed its famed façade, the atmosphere was cold. Bare-legged and bare-headed in my bright summer skirt, Fred in wash-and-wear khakis and tan desert boots, we stood in sharp contrast to the sea of men in dark, dusty jackets and ill-fitting pants who swarmed around the entrance as if waiting for something to happen.

I started when the stone struck my shoulder.

"What's wrong?" Fred asked.

"Somebody threw a rock at me."

Spinning around, I couldn't tell which snickering, staring coward had hurled the stone. Tears welled in my eyes.

Fred's eyes hardened and his mouth drew tight. "How dare you attack my wife!" he exploded at the crowd in angry Persian. "She's a guest in your town, and this is the way you treat her?"

If a crowd can look abashed, this one did. Fred had accused them of being rude to a guest, a horrible breach of etiquette. We strode into the bazaar, followed by several earnest young men, making their apologies in English and Farsi. "Stupid Turks," Fred muttered, impugning the province's majority population. He was in an angry mood. I couldn't wait to leave Tabriz.

"*Khosh amadeed*" ("Welcome"), the bus driver said as Fred and I climbed on board for the six-hour ride west to Erzurum later that day. We were old friends; he'd been at the wheel during that sojourn through the floods the past winter. Two hours out of Tabriz, of course the bus broke down. While the driver replaced a necessary part, the passengers milled around. There was a little bit of everywhere in our group: two German travelers, retracing their route home from India; a Greek seamstress, her voluminous black skirts reaching the ground, going to Izmir for her grandmother's funeral; two brothers from the Gulf Coast, heading for jobs in Rome with several teenage wives—their noses studded with rubies, and their chins, hands, and foreheads attractively tattooed. A brown-robed mullah kept his back toward me, shielding his eyes as he passed.

"He doesn't want to look at your hair," one of the brothers told me. "It might bring impure thoughts." I was having quite a day.

"I don't mean to offend," I said. But it was too damn hot to put on my scarf.

When Fred and I had first plotted our adventure over Hungarian goulash in Tehran's Paprika Restaurant, a voyage from Trabzon to Istanbul along the Black Sea coast seemed the perfect antidote to months in the high desert. These freighters,

Fred said, stopped in towns along the coast picking up and off-loading people and packages, wending their way west to the Bosphorus Straits and Istanbul. The journey sounded luxuriously slow and romantic. It was also impossible to arrange from Iran. "Just go," the man in the Turkish consulate advised. "If there's a boat, they'll let you on." But after all those buses, when we reached the port city of Trabzon, our ship had sailed.

By early afternoon we'd figured out an alternative. We climbed into the back seat of the taxi we were sharing with a Turkish couple as far as Ankara, heading west out of town along the Black Sea coast. Thankful to be moving in the right direction, I leaned back against the seat, breathing in the moist salty air, Fred's fingers grazing mine on the seat between us. No overt signs of affection in this Muslim country, but his touch spoke volumes. "God, it's gorgeous here," he said.

He was right. The drive west along the Black Sea from Trabzon to Samsun was spectacular. The land met the water in a unique way at every turn: sometimes leafy-green hillsides protruded into the rolling sea or sheltered small villages; in other places, sandy beaches were dressed in long streams of brown seaweed. Giving me a nudge, Fred pointed to small fishing boats zigzagging along secluded inlets, their nets extending like arms. Ruins of Christian churches crumbled on high promontories jutting towards Russia. As the sun disappeared into the water's depths, it left an orange nimbus in its wake. Half a century later, that afternoon remained etched in my memory.

Fields of wheat, groves of gnarled olive trees, and prosperous-looking villages stretched across the countryside the next day as we headed inland toward Ankara. Lots of women were out and about, heads covered by flowered scarves, some in clothing masking their lower faces, but only a few were draped in chadors. The men's attire was recognizably

European. During Ottoman times, their headwear had symbolic resonance, the popular fez an indication of wealth and status. Calling it feudal, Atatürk, the father of modern Turkey, banned this raised red cap in 1925, insisting on western-style headgear for the new nation. The ruins of early churches and monasteries were the only sign that the area was part of eastern Christendom until the fifteenth-century Ottoman conquest. In recent memory Turkey had not been kind to its Christian minorities. "You know what they did to the Armenians," Fred whispered as the taxi sped along the road.

After taxis and buses and ships that had sailed, we were finally in Istanbul. Legendary names eliciting the romance of far-away places were everywhere: Bosphorus, Golden Horn, Hagia Sophia, Topkapi Palace. The Orient meets the Occident in this city straddling Europe and Asia. Travelers from the west could feel the pull of the east—mosques and minarets, a grand bazaar, a few veiled women, elaborate mosaics. I saw Europe—couples strolling arm in arm, easy transportation, skyscrapers, museums, heedless crowds, and bustling restaurants.

Fred and I explored the wonder that is Istanbul. I did some of my best dickering ever in the Grand Bazaar on the Asian side of the Bosphorus, buying a green suede coat for myself and a leather jacket for Betsy at fractions of the asking prices. Those merchants, seeing a tall, light-haired foreigner, were not expecting a savvy Kermani bargainer. Visiting the Topkapi Palace, I tried to imagine harem life. Dozens of beautiful rooms housed the sultan's favorites, but the exits were carefully guarded. "You could have been a concubine," the tour leader said, pointing to me. "The rulers preferred white Christian girls." I reddened. "No way I'd share you, not even with a sultan," Fred said, putting his arm around my waist. His girl back home was but a dim thought for me.

Antiquity reaches back to the dawn of time in Turkey, legend the matrix in which history and religion flourish. Exploring the Hagia Sophia, Istanbul's most famous landmark, we learned that its convoluted past reflected that of the region. First dedicated as an Orthodox Christian cathedral in 353 AD, it changed for a few decades to a Roman Catholic church in the thirteenth-century, went back to Orthodoxy until 1453, then was a Muslim mosque until 1931 when it became a museum. Standing in its famed basilica, I felt the pull of history—fields of warriors fighting for an important harbor, a new set of beliefs, or a place in the modern world. And there were the city's residents, struggling to survive the onslaughts, adapting to new realities. How terrifying it must have been to have hostile invaders threatening the gates of the city.

But it was the present that ensnared me in Istanbul: the smells of salty air laced with fresh fish and unfamiliar spices; the blues of the sky, the mosques, the water; the intimacy of lying side by side with Fred while we shared our dreams of the future.

"Now that I know 'It's Istanbul, not Constantinople,'" I said, "I want to see all those immortalized places—travel the 'Road to Mandalay,' go 'From here to Timbuktu,' be that 'Girl from Ipanema.'"

"We'll do it, I promise," Fred said. "We'll visit all the cities we've heard about—Paris, Rome, Hong Kong, Delhi, Tokyo. We'll just take off, teach English wherever we are."

"Native speakers for hire. Have grammar, will travel." It all seemed so simple.

Aboard a ferryboat, we daydreamed our way up the Bosphorus Straits, dining outdoors at a little restaurant along the Asian side. In the distance, the setting sun over Europe silhouetted the Blue Mosque, its minarets rising into the gloom of dusk. We were looking west, but when the muezzins' calls to prayer echoed across the water, the evening rang with the rhythms of the east. Fred and I could live here; we could live anywhere.

We could live anywhere except in our room overlooking the waters of the Golden Horn. Bites—itching—bedbugs. We changed hotels.

The food in Istanbul was so tasty. A little nook on the Galata Bridge had the freshest seafood I'd ever eaten. "Don't you want to try someplace else?" Fred asked after our third visit. I didn't. I wanted to sit at a table outside the restaurant, listen to the water wash against the bridge pillars, and debone another sweet fish. We breakfasted on *chorba*, a thick soup served with big wedges of dark bread; we were welcomed into restaurant kitchens on the Asian side where we could view our dinner possibilities—delicious green beans, tomatoes, and lamb, perhaps; and of course there was flaky, honeyed baklava anytime, anywhere.

When we weren't eating, we were walking. Although Istanbul's transportation system could take curious tourists anywhere, Fred was convinced we could only get to know the city, feel its heartbeat, interact with Turks in their own milieu, on foot. At first I resisted.

"Look, the trolley outside goes straight to the Basilica Cistern. That'll give us plenty of time to explore."

"The Cistern can't be more than a mile or two away. On the map, it looks like one of the city's Byzantine walls cuts through that neighborhood. You'd like to see that, wouldn't you?"

The wall would be interesting, I supposed. When my feet finally stopped protesting, I began to look forward to these hikes around Istanbul. Fred noticed the quirkiest things—styles of wooden doors on the shops we passed, vegetables he'd never met, the footgear of bicyclists. And he happily chased after the things that drew me in, like finding the military museum so I could see the rusty iron chain that had stretched across the Golden Horn, blocking the ships of fifteenth-century invaders. He had such compelling insights about the city's role in the region's complicated history. Perched on a bench or wall, we would piece together the bits of information we'd gleaned over the weeks, weaving them into a narrative that was uniquely ours. I didn't want these moments to end.

But our vacation break was almost over. Our pockets were verging on empty; it was time to go back to Iran, by air if possible. Flashing some dubious student identification, we booked a flight to Tabriz on Turkish Airlines. In the waiting room we met Jack, a volunteer from my Peace Corps training group. "I'd have walked to Istanbul," he said, "but flying is the only way I can face going back."

A month before, Iran was a place I'd also had "to face." After these rejuvenating weeks away it was clear that the past year had been even more difficult than I'd realized. Now I wanted to be more than an observer in the Middle East, do more than just survive. In Turkey I'd been on the outside looking in; in Iran my life was woven into the fabric of the country. For the remainder of my time in the Peace Corps, Kerman would be my Constantinople, my Mandalay, my Timbuktu, my place to belong.

A FOREIGNER'S SPACE IN
A FAMILIAR PLACE

When you travel, remember that a foreign
country is not designed to make you comfortable. It is designed to make its own people
comfortable. —*Clifton Fadiman*

A New Beginning

My first fall in Kerman, I could peek through our curtains at the girls mingling in the daneshsera's courtyard and know classes had begun. A year later, standing on the balcony on Cinema Nur Street, the signs were subtler. Neighborhood women squatted near the water pump across the street, their chadors arranged to free their arms for scrubbing dirty clothes. Their barefoot children scampered after each other, ignoring their mothers' pleas to come help. But here and there, weaving through the familiar scene of donkey carts, bicycles, and herds of goats, were girls of all sizes, chadors firmly clasped, heading toward the paved road and school.

It was the start of a new school year and I had a new roommate. Sixty-six year old Alice Phinney, a New Englander, had spent the last forty years as an English teacher in a teenage boys' boarding school. A year past retirement age, she'd opted for a change of scene and joined the Peace Corps. In my opinion, assigning her to Kerman was a brilliant move. I'd been given a reprieve. A white-haired "woman of years" would add some familial grounding in the eyes of the Kermanis. But Alice Phinney ("call me 'Phin,'" she'd directed) had no intention of chaperoning anyone. Nor was she willing to be led around by volunteers wise to the ways of Iran. She was determined to follow her own path in this unfamiliar place.

"Mary, I'm going," she called from the head of the stairs. "I'm meeting Mr. Sayeed-Nejad at his office; he's going to introduce me to the teachers at—I forget the name of the school. I'll see you at lunchtime."

"You know how to tell the taxi driver 'Office of Education,' don't you?" I asked.

"Don't worry. I had Sayeed write it down."

"Great. Have fun," I said, hoping the cabbie was literate.

I shouldn't worry. Alice Phinney was very resourceful—like the day we'd met, when she described finding food for Willy the Cat.

"I told that girl who was taking care of him not to come back. She'd been throwing his meat on the floor. The kitchen was a huge mess, bugs everywhere," Phin had said. "But then feeding the cat was up to me. I looked up the words for cat [*gorbeh*] and hungry [*gorosneh*] in the dictionary and set off for the bazaar."

"You must have gone to the meat section…"

"I didn't know where to go, so I stopped at the first shop at the entrance and stood there looking confused."

"You stopped at just any shop? That man sells chickpeas."

"It didn't matter. In no time at all, there were five or six young men asking me what I wanted. '*Gorb grushni*,' I told them, but they didn't understand. So I stroked my face where a cat's whiskers would be, and put my hands in front of me like a begging animal. 'Meow, meow, gorb grushni, gorb grushni.' I meowed rather plaintively, I thought. After a couple of tries they figured it out, and one of those handsome fellows went scurrying away. In less than five minutes, he was back with a bag of ground meat."

"Did you know what to pay him?"

"Oh, that was easy. I know to say 'how much', so I asked him '*chandeh?*' He held up ten fingers, so I gave him ten tomans. No problem there."

She'd overpaid a little, but other than that, she was right. There was no problem.

And days later, she was off to the schools, meeting Kerman and the Kermanis on her own terms. I was heading to Parvin Etesami High School, a bag of *kolompeh* (date pastries) for the teachers' in my shopping bag. "Good morning, Miss Mary." "How are you, Miss Mary?" "Where have you been, Miss Mary?" the girls greeted me as I hurried through the school's courtyard.

Mrs. Nahidi, still the seventh-grade English teacher, led the way into a room where seventy students were ready for their first day of English. "Good morning, class," she said, and began writing English's three alphabets on the blackboard: capital letters, lower case letters, and cursive writing. Crossing and recrossing my legs in my place of honor facing the girls, I couldn't wait for oral practice, my place to shine. Finally it was my turn.

"Repeat after me," I said, adding "*takrar koneed*" after seventy girls answered with a blank stare. The students began to utter their first English sentences. "Where am I?" I asked. "Vere am I?" they repeated. "Wuh, wuh, where, where," I said, making the round shape of "w" with my lips. Maybe one or two of these twelve-year olds would actually use the English they were learning.

I was Mrs. Nahidi's shadow, listening a lot, speaking a little, through another beginning class. Did I look as young as these girls when I was in seventh grade? I'd spent that year at Cranford High School in New Jersey feeling gawky and out of place.

"Are seventh grade girls difficult at home?" I asked Mrs. Nahidi on our way to the teachers' room.

"Terrible," she answered. "My daughter—you know her, Parvaneh—sat in a corner playing love songs on the record player. She refused to help, she was mean to her younger brother, she was even rude to her father. Honestly, I didn't know what to do with her. But after a year or so, she started to grow out of it. And now she's a university graduate with a baby girl of her own. I can't wait until her daughter is a teenager."

Mrs. Nahidi's daughter taught history here. We smiled at each other when her mother and I sat down for the mid-morning break, the kolompeh I'd brought the featured treat. Asked about Betsy's absence, my Farsi flowed freely as I explained she was now in Tehran, that she and her financé had postponed their wedding.

"I have a new roommate," I added.

"Yes, we met Miss Phinney," said Mrs. Nahidi's daughter. "Is she your relative? You're taller than she is, but maybe she's your grandmother."

"No, she's another Peace Corps volunteer."

"It's good to have an older woman to advise you," Mrs. Nahidi said.

"It is."

"But Miss Mary has been with us for a long time," my friend Fereshteh said. "She'll help Miss Phinney get to know Kerman."

Early the next morning, the doorbell buzzed insistently. "That might be Mr. Ahmadi," Phin called as I started down the staircase to the door. "Something about furniture, I think. When he came a couple of days ago, I told him you'd be here on panj-shambeh [Thursday], and he could talk to you. I'm not sure he understood me, but I said panj-shambeh very clearly."

It was Thursday, but who was Mr. Ahmadi? It turned out he was the last local employee of the U.S. Agency for International Development, charged with handing over the furniture left by the U.S. Mappers and the AID program to the only Americans in town, the Peace Corps. The guys had rejected everything but a small electric refrigerator; the rest was ours.

"Can I see what you've got?" I asked. Mr. Ahmadi opened the rear doors of the AID truck parked nearby, and I peeked in. Easy chairs, lamps, and a huge stove caught my eye. "Wow. Bring them right up." A real oven! These would be alien objects in most Kermani homes, but I didn't care.

"Phin," I called, opening the doors wide. "They're delivering a lot of furniture."

Mr. Ahmadi's helpers began to unload the truck, hauling this windfall up the stairs to our barely furnished apartment:

2 thick mattresses with box springs
1 huge dining room table with an extra leaf and 6 chairs
2 big easy chairs
1 kitchen table and 2 chairs
2 full-sized dressers
1 standing lamp and 2 table lamps with lampshades
1 corner table
1 armoire for clothing
1 huge rug
1 four-burner gas stove with broiler and oven

"Now for the refrigerators," Mr. Ahmadi said. "I see you already have one. Where do you want the rest?"

"The rest? More than one? I don't want another refrigerator. Someone must need them."

"There are four; one or two even work. I have to leave them with a U.S. Government employee."

That would be me. For the rest of my stay in Kerman, four large white refrigerators stood like sentinels, guarding the unoccupied apartment on the ground floor, symbols of American opulence to all who visited.

Rather than observing young girls struggle with one of English's many alphabets that day, I spent it placing heavy American furniture just so around the apartment. Phin headed to the guys' house in the bazaar for help. Soon Fred and the two Toms were hefting easy chairs into the living room, and pulling Phin's metal-framed cot out of the bedroom Betsy had decorated with such care. I stared at my mattress on the floor of the dusty blue room. Why stay here? The bridal chamber behind the living room was unoccupied.

"Put my new bed against that wall," I said, pointing to the empty room that held only Christopher and Betsy's broken dreams. "I'm getting out of this dark hole."

"About time," Fred said, brushing dust out of his hair.

With a great deal of effort, Fred and Tom Sisul maneuvered the stove up against the kitchen wall and we managed to light it. The stove, table, and chairs transformed the space into a kitchen resembling my mom's. Although Phin claimed no culinary ability, the *Joy of Cooking* was in her luggage. With Rombauer and Becker's "from scratch" recipes at my fingertips, I could make a meal or two.

"I want to learn to cook," I said, "but we need someone who'll shop for food and fix our lunch, do the sweeping and laundry while we're at work."

"Can we afford a helper?" Phin asked.

"From what I understand, a servant who doesn't live with us will get paid about five tomans [65 cents] a day. I think the two of us can swing that."

"It doesn't sound very Peace Corps-ish."

"Phin, every teacher in Kerman has help at home. The system's different here."

"Most of the volunteers have a servant," Tom Taaffe said. "Look, why don't I ask Fatimeh if she knows someone. She works for us, she's honest. I'm sure she'll recommend a woman you can trust."

"Well," said Phin. "I'm no cook. I'm willing to give it a try. But my budget can't stand more than three days a week."

Rubabeh, the mother of two teenagers, arrived days later, brightening our kitchen with her infectious smile.

Relaxing that evening, my legs flung over the arm of an easy chair, it was obvious I had abandoned all pretensions of living like an Iranian. While a servant would fit into the Kermani rhythm of things, those comfortable chairs, a refrigerator stocked with food rather than soft drinks, and an honest-to-god oven were an admission that I was different. But this was news to no one. I could teach girls to pronounce the letter "w," run English clubs, have Kermani friends, speak good Persian, and still sleep on a bed with box springs.

I picked up the *Joy of Cooking* from the end table, switched on a lamp, and opened it to a recipe for pie crust: *Preheat the oven to 425 degrees*, it directed. Whoopee! I can do that now. *Sift 2 ½ cups of flour into a bowl.* I didn't have a sifter, but they sold wire strainers in the bazaar. *Cut ¾ cup of butter into the flour.* I could use two knives. *Mix in 3-4 tablespoons of cold water until the dough holds together.* Done. *Divide into two pieces. Roll each piece out on a floured board.* A beer bottle would be my rolling pin, Christopher's countertop my board. Mary's Delicious American Apple Pie was in our future.

Special Treatment

It was barely light when I threw open the balcony doors, stepping outside to breathe the fresh, cool morning air. The orange of dawn washed over the ragged mountains buffering Kerman, and the empty street in front of our apartment was silent. Yawning, I stumbled into the kitchen to find my roommate seated at our new table, her head in her hands.

"What's the matter, Phin?"

"I'm really sick. I've been up all night with the trots. Squatting over that hole in the floor is usually okay, but at times like this it's exhausting. It's so hard to get up."

The things I didn't think of at age twenty-two. Washing myself with water afterwards was my main complaint about ground-level toilets; my underwear got soggy. Getting up and down was easy for me. For my sixty-six year old roommate, of course it was a challenge. And she did look pale; her rosy cheeks had faded to a dull gray, a pallid contrast to her bright white hair.

"The trots are the foreigners' plague," I said. "Drink lots of tea and eat yogurt. You'll feel better in a day or so."

"This is more than Montezuma's Revenge. I've been vomiting, too. I can't hold down anything. I need to see a doctor."

"Maybe you do. I'll check in with Mr. Sayeed-Nejad when the Office of Education opens. He can telephone Dr. Azari from there." Diarrhea was common among foreigners; nausea was not. I wasn't worried, but my roommate was.

It was almost seven a.m. when I closed the front door behind me and stepped onto the dirt road, glad to be outside on this beautiful October day. After greeting three or four women filling blue and yellow plastic buckets at the pump across the street, I hurried to the pavement a block away to catch a cab. "*Edareh farhang*," I directed the driver, and we chatted cheerfully on the way to Mr Sayeed-Nejad's office. The office halls were humming. Groups of men congregated in front of each office, some in quiet conversation, while others were gesticulating broadly. Here and there a wife stood behind her husband, all but her eyes hidden by the drapes of her chador. Nodding at Hassan-agha, the office's manservant, I turned into the room Mr. Sayeed-Nejad shared with several other men. "Mary-khanum," he greeted me, "you're here early this morning. What's up?" The words diarrhea and nausea were barely out of my mouth when Mr. Sayeed-Nejad grabbed the phone to call Dr. Azari. After a hurried conversation, he hung up. "He's out of town. I have to find someone else." And without even a polite goodbye, he stood up from his desk and sped out of the room.

Why the hurry? Phin wasn't that sick. But Mr. Sayeed-Nejad was now in charge. Strolling towards the bazaar, still keeping to the shady side of the street, I made a mental shopping list: yogurt, meat for Willy, sugar, and one of those wonderful fall melons I could eat, even if my roommate couldn't. The figs at the fruit stall looked luscious, and so did the apples. "Are they tart?" I asked the vendor. Maybe this was the day to try my first pie.

When I got home, Phin was lying in bed, a cloth over her forehead, her eyes closed. Tiptoeing past her room, I headed for the kitchen to put away the perishables. The refrigerator was still open when the doorbell rang. Mr. Sayeed-Nejad maneuvered his way up the stairs and peeked into Phin's room. She blinked her eyes open to hear that as our regular doctor was out of town, Mr. Sayeed-Nejad had gone to the health department; two doctors would be here any minute. "Two?"

I asked. Then it hit me. Cholera. Diarrhea and nausea are its first signs, but it hadn't occurred to me that my roommate could be suffering from this killer. She'd been vaccinated; we all had. But the threat of a recurring epidemic in Kerman, so recently under quarantine for this disease, was very much alive. That every foreigner here frequently suffered from diarrhea was irrelevant.

Minutes later they arrived, four doctors in somber suits parading into our apartment. Crowding into Alice Phinney's small room, the doctors stood around her bed, peppering Mr. Sayeed-Nejad with questions that he translated for the patient. "Have you had any out-of-town visitors with diarrhea?" "How many times have you eliminated in the past twenty-four hours?" "Have you been vaccinated?" Phin grew more impatient with each exchange, but Mr. Sayeed-Nejad's translations smoothed over her curt answers, showing proper respect to our distinguished visitors.

The chief doctor took her pulse for about five seconds, determined she wasn't dying, and concluded his physical examination. It was doubtful she had cholera, he declared, but they needed to take a stool sample anyway. Phin, however, wasn't in the mood to produce. They would return in an hour for the sample, the doctors announced, and marched out our front door to their official health department car and waiting driver. Mr. Sayeed-Nejad got on his motorized three-wheeler, promising he, too, would be back soon.

I had some spare time so I decided to construct my first pie—apple, of course. While I attempted to roll out the crust, Phin ran around in circles trying to get her digestive system to misbehave. "After all this, I just can't be a failure," she said.

My pie was in the oven and Phin's efforts had been successful when the doorbell rang. I skipped down the stairs, sample bottle in hand, but instead of the messenger I expected at the door, the whole troop was there, a nurse wearing a navy blue chador in tow. Looking amazed at the bottle I tried to hand them, they explained that they wanted to take the stool sample themselves.

Having no idea what would come next, I invited everyone inside. We crowded into Phin's room, where she was propped up in her bed, the queen ready to receive her courtiers. Confusion abounded, but my Farsi was good enough to negotiate the Phinney Standoff. No, she didn't need a nurse. Yes, the product in the bottle was actually hers. No, she would not accept the nurse's ministrations. She'd done all she could do. "Take it or leave it," she said, gesturing toward her bottle. The corners of the doctors' mouths began to turn up. The nurse couldn't conceal her giggles. Even Phin's blue eyes were twinkling. Finally, both sides collapsed in laughter. Accepting the sample, the cholera SWAT team traipsed down the stairs again, mentioning on the way out that the decontamination squad was coming and I wasn't to go out or let anyone in until the stool test was completed the day after tomorrow. Good thing I'd gone shopping.

The decontamination squad—three men in white hazard suits—was the next to arrive, hauling in all sorts of disinfectants. Pails in hand, they scoured the entire apartment, with the exception of the patient's room because they didn't want to disturb her. Using a blue bath towel as a washrag, they scrubbed everything with knobs or handles, turning on all the stove's burners, and turning off the oven where my poor pie was trying to survive.

Three hours later, they were on their way out of our bug free residence when the doctors paid their third visit. Before I knew it, I was getting yet another cholera vaccination and swallowing four unidentified pills. "No, another vaccine won't harm you," the chief doctor said. By now, we were old friends, but I hoped he was right. In the midst of this, Mr. Sayeed-Nejad returned, and he, too, had to swallow his medicine.

The patient wasn't altogether forgotten; she took her pills, but refused the shot. "I just had one three weeks ago," she said. The doctors decided to let this stubborn woman be. After they left, Phin declared she was feeling a little better; she'd like some soup for lunch. And didn't that pie smell good!

Days later, a few fumes from the disinfectant lingered, the pie was gone, Phin felt fine, the cholera test was negative, and I was free to come and go. Conservative Kerman had entered modern times on its own terms. Herds of goats populated its streets, and donkey carts its bazaar, but as preposterous as the Phinney Standoff seemed, I knew Kermanis were determined to keep their foreigners safe.

A Little Bird in a Tree

The latest cholera scare behind us, we were settling into classroom routines when Dr. Dorry announced that a regional conference for Peace Corps English teachers would be held in our city. The final sentence of her letter to us jumped out: "I hope you will use this opportunity to showcase your activities in Kerman."

Fred reacted immediately: "Like hell I will! I've got enough to do without putting on a dog and pony show." His housemates echoed his refusal; that left any showcasing up to Phin and me.

In our apartment on Cinema Nur Street, I paced from room to room while my roommate tried to memorize Persian nouns. Finally, she gave up. "Sit down, Mary. You're making me nervous. And stop worrying about Dr. Dorry. We'll think of something." Easy for Phin to say. She wasn't the one who had nearly bailed out and gone home two months before. Gertrude Dorry was throwing down the gauntlet. I had to prove my worth.

Phin, her brow furrowed in concentration, began to suggest options, each unworkable for one reason or another. At last, she brightened.

"How about a play? These girls are really good at memorizing. Don't the girls in your English clubs need something to do? We know they want to speak English."

"Hey, that's not a bad idea. They'd love to show off. We could even have a big shindig and invite all the parents. But where are we going to find a play?"

"We'll write one. We've got almost a month." Me a playwright? It would be a first.

"Okay, if you say so. Let me run this past Mr. Sayeed-Nejad before we change our minds."

Ten minutes later, I was in Mr. Sayeed-Nejad's office regaling him with our plan. "Good idea, Mary," he said. "See if Mr. Tavanah will offer Bahmanyar High School's auditorium for the performance. He doesn't like to be left out, you know."

The early morning chill was still in the air when I knocked on the door of the principal's office. He stood as we exchanged pleasantries in Farsi, looking very much like a London solicitor. Years before, Kerman's English missionaries had trained Mr. Tavanah well; every inch of his demeanor declared, "Rule Britannia!"

"What can I do for you?" he asked. I told him about the upcoming Peace Corps conference, and launched into our plans for presenting a play in English, drawing its actors from my English clubs in the girls' high schools across the city. "We need a room to rehearse in," I said, "and an auditorium for the performance. With your permission, I thought Bahmanyar High School would be perfect. We'll invite all the girls' parents, of course. We're planning the event for Thursday evening, November 18th. Our conference begins the next day."

He pulled out his calendar to check the date. "That would put your program on the twenty-seventh of Azar," he said, citing the Iranian month and day. "That should be fine. I don't see any conflict here. Just tell the gatekeeper to expect the girls for rehearsals."

During the next few days, Phin and I hunched over the kitchen table developing the plot. Because the clubs were under my supervision, I was in charge of the production, Phin helping with the script. The play needed as many characters as possible to give roles to a maximum number of girls, but these roles couldn't be too complicated. And the dialog should be simple if the parents in the audience were going to understand any of it.

"The girls in your clubs have learned lots of songs, haven't they?" Phin asked.

"Yeah, but the songs are pretty simple."

"No matter. We'll have a large chorus, and we'll work the songs they know into some kind of plot."

Slowly, the drama took shape. Each evening I sat cross-legged on my bed, pen in hand, working out the dialogue, calling Phin into my room for her suggestions. Back and forth we went, until we'd composed Kerman's first, very short, English language musical. With less than three weeks before the conference, the play was almost complete; only the title and a few finishing touches remained.

The evening before tryouts, Phin and I got home late. Crown Prince Reza's fifth birthday celebration had gone on forever, its laudatory speeches in formal Persian almost incomprehensible to me. I was hungry, and exhausted from acting polite and interested. Tossing my coat on the dining room table, I hurried into the living room to light our kerosene heater. It was already two-blanket weather; we were fast approaching Kerman's eternal shivering season.

Chicken soup was heating on the stove when the electricity in the apartment went out for the third time in four days. Phin felt her way into the kitchen to find the matches and candles. "If our appliances were electric, we'd be out of luck," she said, leaving a flaming candle on the table, and carrying the other to the living room. Following, I tried not to slosh the brimming soup bowls.

The soup was gone, we'd polished off the remainder of Mary's Pretty Good Chocolate Cake, but the lights were still off. "We've just got to wrap up this play," I said. "Casting starts tomorrow, and we don't even have a name for the thing."

Phin hunted down her handwritten copy while I searched for more candles. We huddled over a flickering flame trying out titles. "The Animals on the Farm?" Too bland. "Our Family Practices Its English?" Snore. After three or four more uninspiring suggestions, we went back to the script for ideas. "Look," Phin said, "the play starts out with Little Bird. Let her carry the show." We added a few Little Bird transitions, and by the end of the evening we had a full draft of A *Little Bird in a Tree*.

"Our program has a childish simplicity about it," Phin said.

The electricity was still down when we turned off the heater, blew out the candles, and crept under the blankets in our beds.

Tryouts were a madhouse, but over the next few days I winnowed down the contestants to a cast of twenty. Rehearsals began in earnest at Bahmanyar High School, actors and stage crew from other schools rushing over after class to participate. Preparations were not going like clockwork. Someone on scenery detail spilled red paint, no one at the Office of Education could locate the invitation mimeograph, Little Bird came down with laryngitis, and the cardboard bird in the tree looked more like a pterodactyl.

But days before the performance, the invitations finally had gone out, and the girls and I had remedied everything but the star's laryngitis. Little Bird was whispering her lines when Mr. Tavanah marched into the rehearsal room, a scowl on his face.

"With your permission, I need to talk to you," he said, heading for the door. I followed him outside.

"I understand girls from other high schools are practicing here. I cannot be responsible. They must go," he said.

"But, I asked you…"

"And," he continued, waving one of our invitations, "I know nothing about this program in our auditorium. I have spoken to the director of education. He knows nothing about it either. I will not open this school in the evening to just anyone."

"But you agreed…"

"I agreed only on the possibility of students from this school performing a play. Nothing more. Please send the other girls home." He turned, and strode across the courtyard.

Opening the door to the rehearsal room, my heart was pounding. "We have to stop early today. There's been some confusion that I must straighten out. I'll let your principals know if you are to come back tomorrow," I informed the cast in Persian. "Remember to practice your lines. We have to be ready by Thursday."

The girls gone, our props stored safely, I banged the classroom door shut, passed Mr. Tavanah's office without a glance in his direction, said goodbye to the gate keeper, and hailed a taxi. *Edareh farhang. Zood bash!*" ("The Office of Education, and be quick about it!") I ordered the driver. Just when I was finally tuning in to the Kermanis, something like this happened. Mr. Tavanah couldn't have misunderstood; his English was perfect. I knew I'd been clear when we first spoke. The naysayers were right: Iranians told us what we wanted to hear; they had no intention of following through.

The driver screeched to a stop, and I barged into Mr. Sayeed-Nejad's office. Skipping the usual polite preliminaries, I towered over his desk, giving him a blow-by-blow account of my encounter with Mr. Tavanah.

"If he didn't want to have our program, why did he say he did? Why do people always agree when they really don't mean it? I never know what to believe."

"There, there. This is just a misunderstanding. Why don't we speak with the director of education?"

When he picked up the telephone, a stream of very polite Persian followed. "Good, thank you, Mr. Manucher. We'll be there in fifteen minutes," I understood him to conclude.

Mr. Manucher's office was full of petitioners when Mr. Sayeed-Nejad and I arrived. We took seats by the window, sipping tea, waiting to be called. Fall leaves were blowing around the courtyard, much as they had a year earlier when

Betsy and I first sat in this office. But this time I wasn't feeling intimidated; I was furious—with Bahmanyar's ridiculous principal, with the director of education for taking his side, with Mr. Sayeed-Nejad for simply being there. Mr. Sayeed-Nejad nudged me. "He'll see us now. Remember, be nice. Let me do the talking."

The exchange of ta'arof was brief; a few mumbled pleasantries, good wishes for everyone's health, and then we were seated across from His Excellency. Mr. Sayeed-Nejad began his explication in elegant Farsi. I listened as closely as I could, hoping he would express my dismay, give a good reckoning of Mr. Tavanah's duplicity. But after apologizing for not informing the director about using the school's auditorium, he recounted how the principal had been nothing but cooperative since I arrived; how he had offered his school unselfishly for my adult classes; how he had been very supportive of his school's English club; how he had even agreed to let his students practice for our play after school. Unfortunately, there had been a minor misunderstanding. Miss Mary's plans for a performance that would spotlight Kerman's students and its forward-thinking department of education would be compromised if Bahmanyar High School's auditorium could not be used. He begged his Excellency to persuade Mr. Tavanah to change his mind.

"Did you understand?" he asked me in English, when he had finished his plea. I nodded.

Clearing his throat, Mr. Manucher began to speak in polite, straightforward Farsi. He appreciated all that Mr. Sayeed-Nejad had said. And the Office of Education was truly grateful for the impressive work Miss Mary was doing with the students and teachers. But as Mr. Sayeed-Nejad knew, the schools were on a very tight budget. Mr. Tavanah could not find the funds to keep the caretaker late and offer tea to the program's distinguished guests. Perhaps the Peace Corps had money to pay for all this.

This was blackmail. Without giving my mentor a chance to translate, my anger poured out in English. Kerman had my services at absolutely no cost to the Office of Education. The U.S. Government paid my rent, technically the department's responsibility. The Peace Corps had funded the summer camp's craft supplies, and the props for this play, I continued, my voice shrill and shaking. It covered the cost of anything the English clubs needed. If the director, with all his resources, could not find the few tomans it would cost for tea and the caretaker, perhaps I should go back to America. It was obvious my work was not valued here.

No translation was necessary; my frustration was apparent in any language. A magnanimous smile spread across Mr. Manucher's face, and he addressed me in Persian. He was dismayed that I was upset. Above all things, he did not wish me to be uncomfortable. Because the play was so important to me and to Kerman's students, he would be happy to see personally to the costs of the program. He was certain Mr. Tavanah would allow performers from all schools to keep practicing at Bahmanyar High School. We could resume our rehearsals tomorrow. And, he added, he and his wife were looking forward to attending the play.

"*Teshakor meekonam*" ("I'm very grateful"), I said, my knees knocking.

Mr. Sayeed-Nejad and I left the building together. A cool breeze had driven away the warmth of the day; Kerman's mountains were dramatic silhouettes against the clear blue of late afternoon. "Thank you, thank you," I said. "There was never any real problem," he said.

Four nights later I hovered by the door to the stage, whispering last-minute instructions in Farsi to the jittery cast. Iran's empress of English, Dr. Dorry, was in the third row, flanked by the director of education and Mr. Sayeed-Nejad. Several rows behind them, Alice Phinney's fluffy white hair caught the light. Absent among the Iranian English teachers in the audience was Mrs. Mesbah, who had moved to Yazd. Her replacement, Mrs. Noruzi, was seated next to her husband, a handsome military officer. The visiting volunteers, their bare heads and khaki pants announcing the presence of foreigners, were scattered among chadors and somber suits. Seniors from Bahmanyar High School went up and down the aisles, offering steaming tea in silver filigreed glass holders to members of the audience.

A hush fell as Mr. Tavanah took the stage. He opened the program in English, expressing his pleasure that the Peace Corps had chosen his school auditorium for such an illustrious occasion, and welcoming Dr. Dorry and the other visitors to Kerman's fair city. Begging the English-speakers' pardon, he switched to Persian, the round tones of formal Farsi rolling off his tongue. He concluded with a flourish in English: "Now on with the show!"

The lights dimmed, and the rustle of actors taking their places echoed through the hall. When I flicked on the stage lights, a few nervous giggles trickled across the platform. A large cutout of a tree, green crêpe paper leaves dangling from its branches, dominated the scene; peeking out from its perch high on a limb was a delicate blue bird. Chorus members, dressed in their best, squirmed in the background, their eyes darting about to find parents in the audience. A chorus member holding a large oak tag sign and trying not to smile moved front and center. "Welcome to our VERY short program," the sign read. The audience clapped. The lead character, her voice still foggy from lingering laryngitis, came forward; the sign around her neck read "Little Bird" in both English and Persian. "I am a little bird," she said, plucking at her pink party dress with one hand, holding up a cutout of a blue bird on a stick with the other. "Welcome to my tree."

An explanatory monologue followed. Then Little Bird, forgetfully dragging her cutout across the floor, led the chorus in "Old MacDonald Had a Farm" before turning the stage over to a young family: a woman in a business suit; her husband, also in office attire; and their daughter, a student studying English and wearing green taffeta. Their short spurts of dialog wove various characters into the drama: a hat, a boat, a sheep, even a cowboy; all were wearing identifying signs and holding up cutouts. The chorus responded throughout the act, singing and acting out "My Hat It Has Three Corners," "Row, Row, Row Your Boat," "Baa, Baa Black Sheep," and an absolutely murdered version of "Red River Valley." The girls in the chorus grinned and waved to their parents, and the stars stumbled over their lines. But at the end of part one, all of fifteen minutes long, they took their bows to thunderous applause.

Part two was even shorter. Little Bird invited the audience to participate in the "Hokey Pokey" while the cast performed it on stage. We'd done this at the orphanage, too. (My repertoire was limited.) But in this setting no one budged; not Miss Phinney, not even Dr. Dorry "shook it" out there in the audience. The final "that's what it's all about" resounded loudly through the auditorium. Another sign-bearing chorus member made her way stage center: "The End. Thank You for Coming." Cast members proudly took a bow, and the production of the year was over.

"Pretty cute," Dr. Dorry said as we stepped out into the star-studded Kerman evening. "And the director of education was here. Good for you." Coming from her, this was high praise.

Phin and I stood by the courtyard gate, congratulating cast members as they pulled on their chadors and followed their proud parents out into the street. We'd done it! I was giddy with relief, and so proud of the girls.

"Good job," Fred said, leaving with a group of out-of-town volunteers. "You got us off the hook."

"Be sure to thank Mr. Tavanah," Mr. Sayeed-Nejad said.

Mr. Tavanah was speaking with a group of parents in the courtyard. When I paused a few feet away, he called me over.

"This is Miss Mary, our excellent director," he said.

I took a deep breath. It was time to let it go. Like Mr. Sayeed-Nejad had predicted, everything had worked out.

"Bahmanyar High School was the perfect setting for our play. Thank you for making it possible."

"I am always at your service."

Belonging

A week after *Little Bird*, Phin and I invited our colleagues to a tea party. I'd spent every spare moment deconstructing the *Joy of Cooking*'s baking section. Using tart limes, I made lemon bars; with my hoarded stash of cocoa powder from Esfahan, I baked America's favorite treat, dense chocolate brownies packed with walnuts. No bland, crumbly rice flour cookies from the bazaar for my guests. Bowls of fruit were lined up alongside the plates of cookies on our kitchen counter: bright red pomegranate seeds; small, sweet apples; and tiny fall pears. Although it was early in the season for oranges, I splurged on the largest ones—four rials apiece (six cents) which, belying their name, were still November green. Pistachios and salted pumpkin seeds rounded out our repast. Rubabeh, her white headcloth draping over her shoulders, waited in the kitchen, ready to rinse out tea glasses, replenish the cookie trays, and attend to the dirty plates. With four minutes to go, I couldn't think of another thing to do.

I shouldn't have worried. The party, a chance to show off our new apartment and furniture, was such a success even I had fun. Our guests ran the gamut in age from Mehri-khanum, already a mother at nineteen, to Alice Phinney, a white-haired senior. The talk was easy, flipping back and forth between English and Persian, Mrs. Nahidi, Mrs. Farvahari, and our new teacher, Mrs. Noruzi, all translating when necessary.

Maryam-khanum, a grade school teacher and one of my adult students, attempted both languages, while Fereshteh-khanum and her sister-in-law, Mehri, stuck with Persian. Phin smiled a lot. That used to be my role as well, but at this point I could gossip a little with the rest: Was Bahmanyar's English teacher, Mr. Heydarshahi, really going to get married? None of us were sure. We delved into our families, exploring way beyond last year's opening gambit of "How many sisters have you?" and peered into the future, divining our fortunes from Hafez's poems. Phin and I offered tea, fruit, and sweets again and again: "Befarmayeed, befarmayeed, befarmayeed...."

Somewhere between the small pears and the third glass of tea, I realized I wanted a chador. This hadn't crossed my mind before, but in this room, with these women, a chador spoke more tangibly about Iran than anything else I could own.

"Where can I get a chador made?" I asked the group in Persian.

"Why do you want a chador?" Mrs. Noruzi, a Tehrani, asked. "I only wear one because everyone here does."

"That's exactly why I want one," I said, not sure I was saying "exactly" exactly right. "I wouldn't wear it every day, just on special occasions."

"We all sew them at home," said Mrs. Nahidi.

"This is nothing," Fereshteh chimed in. "I'll make one for you." Minutes later, I'd learned about the best fabric shop in the bazaar, and knew I should wash and iron the requisite six meters of cloth before handing it over to my friend.

The party was almost over, but I had one last treat to offer. I stood in front of each guest, the plate of brownies in my hand. "Americans love these. Befarmayeed." Reluctantly, each guest helped herself. They reacted as one: a small nibble, a repressed expression of distaste, the barely touched brownies ending up on their plates.

"I've eaten too much already," Mrs. Nahidi said.

"It's time for me to prepare dinner for my family," added Maryam-khanum.

"We don't eat much cacao in Iran," Mrs. Noruzi said. Thinking about it, the only chocolate I'd encountered here was a pale, pasty confection, bearing almost no resemblance to the dark-colored brownies rejected by my guests. I was about to regret the whole thing, when Fereshteh changed the subject.

"We've had such a good time today, why don't we form a *dooreh*?

"*Dooreh chee-eh?*" ("What's a *dooreh*?") I asked.

"It's a circle of friends who get together on a regular basis," Mrs. Nahidi said. "This sounds like fun."

"I think it's a terrific idea," said Mrs. Farvahari.

"Can I come?" asked our youngest, Mehri-khanum.

"Of course," we all answered.

"We can meet at each other's houses," said Mrs. Noruzi "How does every two weeks sound?"

It sounded perfect. Our visitors donned their coats and chadors and tromped down the stairs and out into the dusk of late afternoon.

"I think that went pretty well," Phin said. "They seemed to be having a good time."

"Do you realize what just happened?" I asked. "We're part of a group—these women aren't just being polite. They really want to spend time with us."

"And why wouldn't they? We're perfectly nice people." If only it were that simple.

"Should we give these brownies to the new volunteers?" I asked, changing the subject.

"Good idea. I'll bet they're longing for a piece of home about now."

Two architects fresh out of college had arrived in Kerman, raising our number of volunteers to seven. Wayne was a tall, soft-spoken blond from the Midwest; his roommate, Ed, another Californian, was edgier, full of complaints that failed to garner much sympathy among us old Iran hands. Attached to the province's city planning department, their liaison had found them a small house with a courtyard at the end of a quiet lane—a great place but they still didn't feel at home.

It crept up on you, this confidence of place. Just a minute ago, I was fleeing Kerman, headed anywhere but here. An instant later, riding the wave of a new beginning, I was comfortable gossiping in Mayel High School's teachers' room, struggling for the attention of sixty-five seventh graders at

Parvin Etesami, drilling uninterested nursing students on the past-perfect tense. The girls' schools, unfamiliar just a year earlier, were now my anchors, tethering me to places and people that provided the rationale for being in Kerman. This year was different. This year, I belonged.Some places just got better, and the bazaar was one of them. A cool haven in the summer, it was actually cold in the fall, but so alive. The beggars had given up on me so I shopped for chador material in peace. My mind was peaceful too. Almost automatically, I filtered out the scenes of despair that passed by; it was now clear there was nothing I could do. My two or three rials wouldn't cure the cloud of milky glaucoma creeping across a young boy's eye, or straighten a child's twisted limb. I barely noticed I had accepted Iran's poverty. Instead, I reveled in the amazing tableau of people in this, the heart of the city.

A shop in Kerman's copper bazaar.

"Did you see all those Baluchis in the bazaar this morning?"
I asked the newcomer Ed. He paused a moment to pour a glass
of tea from the pot sitting atop the bubbling samovar, then
strolled over to join me on Fred's living room floor. There was
something so American about the way Ed walked. And young.
There was still peach fuzz on his chin. Did we look so well-
scrubbed, so white, when we arrived?

"Baluchis? All I saw were the same bunch of guys I always
see. You'd think they'd wash their clothes once in awhile." Ed's
sensory overload was familiar. Last year at this time I hadn't
been able to distinguish the unusual from the normal, the
beautiful from the mundane. It was all new. But even then,
I couldn't have missed the Baluchis, proud tribal men from
Iran's southeastern borderlands, their heads held high, striding
down the solid dirt pathways, yielding to no one. Had their
expertly-wrapped turbans been dirty? I hadn't noticed. Instead,
the billowing pants, long tunics, and black vests caught my
eye. Uniformed soldiers, guns slung over their shoulders, were
never far away, present to quell any disturbance these fiercely
independent visitors might incite. The Baluchis appeared up to
any challenge, but trade, not disruption was their intent. Their
homeland, adjacent to the province of Kerman, extended into
Pakistan and Afghanistan, its porous borders providing untold
opportunities for smuggling. This day their arms were loaded
with dozens of overcoats. Heading deep into the twisting alleyways of the marketplace, they ignored the village women, foreheads adorned with thin gold coins, who were hunkering in
rays of warm sunshine streaming in from the light wells in the
domed roof. "*Noon, noon*" ("Bread, bread"), the women cried
as I neared. But I had another purchase in mind. We were all
in the bazaar for a reason: the Baluchis, the village women, the
soldiers, and me.

Spicing up the city with a bit of modernity, like refrigerators and Pepsi Cola, was fine, but it was the donkey carts, the herds of goats, the ruins on the hill, the Baluchis, the bazaar that drew me in. "Mary-khanum," Mrs. Nahidi once said to me, "some of the teachers are upset that you don't notice the new, modern things we have here in Kerman. They worry you think we are primitive." Before I could comment, she'd added, "But I told them you enjoy seeing things you can't see at home. Isn't that right?" What a sensitive way to explain my enthusiasms. "I have so much to learn," I said. "There's nothing primitive about Kermanis."

That day, I didn't give our conversation much thought. Of course I was more drawn to the old, the unfamiliar. They were among the things that differentiated Kerman from other places, even Iranian ones like Esfahan and Tehran. To me the place of Kerman and the people who lived there were the real Iran, more genuine than Iran's more modernized cities with their sophisticated residents. Of course, I lived among the Kermanis; had I been working in Esfahan or Tehran or Tabriz, my definition of genuine could have been quite different. But I had learned what to expect from the Kermanis, how to behave; their big-city compatriots, on the other hand, frequently confused me. Just when I thought I should play the modern western woman role—suggesting getting together for tea on a minor Muslim holiday, or confessing to dating a number of men in the States—those same westernized women would switch gears, showing their more religious or conservative sides. The chameleon I had become didn't know which color to turn.

So there I was, an agent of change who was indifferent to Kerman's efforts to modernize. I reveled in the fact that a mule pulled the tank full of drinking water from Hussein's spring, and that the man who delivered it climbed our stairs in hand-woven shoes. I didn't want him to be wearing Keds. If the city had clean piped water, he would disappear. And that was the problem. Better education, safe water and fruit, good medical care, paved roads—things that would benefit the populace as a whole—were the desirable elements of a more modern life. But what would Kerman—Iran—sacrifice in achieving them?

Part of me realized, even then, that Iranians could sacrifice whatever they chose. This was their country, not mine. How presumptive of me to mandate, if only in my mind, the shape of their future. Quaintness was unlikely to be a developing country's objective. But I would go back to Homewood, no longer oblivious to its clean piped water, the tennis shoes on my feet, the car I drove, remembering what was different about Kerman, freezing it forever in the present I had experienced.

My new chador, a true Kerman icon, was almost ready. On the day the Baluchis had swarmed into the bazaar, I had located that best fabric store, one among dozens lining a broad pathway deep in the interior of the marketplace. The shopkeeper, grinning broadly, proffered an overwhelming selection. I finally settled on a mid-priced navy blue cloth patterned with small red roses. Rubabeh, complaining about extra work, washed the long swath of material in a shallow plastic tub on the kitchen floor. After it dried, I pulled out my iron and went to work. Phin helped me fold the cloth into a compact bundle. Wrapped in newspaper and tied up with string, it was a discreet, Kerman-style package ready for delivery.

Only two measurements were necessary to make my half-moon shaped chador: the first spanned the distance from the floor a few inches from one side of my body, over my head, to the same place on the floor on my other side; the second led from the middle of my forehead to the floor in back of me. My friend would make this chador like all others: joining two pieces of material, the seam running horizontally across the back; cutting it into a semi-circle that reached the floor on either side and in the rear; and finally hemming it all the way around.

Fereshteh ripped off the newspaper to inspect my purchase, holding the cloth up for everyone in the teachers' room to see. "*Khalee ghashangeh,*" she said. ("Very pretty.") "How much did you pay?" Automatically, I subtracted two tomans a meter from the price. "Oh, didn't she do well!" Mrs. Nahidi said. "I actually paid a toman more a meter at that shop. My material must be a better quality."

"She chose well," I heard a teacher comment in Farsi. "Yes," agreed another. "Pretty, but not bold."

"Mary-khanum, you'll have your chador next week," Fereshteh said. "Isn't it great? She's going to look like a real Kermani woman."

Stormy Weather

Journal entry

> What a sad time. I just found out that Mrs. Mesbah and her husband were killed last week in an automobile accident. She was no more than a year older than me. I don't know what to think. I hadn't seen her since she moved to Yazd more than a year ago. The teachers at Parvin Etesami seemed so accepting—but maybe they were trying to make me feel better. What will happen to Baby Mohammad?

It was only a little after noon, but the sky was a deep, murky yellow as I hurried home. In Illinois, a thunderstorm would be headed my way, but these clouds weren't full of rain and lightning. Instead, a fierce wind was steam-shoveling a wave of dirt from the outskirts of town down Cinema Nur Street, heading straight for me. Dashing to my door, I fumbled with the key, trying to get inside before the dust storm hit. A gust slammed the metal door shut behind me. I stood in the hallway, trying to catch my breath, an eerie howl creeping in around the door cracks. "Khanum, khanum," Rubabeh called from the stair top. "The wind and dust are coming. I have to go home right now." Our housekeeper pulled her chador over her head and rushed past me on the stairs. "I'll finish up tomorrow," she said, forcing the door open with the weight of her slight body. "Take a taxi," I called. "I'll pay for it." The door banged closed; I didn't know if she heard me.

When I took off my suede coat, its green was the color of a stagnant pond. By every window and door fine brown grit was mounding along slender cracks, and a dense cloud of dust-laden air surrounded me. Meowing, Willy crept into the living room, his gleaming white fur now a dirty brown. Peering out the doors to the balcony, I couldn't see the water pump twenty-five feet across the street. And what a racket the storm was making. Holding a damp washcloth over my mouth and nose with one hand, and Willy with the other, I kicked the doors to my bedroom shut. My bedspread wrapped around me and holding Willy close, I propped myself up in a corner of my bed and shut my eyes.

This storm fit in perfectly with the week I was having. First, the terrible news about Mrs. Mesbah: it wasn't that I missed her—she'd left Kerman more than a year before—but she and her students had been such a big part of my first year in Iran. I missed who we'd been together. People so young, people that I knew, weren't supposed to die.

And then there was my roommate: Alice Phinney had become as stubborn as the donkeys braying in the bazaar. With a year of doing things wrong behind me, I'd thought I could help her avoid some of Kerman's pitfalls, but she was determined to make her mistakes her way. Just last week, trying to boil water for tea, she discovered that there was no propane for the kitchen stove. "No point going to the gas man now," I said. "It's one o'clock in the afternoon. He'll be at home, napping. He should reopen about four." But Phin insisted, even after Fred agreed that every store closed this time of day. Down the stairs she went, lugging the heavy propane canister. A half an hour later, she and the empty tank were back. "The store was shuttered," she said, stalking into her room.

She was beginning to worry me. Whereas I'd put on pound after pound my first months in Kerman, Phin was shedding them. She didn't much care for rice, she said. Okay, but why reject my newest creation—a tasty meat pie made out of ground beef, onions, raisins, and yogurt? She really wasn't eating very much. And she was too tired to last even the morning observing English classes. They bored me to distraction, too, but I wanted to run around, not go home and go to bed. At 6500 feet above sea level, Kerman's altitude often exhausted newcomers, but her weariness was lasting a long time. To top it off, she was sick all the time. For the past two days she'd been in Arjomand Hospital with a horrendous sore throat—almost a year to the day after Betsy and I had shared a room there with a similar malady. Come to think of it, I was sick a lot my first year. But still... She was lonely, too, missing the companionship of native English speakers her own age. Mr. Sayeed-Nejad understood this—or perhaps she told him—because the women he introduced her to were older than those I'd met. She'd been the guest of the female director of the Lion and Sun (Iran's Red Cross), and of Mrs. Nouri, the head of Kerman's women's committee. But even with these accomplished women, language was a problem. I tried to be sympathetic, but I didn't understand why the company of six Americans in our twenties wasn't enough. Sitting on my bed, dust whirling around, I decided to write the new Peace Corps doctor if she didn't perk up.

Fine grit showered against the bedroom window as the storm hit from all directions. There had been dust storms when I lived at the daneshsera, but there the walls and garden had buffered the worst effects. Here, the storm raged around my unprotected apartment building.

Closeted in my room with the cat for company, I remembered how lonely I had been at the daneshsera, with Betsy not five feet away and the courtyard outside full of future teachers. With Fred in my life, that emptiness had vanished. Surely, our growing relationship compounded Phin's sense of isolation. We spent all our free time together, either at Fred's house or my apartment. Choosing to focus on his ready wit, his intellect and his popularity with Iranians, I shoved his awful temper tantrums into a dark recess of my mind. Sitting quietly together, we wrote letters, read books, or perused the *New Yorker* magazines that arrived only a couple of months late. "I'm going to be a Peck & Peck girl when I get back to the States," I announced, gazing at the chic young lady modeling a red plaid Pendleton skirt in front of its Chicago department store. In clothes just like hers, I would stride along Lake Shore Drive on my way to an important job in a towering building. Or I'd climb behind the wheel of my sporty Triumph, a handsome boyfriend in the passenger seat.

But with Fred by my side, my daydreams were evolving. He was the Peace Corps' golden boy, so good at languages, so adept with ta'arof that his manners impressed every Iranian he met. On his last visit to Tehran, the Peace Corps director had called him in to his office. "Would you consider being a field officer here in Iran next fall?" he asked. Would he consider it! He'd have to interview for the position in Washington after he finished his service in January, but it sounded like Fred would be returning in the fall to work for the Peace Corps. Where did that leave us?

Maybe the problem was a step closer to a resolution. Just days before this blanketing dust storm, Fred revealed he'd written to his girlfriend Maria, breaking off their engagement. With tears in his eyes, he'd said, "I told her I was in love with someone else."

Their engagement had seemed like a loose strand for months. I was glad it was resolved. Still, I was uncertain was how our future would play out. I was leaving Iran in June; Fred would be returning to Tehran in September. We had edged around the subject days earlier. "Maybe I can go to graduate school at the American University in Beirut," I'd said. Fred thought that was a good idea. But Beirut wasn't all that close to Tehran. Sitting on my bed, the wind howling, Willy snoozing on my lap, I knew that Fred was committed to our present together, but his volunteer service was over in January. Then what? My head spun in stormy circles trying to tease out the possibilities.

Fred aside, Iran was starting to feel like home. I wasn't ready to leave, to abandon all my hard-won understanding, my newfound comfort, my increasing facility with the language. I couldn't be a Peace Corps field officer. A woman just couldn't; a single woman *really* couldn't. If I were to return to Iran after the Peace Corps, it would have to be with Fred.

Willy began to stretch, then leapt off the bed meowing. It was way past his lunchtime. The storm had subsided and my stomach was growling, too. Leaving a trail of footprints in the dust, I followed him into the kitchen, opened the refrigerator door and pulled out his food and the leftover hamburger pie. Willy purred, rubbing against my leg while I rinsed out his bowl. Keeping up a loud cat-conversation, he kept bumping into me while I bent down to put his meal on the floor. Then all was quiet as he gulped down dinner. I had sliced a piece of cold pie, and was seated at the kitchen table when I heard the downstairs door open.

"I'm home," Phin called, her footsteps echoing on the staircase.

"Hi, I'm in the kitchen."

"My temp's gone, the storm's stopped, so they let me out," she said, doffing her coat.

"Great, you're just in time for either a late lunch or an early dinner."

Phin cast a wary eye in the direction of my meal. "Thanks. I know your pie's delicious, but I think I'll just lie down for a while. I'm exhausted." Tossing her bag on the hall table, she disappeared into her room.

The pie went back into the refrigerator. I washed Willy's bowl and my plate and climbed back up on my bed. Phin had been asleep when I'd visited her at the hospital this morning. Something must be seriously wrong. No one needed this much rest. Pulling out pen and paper, I started to write:

Dear Dr. West,
I'm really worried about my roommate, Alice Phinney...

On the Road

Yazd
Letter home

> Yazd is famous for its cloth, and some of it is very
> lovely—like the beautiful green and lavender brocade
> I bought. Phin says that when I have it made into a
> jacket, I'll be so elegantly dressed the shah will have
> to invite me to dinner.

The Kerman volunteers were on the road—at least
some of us were; Phin had decided to stay home and
study. In her spare time, she was reading the Bible
in Persian under the tutelage of my least favorite person in
Kerman, the reverend Mr. Ardibili. "He's not so bad, Mary,"
Phin said. "He's spending a lot of his valuable time helping
me." True, and I still didn't like him. After her hospital stay,
Phin seemed more energetic. Maybe Dr. West was right. He'd
answered my letter, suggesting I stop worrying about my roommate. Everybody gets sick; as she'd been a little plump, losing weight was a good thing. But she wasn't going to Yazd for
Thanksgiving with the rest of us; maybe she was looking forward to some time alone.

Celebrating this day with the volunteers in Yazd had been
in the planning for several weeks. The three American teachers there, two men and a woman, had convinced the Yazdis it
was okay for mixed sexes to live together, so they had a house
big enough to accommodate us all; we often stopped there on
bus trips to and from Iran's bigger cities.

Tom Turkey, central to the Yazd festivities, was coming
with us. A rare fowl in this part of Iran, he'd spent his first

months at the agriculture school, Tom Taaffe's home his first
year in Kerman. A couple of weeks before T Day, someone
transported Turkey Tom, fine figured and fully grown, to the
house in the bazaar, bringing the Tom count there to three.
For days, he chased Fred and the other Toms around their
courtyard, gobbling for all he was worth. (Iranians have the
perfect word for turkey, *boogalamoo*, which sounded just like
him.) His sad end came when the helper Fatimeh hired for the
job faced Tom towards Mecca, offered him a drink of water,
and whacked off his head. When the carcass finally stopped
running around the courtyard, Fatimeh gutted and plucked it.
Turkey feet, floating eerily in broth, were the base of the soup
she made that day.

The adventure was just beginning. With Thanksgiving
more than a week away, we were afraid Tom would spoil. Fred
and I tied his legs and wings together in roast-turkey fash-
ion, turned the electric refrigerator up as far as it would go,
and froze him solid. Fatimeh got the biggest kick out of this.
"*Bebeen, mehmun dareem!*" ("Look, we have a guest!") she'd
announce to friends, throwing open the refrigerator door to
expose poor Tom, a huge grin on her face.

Transporting the turkey to Yazd was yet another challenge.
Fred, fearing frozen Tom might shatter during the trip, wrapped
him tightly in a mattress and insisted the driver's assistant stow
him on the roof of the bus on top of everything else.

Taking our seats, soon we were traveling along the dirt road
that led northwest to Yazd and beyond. The unchanging view
was lulling me to sleep when the bus slowed to a stop at a small
adobe structure flying the green, red, and white Iranian flag.
Murmurs spread among the passengers as the driver opened
the door to admit a soldier, gun slung over his shoulder, followed by a man in a white lab coat—"Doctor" the driver

called him. This was one of the infamous pill-taking stations that had sprung up around the province of Kerman after its cholera quarantine.* Travelers leaving the area had to swallow capsules that reportedly cleaned all the bacteria out of their systems for twenty-four hours. But according to a Peace Corps circular, these same pills did dreadful things to one's bone marrow. "Peace Corps Volunteers are not authorized to take these capsules," the bulletin concluded, but the soldier hadn't received the memo. Pulling himself to his full height and holding his rifle firmly, he and the doctor threaded their way up the aisle, the doctor handing out pills, four to a passenger, along with water in a common cup.

"It's time for good ole American ingenuity. I'm just gonna pretend." Tom Taaffe drawled in our secret language, English. "Nobody's gonna make me down that stuff."

"Naah," Tom Sisul agreed. "Don't wanna mess with the old bone marrow."

It was fun, if a little risky, to voice rebellion in conversational English. Fred changed the pattern: "*Ob kasifeh*" ("The water's dirty"), he said, pushing the cup away. The doctor handed us our medicine anyway. When he and the soldier turned away to administer to other passengers, we slipped the capsules into our pockets. The doctor had left; the soldier was chatting outside with the driver, when the woman across the aisle commented loudly that everyone had to swallow the capsules, even the foreigners. "They did not," her son said in a high, child's voice. "They put the pills in their pockets." The

---

* Cholera came to Iran by way of Afghanistan and Pakistan where officials were unable to prevent its spread. Iranian efforts, however irrational they appeared to those experiencing them, successfully stopped the epidemic at its western borders. Turkey, Iraq, and countries further west were spared this scourge.

old man sitting next to us corrected him gently. "They swallowed them, son. They swallowed them."

Crossing the divide between Kerman and Yazd provinces was like going from Illinois into Iowa—one place looked pretty much like the next. Known all over Iran for its baklava and fine silk textiles, Yazd, just six hours away by bus when all went well, was the nearest metropolis to Kerman. Both cities had significant Zoroastrian populations, the only places in Iran where this age-old religion had survived the upheaval of Muslim conquest and conversion. When I asked Mr. Sayeed-Nejad about this, he gave me one of his knowing smiles. "Mary-jun" ("Mary dear"), he said, "you forget we're on the edge of the desert. If Kerman seems far away from Esfahan or Shiraz or Tehran now, imagine how remote it was when everyone traveled by horse or donkey. It was a safe place to seek refuge." Yazd, whose Zoroastrian population was even larger, was also far from the center of things. Today, the road beyond Yazd was paved; our bus driver should be able to make it to Tehran in another thirteen hours or so.

The assistant pulled Tom Turkey off the roof after the bus drove into town, setting him beside our suitcases. New passengers filled our seats behind the driver, and I watched the bus get smaller and smaller as it headed northwest: first to beautiful Esfahan, with its stunning mosques and renowned gardens; then skirting Qom, Iran's conservative religious center where the devout studied and interpreted Islamic law; and finally to Tehran, the seat of government, the home of the shah, the place where everything started.

Loaded down, we stuffed our bags and frozen passenger into the trunk of a taxi for the short ride to the volunteers' house. On the surface, the city resembled Kerman, its high, chimney-like *bod-girs* visible above the walls of many homes.

These wind-catchers, ventilation systems where open, narrow slots funnel cool breezes through the house, were even more common here than they were in Kerman. Yazd, which borders both of Iran's deserts, the Dasht-e Lut and the Dasht-e Kavir, is one of the country's warmest cities during parts of the year, but not in November. Tom Turkey spent the night on the living room floor with the other guests from Kerman, next to the heater which was turned up full blast so he would thaw.

Thanksgiving dinner was all that I had hoped for. When I woke early that morning, Fred was in the kitchen dicing onions, the chop-chop of his knife resounding off the cutting board. The turkey was but a wrapping for the pièce de résistance, his Uncle Al's famous stuffing, which our master chef crammed into Tom's cavities. The turkey roasted for hours in an oblong black box oven on top of a two burner propane stove, basted every fifteen minutes with butter and Zoroastrian wine. At precisely 6:15 in the evening, Fred declared the beautifully turned bird done. Seven of us sat cross-legged around the sofreh on the living room floor, awed by Uncle Al's stuffing and thankful for Tom, and the mashed potatoes and creamed carrots that accompanied him.

What a lot of trouble we went through to celebrate our American-ness on the holidays, as if we were telling the world, and ourselves, "Look, we haven't changed—we're still Americans, good Americans. See how resourceful we are in recreating a small part of home here." If I'd been able to look into the future, I would have been shocked to see myself in my American kitchen preparing fesenjun, chelo kebab, or ghormeh sabzee, steaming rice the Persian way, struggling to create a small part of Iran back in the States. "Look," I'd be saying, "I'm not just any American. I've lived in Iran. It changed me forever."

Peace Corps volunteers mount camels for their trek in the desert.

I passed up a camel ride in the desert the next morning, remembering all too vividly my brief encounter a year before when sheer luck had kept the beast from biting me. "Are there any Zoroastrian sites I can visit while you play Lawrence of Arabia?" I asked our hosts as the adventurers packed water, turkey sandwiches, and cameras for their camelback outing in the desert.

"Well," said Rick, a Yazd volunteer, "once we hired a taxi and drove way out of town to visit a tower of silence, but there was something going on so we couldn't get in."

If Zoroastrians were known for one thing, it was exposing their dead to carrion-eaters and the elements, laying them out on circular brick structures built on high, remote mounds—towers of silence—so the dead would never contaminate the earth. This practice was diminishing, but there were still towers in use around Yazd.

I wasn't anxious to spend my day contemplating death. "Isn't there a famous fire temple here?" I asked.

There was. According to a Zoroastrian colleague of the Yazd volunteers, about thirty years earlier, rich Parsees* in Bombay purchased land for a temple in Yazd. The fire itself originated from lots of different sources—lightning, cooking, forest fires—and had been burning for more than fifteen hundred years. It was transported from India to Yazd with great fanfare when the temple opened. Only a few Zoroastrian fires are so historical.

Deciding to visit the temple, I pulled on my coat and locked the gate behind me. "Taxi," I called, and a blue Peykan, the Iranian-made car that was everywhere, rolled to a stop. "Atash Behram" ("The fire temple"), I said, squeezing into the Peykan's narrow back seat.

Sometimes, things simply fall into place. The driver was a Zoroastrian from Sharifabad, a village some distance from Yazd. "My village is a very special place," he told me in precise Persian. "There was a fire temple there even before Islam came to our country. My grandfather and uncle are priests of our religion, but my father was more interested in business."

"Do the people in Yazd treat the Zoroastrians well?" I asked, remembering the narrow escape of those in Kerman centuries before.

"They do today," he answered, turning down one street after another. "But over the centuries we've had lots of problems. Zoroastrians everywhere had to pay more taxes than the Muslims. This was very hard for us because we couldn't have good jobs. We were so poor." His eyes caught mine in the rear view mirror. He had an eager listener.

---

* Parsees are Zoroastrians whose ancestors immigrated to India in the tenth century to avoid conversion to Islam.

"And in those days," he continued, "the Muslims in Yazd made us wear special clothing. Zoroastrian men were always in white. Our women had to sew their dresses from many different fabrics. But they were very clever. The things they made were so beautiful, even today our daughters wear these dresses for special occasions. My sister, Mahnaz, chose twenty different silk swaths for her wedding dress. She looked so beautiful in those reds and greens."

I peered out of the car window. It was Friday, the day of rest, so the usually busy streets were almost empty. But if I'd happened to catch a glimpse of a woman, the ever-present chador would have concealed her clothing, multicolored or not.

Growing up in the era of civil rights, the Zoroastrian response to threats of violence sounded very familiar to me: keep a low profile, stay out of trouble, be polite—prudent actions for a persecuted population. In the past, I later learned, even touching a Muslim could draw a severe fine, beating, or worse. At one point along the wide spectrum of discrimination, they weren't permitted to wear eyeglasses, of all things.

By the time I arrived in Iran, Zoroastrians, emerging from dark times, had won the respect of many of their neighbors. They were noted for cleanliness, honesty, helpfulness, and educating their children, according to my friends. Mrs. Farvahari, the only Zoroastrian in our dooreh, was proud of this reputation.

The cab driver pulled to a stop in front of a nondescript adobe wall, with a standard red metal gate. "Please don't go to any trouble," I said. But there was no persuading him that I was fine alone. He waited with me until a slight man, bent with age and dressed all in white, opened the creaking gate. The driver took the lead, speaking so quickly and softly I didn't catch what he was saying. The man answered him just as incomprehensibly and shut the gate, leaving us standing alongside the road. "The temple's closed," the driver said, "but Darioosh-agha—he's the gatekeeper—is asking if you can see the courtyard.

The gate squeaked open, the old man motioning for me to enter. I knew my taxi driver would be right behind me. I stepped into a modern Iranian setting. Only the temple itself—a colonnaded rectangular yellow brick building—hinted that this was a religious site. Contemporary paving stones covered the temple's large courtyard, and large copses of bare trees flanked its sides, their gray reflections shimmering in a circular pool that was raised several feet above the pavement. Standing in the center of this scene, a tall man in a dark suit called out: "Welcome, Reza-agha." A flurry of ta'arof followed before my driver, Reza, turned to explain: "This priest is from my village."

Often in Iran, it was the place that drew me in—a fragrant garden; the majesty of a tall minaret stretching to the sky; the loneliness of a single tree decorated with bits of colored cloth—but this day, the complexity of a people whose religion extended back into history's dawn held my attention.

"We believe in three basic things: good thoughts, good words, good deeds." I was seated on a bench at the side of the courtyard, listening to Mr. Esfandiari, the Zoroastrian priest who'd been waiting in the courtyard. "You know, our religion is the oldest in the world to worship only one god, Ahura Mazda. He leads us along the path of goodness. In the distant past, at the time Alexander the Great burned Persepolis, most people in the land were Zoroastrians." As he spoke in a quiet, assured voice, he pulled a strand of ivory beads from his pocket. "But we suffered greatly," he continued, "first when Alexander's troops burned our libraries and destroyed our places of worship; then centuries later at the hands of the Muslims who forced most Iranians to convert; and everyone suffered when those awful Turks invaded." The small beads slipped through his fingers as if he were counting the sins of the oppressors.

Mr. Esfandiari, his middle-aged paunch pulling at the buttons of his vest, resembled a businessman more than he did a priest, not that I had any idea what a Zoroastrian priest should look like. My life in Iran was so full of incongruities, yet so privileged. Two days before, I'd been sneaking malevolent pills into my pocket under the nose of an armed soldier. Today, by chance, I'm seated in a garden, exchanging views in Persian on the nature of good and evil. God, or Ahura Mazda, if I understood Mr. Esfandiari correctly, embodies the good we strive to achieve. Fire is his light, the light of God, and for millennia the Zoroastrians built fire temples in Ahura Mazda's honor. Their ruins punctuate the stark Iranian landscape, hillocks of crumbled mud walls that evoke a remembered past.

Unfortunately, the doors of the active temple just yards away were closed. "I'm sorry, it's unsafe," Mr. Esfandiari said. "It's a fairly new building, but still in need of repairs. Maybe the next time you visit, you can observe the fire. It's a very old, very important fire, you know."

Standing up to leave, I noticed a familiar image mounted over the portals of the temple: the profile of a man's upper body atop the spreading wings and tail of a bird.

"I saw that same figure at Persepolis," I said. "Is it a Zoroastrian symbol?"

"Yes," Mr. Esfandiari said. "It's a *farvahar*, a sign of Ahura Mazda, who is always moving forward toward the goodness of light." *Farvahar?* My friend Mrs. Farvahari had a heavenly connection.

Buttoning his jacket to ward off the chill of the wind, Mr. Esfandiari walked with Reza and me to the temple gate.

"Everywhere you look in Iran," he said, "you see evidence
of its Zoroastrian past—ancient fire temples and villages, or
great pavilions like Persepolis—but don't forget that we are
a modern people. We educate our children and contribute to
our communities; we are convinced that Zoroastrian beliefs—
good thoughts, good words, good deeds—are as important
today as they were then."

I felt a sudden shiver. Maybe it was the wind. Thanking
Mr. Esfandiari for his time and his insight, I got back into the
taxi. The sun was noon-high in this late November sky. As
Reza drove through the city, the streets and structures looked
the same as they had an hour before, but now the people of
Yazd—their lives, their histories—enlivened the drab adobe
buildings, the empty streets, the wind-catchers, the bazaar. I
imagined Zoroastrians here, Muslims there, drawing closer at
times, distancing themselves at others. The past was pulling
me back, the present luring me forward.

Reza pulled up in front of the volunteers' house—surrounded by yet another wall concealing the lives behind it.
Pressing extra payment in his palm, I told him how grateful I
was. When the gate banged closed behind me, I stepped back
into my world.

Bandar Abbas

A week or two later I was lying in an upstairs hotel room,
exhausted from yet another long bus ride. Shadows from
the ceiling fan crept across the walls, my imagination filling
them with images of dissolute Oriental intrigue, like a Sydney
Greenstreet moment in a B movie:

Think Shanghai *or* Casablanca. *Remember The Fat Man in a*
white suit and red fez selling forged letters of transit in his bazaar

office. Carry your suitcase up the stairs to the seedy hotel room you rented with your last tomans, pause on the balcony to watch the dhows sailing on the Persian Gulf, and despair of ever seeing Paris again. Unlock the door and throw yourself down on the creaky cot. Feel the faint breeze from the decrepit ceiling fan, keeping the flies at bay but doing nothing for the oppressive afternoon heat. And exhausted by your narrow escape from evil diamond smugglers, fall asleep in Bandar Abbas.

Of course, there were no diamond smugglers, just Americans from Kerman. Sharing a large room—six tomans a bed, with a view of the Persian Gulf— the five male volunteers and I had collapsed on our cots minutes after we walked in the door. In the smothering mid-afternoon heat, our decision to escape Kerman's December cold and spend the four-day school holiday in balmy Bandar Abbas, didn't seem quite so brilliant.

Arriving earlier that afternoon, we'd stepped out of the air-conditioned bus into the suffocating humidity of the gulf, my blouse immediately damp and clinging. If the weather was this oppressive in December, it must have been unbearable in July. No wonder former shahs banished dissidents of the realm to this remote location.

I was slightly behind Fred and the others when *she* strode past, her head moving neither right nor left. Slight in build, her dress was a riot of bright colors draping over loose pants intricately embroidered at the ankles, orange plastic sandals flapping on her brown feet. But it was the shiny, bronze-toned mask that stopped me short. Obscured from hairline to lip, her face resembled a prehistoric reptile.

"Hey! Did you see that?" I asked, catching up with the guys. But they hadn't. Minutes later, another masked woman, balancing a jug of water on her head, rounded the corner.

"Wow! She's something else. This sure isn't Kerman," Tom Sisul said.

Shifting our overnight cases from hand to hand, we had trooped through the streets toward the waterfront, looking more like a group of wide-eyed Boy Scouts than the hardened, strung-out ex-patriots of my fantasy. The hotel proprietor hadn't blinked when the six of us rented just one large room. The people in Bandar Abbas were used to strangers and strange ways.

But soon it was cooler and I had awakened from that afternoon nap. Walking out onto the balcony, I leaned against the rail, the gulf waters spreading endlessly beyond, the scent of the salty sea mingling with the odor of freshly caught fish. The vastness of the ocean had always been a siren beckoning me to the unknown, an ebb tide pulling me beyond the horizon. But here on the balcony in Bandar Abbas, it was as if I'd blown in with the sea breezes, riding the crest of a wave to a mysterious place.

The sun was shooting daggers of orange and pink onto the calm gulf waters when Fred stuck his head out the door, cleaning his eyeglasses with the hem of his shirt. "There you are, Mary. We wondered where you'd gone. Want to take a walk before dinner?"

In the early December twilight, the six of us ambled along a nearby pier watching men in Arab dress tie up their boats for the evening, their long *jalabiyahs* brushing the tops of their worn sandals. Dhows, with their triangular sails and long spars, had been sailing in and out of Bandar Abbas for centuries, but the town was still relatively small. With American dollars, the Iranians were dredging the harbor so tankers and warships could enter the area, but in late 1965 big ships were yet to come.

Vines of deep purple bougainvillea hung over the balcony of the restaurant where we dined on sweet fish kebabs. Looking out over the harbor, I watched small fires glowing on the boats at anchor, sailors hunkering over smoking charcoal braziers, grilling their own savory fare.

A market in Bandar Abbas. Note the masked woman seated in the foreground; a wind tower rises in the background.

There wasn't much going on in Bandar Abbas at night: no bars where sailors could drink away their pay, no night clubs where shady businessmen could close deals in smoke-filled back rooms. The dhows were dark; a blanket of black lay over the water. A streetlight here, one there, lit the way as Fred and

I strolled together after dinner, our shoulders brushing now and then. In a month he would be gone, his term of service as a Peace Corps volunteer complete, while mine had another five months to go. There were so many unknowns in our future.

The streets were bustling with activity when we woke the next morning. We met up with Mehdi, one of Fred's students from Kerman, and set out to explore the town. Mehdi, who was visiting his uncle, took his role as our guide very seriously. Tall and slender, the hint of a mustache darkening his upper lip, he blushed every time I spoke to him.

"Can we go to the bazaar?" I asked. In every part of Iran I'd visited, the bazaar was one of the highlights.

"Bazaars here aren't like the ones in the rest of Iran," Mehdi said. "They're outdoors, so they can catch the sea breezes."

As we sauntered toward the marketplace, Baluchis and Indians, Pakistanis, and Arabs, boxes on their backs, merchandise slung over their shoulders or tucked under their arms, were all looking to make a deal. Iranian men in suits and jackets mingled with the throngs, passing a word here, a signal there, their eyes expertly scanning the crowd—for government agents? For easy marks? The undercurrent of lawlessness flowing through the streets was palpable. In this city of exile, anything was available for a price. Boats from as close as the Arabian Peninsula or as far as India could land anywhere along the coast, ferrying in illicit goods from all over the world.

"Veenston," an Arab in a long, white jalabiyah crooned in Tom Sisul's ear. Tom jerked up his head. No. He wasn't about to buy Winston cigarettes on the street. They were illegal, smuggled in. He could get in trouble if one of the shah's men was watching. "Veeskee," a turbaned Pakistani whispered to Fred. Fred, too, shook him off. "Too bad. I could do with a little Johnny Walker," he said.

Mehdi's eyes went wide. "Not here! If you want whiskey, my uncle can get you some."

Minutes later, we were standing in the middle of a wide, open pathway, edged on both sides by small shops, their tin or rattan roofs shading the merchants from the sun. "This is the bazaar," Mehdi said. Trellises of scarlet bougainvilleas lined the area; the vast sky was its ceiling. At various places along the lane, women sold turnips or bread, potatoes or oranges. Light, floral-patterned chadors were draped casually over their heads and shoulders; the shiny masks covering their eyes and nose blocked the annoying, buzzing flies that seemed to land on everything. For once, I was the one who was staring. Those masks, the short chadors so perfect for this climate, the strips of colorful embroidery decorating the ankles of their loose pants—it was mesmerizing.

"Why do the women wear masks?" I asked Mehdi.

"Who knows?" he said. "Women in Bandar Abbas have always worn them."

"They must sell them here someplace. I've got to have one."

"Whatever for?"

"Women," Fred said, shaking his head in sympathy. "We can find a mask now, or we can find one later. She's not going to let this drop."

After a few inquiries, I was the proud owner of a shiny mask and several brightly embroidered narrow strips of cloth. For the next fifty years, they would remain neatly folded in a green box with yellow polka dots in the top drawer of my dresser.

Every week, Mehdi explained, there was a camel market on the beach just west of the harbor. On our last morning we headed toward the market, enjoying the cool breeze blowing in from the water. Above my head the date palms were swaying, their green tufts curtseying to the crowd below. Hundreds of camels knelt on the sand chewing huge cuds, or stood stamping their feet, while Baluchi men extolled their virtues to doubtful buyers dressed in Arab whites. "The Baluchis are big camel traders," Mehdi said. "They sell to men from the Emirates and to the caravan drivers who carry goods across the desert into Pakistan."

The Peace Corps men, experts after their recent outing in Yazd's desert, took the camels in stride. But I knew they were ill-tempered beasts, just waiting for a chance to land a well-placed kick. When Fred and Mehdi stopped to talk with a Baluchi merchant about his animal, I backed away—but not soon enough. The camel voiced his disapproval with a loud grumble, hissing and spitting warnings in my direction; the nearby men broke into laughter.

The bridle of that unpleasant beast was decorated with blue beads, a common guard against the evil eye. While camels always looked a little ragged up close—their knees needing patches, their coats mangy—there was something majestic about these fabled animals that could cross deserts carrying heavy loads, going for days without water. Which of those on the beach at Bandar Abbas would end up toiling on the Arabian Peninsula? And which would be traversing the old silk road into Pakistan? Only the buyers knew for sure.

The sun was high in the sky when we left the camels and the increasingly smelly beach. Walking toward our hotel, Mehdi pointed out the town's Hindu temple, the only one in Iran as far as he knew. I peered over a mud wall at its ornate facade, a most un-Iranian spiral rising up from its dome. What a big, showy building! The churches and synagogues I'd seen in Iran were much more discreet.

Turning down a street we hadn't traveled before, Mehdi stopped. "There it is," he said in English, pointing at a mosque across the road. "There it is, the most evil place in Iran." From my perspective, it resembled most Iranian mosques: elaborately tiled minarets reached high above the central domed structure, its arched doorways beautiful and welcoming. Yet here was Mehdi, the same young man who minutes before had cheer-fully shown us a Hindu temple, declaring a mosque to be evil.

"Why is it evil?" Fred asked him in Persian.

"It is Arab, Sunni. They murdered Hussein. They are evil, their religion is evil, this mosque is evil."

We had been passing Arabs in the street for days now with-out any kind of reaction, but in seeing a Sunni mosque, Mehdi was overcome. Here it was again, the raw immediacy of history in Iran. We walked the rest of the way to our hotel in silence.

We left Bandar Abbas—and Mehdi—on the one o'clock bus for Kerman. Four hours later, less than a third of the way home, we were in the small town of Hajiabad—literally, the "place of a *haji*," one who has made a sacred journey to Mecca, the holiest place in all of Islam, located in the middle of Sunni Saudi Arabia. Sipping tea in Hajiabad, waiting for a flat tire to be repaired, I wondered how Shi'a Iranians like Mehdi con-tained their anger during the holy pilgrimage. Most Iranians were Shi'as; Bandar Abbas, however, was on the edge of the Sunni-Shi'a divide—a cauldron of peoples and religions from south Asia and the Middle East, a place where the beliefs one took for granted could be challenged. And in Mehdi's eyes, or so I thought, the most dangerous challengers were those who were most like oneself.

It was dark when we pulled into a restaurant along the road near the town of Sirjan, more than halfway home. I followed my friends through a room full of metal tables and chairs. There, men wearing everything from black baggy pants to crisply cut suits were shoveling in platefuls of steaming rice, rounds of hot bread, and skimpy helpings of khoresh. Tom Taaffe pulled aside the curtain that walled off the women's area, and we sat down at one of its few tables. I'd just given my order to a teenage waiter when the curtains abruptly parted and two armed soldiers entered. "Come outside," the shorter one barked. "This is a customs inspection. You must identify your bags."

Chairs scraped along the floor as everyone in the restaurant rose to obey, amid a mumble of complaints. "They never let us alone." "Who do they think they are?" "If we were important, they wouldn't be stopping us."

The investigation began. "Who does this belong to?" the taller soldier asked, holding up a bag for all to see.

"It belongs to me," came from somewhere in the crowd, as a man with a three-day growth of beard wound his way to the front to claim the bag.

"Open it," the soldier demanded; then he pawed through the contents, searching for something illegal—like cigarettes or whiskey or drugs, I thought—but finding nothing.

This routine was repeated again and again. When the taller soldier waved my pink suitcase in the air, I said: "*Mallehman-eh*" ("It belongs to me.") "What's in it?" the soldier asked. When I answered clothing, he put a big check in white chalk on its side and didn't ask me to open it. "Foreigners, they're foreigners," rumbled around the crowd.

Things got more serious. Pulling a bulky burlap bag from the bus, the short soldier asked the owner to identify himself. No response. "Tell me, who does this belong to?" he asked again. A shaky voice answered, "It belongs to my uncle." Everyone laughed. "Well, with the permission of your uncle, I'm going to open it." Pulling a long knife from a sheath on his belt, he sliced the bag from stem to stern. Fifty or more half-kilo bags of Gulabi tea tumbled to the ground, good tea, the tea we all drank in Kerman, the one with brown label, straight from India. "Do you have tax receipts for these?" the soldier asked. The "nephew," now trembling, shook his head. The soldier smirked. "Your uncle is a big tea drinker. I'll make it easier for him." With that, he slit open each bag, dumping the tea into a sack. It was still drinkable, but its resale value had vanished.

It took over an hour for everything to be inspected. Much to my surprise, tea was the only contraband. Rich Kermanis might indulge in smuggled Winston cigarettes or Johnny Walker scotch, but everyone drank Indian tea. I could hear Mrs. Nahidi admonishing me: "Mary-jun, I know your package says Gulabi tea, but it's not the real thing. Only packages with the brown label are from India."

Back on the bus heading for Kerman, I realized the customs revelations weren't surprising. The little guys were easy picking for law enforcement, unlikely to be well-connected. Big time crooks, who ferried in drugs, whiskey, cigarettes, and other contraband, had "partee," strings tying them to influential people. The grumbling men in the roadside restaurant had it exactly right: if they had been big time smugglers, the gendarmes wouldn't have bothered them.

7

TURNING FOR HOME

I just don't know where home is. There's this
promise of happiness out there. I know it. I
even feel it sometimes. But it's like chasing the
moon – just when I think I have it, it disap-
pears into the horizon. —*Sarah Addison*

My Elephant Thinks of India

Letter home

> I got your letter the other day. I'm still smiling
> about "paté." If you eat it, Mom, it'll be one of the
> most expensive dinners you've ever had. Pateh is
> a Farsi word, a beautiful embroidered cloth, used
> mainly as a table covering or wall hanging. It's
> hand sewn and some of them are exquisite. They're
> particularly from Kerman, and I like them better than
> the carpets. The one given me for you isn't one of the
> best, but I'm trying to buy some beautiful ones to
> bring home.

When my twenty-third birthday arrived in early December, wedged in between Thanksgiving turkey and the masked women of Iran's gulf coast, we stopped our travels to celebrate. Fred produced a light, fluffy delicacy from a box of Betty Crocker yellow cake mix he had unearthed in Esfahan. Declaring it to be the best cake he had ever eaten, Mr. Sayeed-Nejad asked for seconds.

While Fred was in the kitchen, Alice Phinney had scurried around the bazaar, shopping by mime, as only she could, for my gifts. "Wow! How did you ever find this? I've never seen an egg beater here," I said, opening the oddly shaped package.

"Well, I knew you needed one. I found a sympathetic-looking merchant in that section where they sell pots and pans and silverware," she said. "When I had his complete attention, I just turned into an egg beater, that's all, moving my hands and arms, trilling my lips. I think my shoulders got into the act as well." Thank goodness I wasn't there. Solo trips to the bazaar

worked better for both of us. Her antics made me want to sink
into the floor; she complained I cramped her style.

"At first, the man in the kiosk just looked confused," she
continued, her eyes teasing, "but all of a sudden, he got it. The
little boy who works for him—don't they look like little men
in those suit jackets?—led me down the lane to another seller.
Voila!" With such a back-story, this gift would hold a unique
place in my culinary collection.

But *del-am tang shodeh* (my heart tightened), as the Kermanis
would say, when I opened the birthday box from my parents.
Along with a book and underwear was a *National Geographic*
magazine. Among its pages, pressed between sheets of waxed
paper, were the leaves of fall: bright red maples, dusty brown
oaks, yellow sycamores, even a green-needled sprig from the
California redwood my father had planted in our Illinois front
yard. I unwrapped my mother's gift, a Styrofoam Christmas
tree ornament striped in pale blue velvet ribbons, and adorned
with bright red and silver sequins. Holding it in my hands I
could picture her at the kitchen table, chewing on her lip while
she concentrated on the proper place for each piece of glitter,
careful not to let the tiny pushpins fall to the floor where our
dog, Spike, might find them. Soon it would be Christmas. I
would be here in Kerman. They would be in Homewood.

Kermanis have a special way of expressing the loneliness
one feels when reminded of home. "*Fil-am beh yad-e Hindustan
oftad,*" they say—"my elephant just remembered India." As
summer changed to fall, and fall transformed into winter, my
elephant had been thinking about India with disconcerting
regularity. I didn't miss Illinois where my parents now lived;
it was just the last in a string of addresses. But my heart tightened in the Persian way for my mother, my father, my brother,

my grandfather, and grandmother, for the shared experience that made us a family.

When I left the States more than a year earlier, the family dynamic was in an awkward, stilted place. My politics, choice of friends, and the way I spent my time were all issues for my father. He couldn't remain silent, and neither could I. But separated by continents and an ocean, it had been a healing time. I had not been abandoned to Iran, nor had I ignored my family in Illinois. My mother sent typed transcripts of my letters to her friends and relatives. Determined to beat Iranian censors, my father cut a hole in a book to smuggle in an audio tape from all the family. He sent New Year's cards to my friends, and even wrote Mr. Sayeed-Nejad to thank him for helping his daughter. My Iranian colleagues understood my family cared about me. I knew I was loved and, without saying so, my parents and I made peace.

That fall, when questions about being away from home came up yet again, I couldn't dismiss them. Sitting at long tables in a Bahmanyar High School classroom, my six women students were discussing the hugely popular movie *Seven Brides for Seven Brothers* that, dubbed in Farsi, was playing at the local cinema. Mrs. Homayunfar felt sorry for the young women who had been kidnapped by the brothers to become their brides. Taken away from their families, she knew they missed their mothers.

I could feel it coming. "Don't you miss your mother, Miss Mary?" asked Mrs. Faroukpay. Before I could respond, Mrs. Azari chimed in: "I couldn't bear to be so far away from my family. When did you last see your mother, Miss Mary?"

"It's been more than a year. I haven't seen my parents since I came to Kerman. I especially miss my family during the holidays," I added, startled by the strength of my feelings.

"Perhaps you can call them at Christmas," said my new friend Maryam-khanum. "You know that my husband works for the telephone company."

"That would be nice," I said, dismissing the idea. Telephones were a rarity in Kerman in 1965. I hadn't spoken on one more than twice since I'd been here. When away from home, even Americans kept in touch by letter; my family worried about the cost if long distance calls exceeded three minutes.

It was mid-November, cold enough to turn on the kerosene heaters, when Maryam invited me to lunch, a casual affair, she explained. Her husband Mohammed wanted to talk to me about the holiday phone call.

Phone call? Was it really going to happen?

The taxi stopped in front of Maryam's house, a walled-in abode at the other end of town from my apartment. The Elahis' elderly manservant answered my ring, leading me through the bare garden into the house. Maryam and I were standing by the window chatting, her two-year-old son in her arms, when her husband came in. As we said our hellos and settled down on the floor to eat, I realized I'd never been in such an informal situation in Iran with a woman's husband present. Mohammad Elahi, like every professional of either gender I'd met, worked for the Iranian government. A tall man, with a moustache of course, his English was only slightly better than his wife's. Our luncheon conversation was bilingual—when he couldn't find the right word in English, we tried Farsi. If I couldn't talk around the idea I was trying to express in Farsi, I switched to my native tongue. This half-and-half communication was my way of life these days.

While we ate, Mohammad explained that to schedule the telephone call from his office he needed my family's number. Maybe this was for real! There was one thing yet to be resolved.

How much was it going to cost? When I posed the question, Maryam and Mohammad gave each other a look. This was no time for ta'arof, no polite refusals. It would be expensive, Mohammad acknowledged. Two hundred tomans. Twenty-six dollars, I calculated quickly, almost a third of my monthly Peace Corps living allowance. But I had some savings—living in Kerman didn't cost very much. "That's fine," I said, gulping.

I danced out of the Elahi house that afternoon. I was going to get to speak with my family. They would be so excited. If I called them on Christmas Eve at five-thirty in the afternoon, Kerman time, that would be 9 a.m. in Homewood. I puzzled over the correct phone number. Sycamore 8-5746; that was SY 8-5746. How did SY translate into numbers? There were no letters on the 1, I was pretty sure, then three letters each until we ran out—798-5746. I wrote home immediately. December twenty-fourth was less than a month away.

Christmas Eve day took forever to pass. I counted and recounted my money, then checked the clock: one p.m. I tried to take an Iranian siesta, but sleep wouldn't come: one-thirty. I wrote letters to occasional correspondents—my aunt, my grandmother, an ex-boyfriend: two-thirty. I baked Christmas cookies: four-fifteen.

At last it was five o'clock, and time to go to the telephone office. I checked again that the 200 tomans were wrapped safely in my pocketbook, and hailed a cab.

"I'd like to see Mr. Elahi," I told the doorman at the phone company in my most assured Farsi. "He's helping me make a call to America."

"Mr. Elahi has gone home for the day. He said to tell you it is not possible to call today."

"That can't be. My parents are waiting. They'll be very upset."

"I'm sorry. I can't do anything to help you."

A dusty winter wind peppered my face as I trudged home down the unpaved street—past the movie theater, past the bakery, past the communal water tap. Iran was an impossible place to live. And, like every Iranian in the world, Mr. Elahi was impossible, too. He deserved to live here.

"I knew it! I just knew this would happen," I said to Phin. "These people make promises they never mean to keep. I got my family's hopes up that I'd call them on Christmas Eve. I even gave them the exact time, and what happened? Nothing—a big nothing."

"It may still work out," Phin said.

"No, it won't. It never does. They just say what they think you want to hear. Maryam's husband never had any intention of actually letting me make the call."

With that, I stalked into my bedroom, banged the door shut, and threw myself down on the bed. Not only was this botched phone call ruining my Christmas, but it was messing up my family's as well. I should have known better.

I couldn't stay put. Pacing up and down the long, narrow room, I finally ended up at the window where Willy was sleeping, sprawled across my writing supplies. "Hey there, sweet kitty," I cooed into his ear, picking him up and hugging him close. "You wouldn't do this to me, would you?" With that, Willy jumped out of my arms and headed for the door. Fickle kitty, I thought, letting him out of the room. I selected a blue aerogram from my stationery stash, found a black ball point pen, and crawled up on my bed to pour out my frustrations in a letter to my parents: "Iranians promise the moon and give nothing!"

My phone funk continued through Christmas Day. My poor family. What would they think? Reluctantly, I helped Fred with yet another turkey. My mother's ornament dangled over our dining room table that afternoon as the Kerman volunteers and a couple of others from nearby towns feasted on American bounty and my homemade cookies. But for all the camaraderie, the day felt flat. I was angry—especially with myself for letting down my guard.

I was still moping around on New Year's Day when Mr. Sayeed-Nejad appeared at the door to our apartment.

"Come on, Mary-khanum, let's go," he said, motioning toward a waiting taxi.

"Where?"

"To the telephone company. You can make your call."

"It's too late. Christmas is over. My parents won't even be at home."

"Mary-jun, Mr. Elahi has gone to a lot of trouble so you can call your parents. You must come."

"I don't have to do anything of the sort."

But I got my coat and money and followed Mr. Sayeed-Nejad into the cab.

"So how come I can call today, and I couldn't call on Christmas Eve, when it was all arranged?" I asked, as the cab bumped along.

"The telephone lines were all busy. Everyone wants to call home at Christmas."

"We made these arrangements a month ago." I stared out the window at a flock of goats and sheep being herded down the street. "And why didn't Mr. Elahi tell me it wasn't going to happen?"

"He did, Mary-jun, he did. Remember, the doorman at the phone company had a message for you."

Before I could protest further, we reached the telephone
company. I nodded briefly at Mr. Elahi when I was led into
his office but didn't say a word, staring at a spot on the wall
behind him. He was gracious, ignoring my bad manners and
directing me to a nearby booth. Minutes later, he signaled to
me to pick up the receiver.

"Hello, Mother?"

"Hello, hello, I can barely hear you, Mary," she said.

"Well, you're as clear as a bell," I said.

"What did you say? All I can hear is a word or two, and a
lot of static."

"I can hear you fine. Is Daddy there?" She must have heard
"Daddy" for then my father was on the line.

"Hello, Mary, did you get our package?" he asked.

"Not yet. How are you?"

"Mary, I can't hear you. What did you say?"

And so the conversation went for three whole minutes.
Then the line went dead. Struggling to hold back my tears, I
apologized to Mr. Elahi for my abrupt behavior. "I didn't understand that you were working on the call," I said, fishing in my
purse for the 200 tomans—a lot of money for "I can't hear
you." But there was something comforting about sharing real
time with my parents. And for the next few days, my elephant
grinned every time she thought of India.*

---

*   My mother described the process of receiving this call in a letter to
    me:
    Yesterday we got a call from the Paris operator saying you would call today.
    Oh happy day. Don [my brother] handled most of that call, and kept
    asking, "Who is calling from Tehran?" as if we knew dozens of people who
    might be calling. He was pretty excited to even be talking to Paris. Then this
    morning the phone rang, just when they said it would, 8:30 our time, and
    we could hear the Paris operator trying to get Tehran to come on, and they
    tried to get you. It seemed to take ages, but it wasn't more than ten to fifteen
    minutes. Then you were there....

Phin's Story

The new year was a few days old when my roommate banged the front door closed and began to climb the steps to our apartment—up a stair, pause; up another one, stop. Her hesitant pace drew me to the head of the stairs.

"Anything wrong?"

Phin held out our trashcan full of Christmas turkey bones. "She's not there. Our rubbish lady's nowhere to be seen."

Phin had taken over the problem of garbage disposal when she first arrived. Foreigners in Iran produced waste—paper, tin cans, leftovers; Iranians, as far as I could see, did not. Paper was recycled into small bags, nothing was purchased that came in a can, and leftovers were fed to someone's goat. Consequently, there was no garbage pickup. Before Phin, my approach had been to sneak across the street when no one was around and dump the trash behind a crumbling adobe wall. Safely out of sight upstairs, I would watch the neighborhood women swarm to my dumping ground, pick over my discards, stow newfound treasures under their chadors, and hurry home to the warren of households extending back from the street. Phin opted for transparency. "I just stand outside our door and look helpless. Someone always comes, takes the can away, and brings it back empty."

She developed a relationship with one special woman, "the rubbish lady," she called her. "She's different from the other women at the pump across the street. She looks at me with intelligence instead of a blank stare." It wasn't long before Phin added a few ripe tomatoes, an orange or two, even a hunk of lamb to the trove, just for this special woman.

"Your rubbish lady's probably fixing dinner," I said. "I wouldn't worry about it."

"No, Mary. I am worried. It's been three days. I tried to ask one of the women where she was, but she didn't understand. Maybe if you talk to someone we can find out what's happened."

Alice Phinney, Mr. Sanaati, Tom Sisul, and Mr. Sayeed-Nejad.

It was not often my roommate asked for help. We had been sharing this apartment for almost five months, each of us with our own areas of expertise. Alice Phinney's sixty-six years of life experience easily trumped my year and a half of living in Kerman, but she never played that card. I would have happily led her around, showing her this and that about Iran and its people, but she was determined to make her own discoveries. She was drawn to people through her sense of their character, she told me, making friends at both ends of the social spectrum. Mrs. Nouri of the Kerman Women's Club exemplified the elite. Always elegantly attired, she invited Phin to the best Kerman's leading women had to offer. Whereas Mrs. Nouri was progressive, educated, and affluent, the rubbish lady of the water pump across the street could not have been any of those things. But she scrubbed her pots and pans, washed her clothing, and minded her children with a dignity that engaged my roommate. While Phin was curious about both these women, there was more intensity in her relationship with the woman across the street.

"Wait right there. I'll get my coat," I said.

Minutes later, skirting the muddy pool by the water pump, I could see the glint of the setting sun bouncing off the glass doors to our balcony. A strong winter wind blew Phin's white hair into a back-lit halo as children in flip-flops and ill-fitting sweaters scampered around us, reveling in our foreignness. Their mothers and sisters drew themselves up from their laundry basins, pulled their chadors more closely around their narrow bodies, and approached. "*Chee meekhand?*" ("What do they want?") floated through our audience. After waiting for a lull in the chatter, I explained that the woman who often helped Miss Phinney hadn't been around for the past few days; my friend was worried about her. The women knew exactly whom I meant. Sultana, they agreed, had been sick with an upset stomach and a fever. Today she seemed a little better. I translated for Phin, who looked relieved. "There's still some turkey soup in the refrigerator, isn't there? Tell the women to wait while I get her some."

Back upstairs, I ladled our leftovers into a plastic container, then watched from the balcony as Phin strode purposefully behind the neighborhood women. Soon the group—one London Fog clad New Englander among a bevy of flowing chadors—disappeared into the narrow walled lanes across from our apartment.

I closed the balcony doors and flicked on the kitchen lights, considering how the very presence of Phin and her venerable years had eased my life in Kerman. Our apartment on Cinema Nur Street put more distance between my observers and me than I'd had at the daneshsera, but Phin's presence added a vital soupçon of familial stability. That we were not family and she had no intention of acting as a chaperone were immaterial.

I stuck the potatoes in the oven and put the kettle on for tea. Phin was like no one else I knew. She didn't speak Farsi, yet here she was setting off on a mission of mercy where little if any English was spoken. Somehow, she would make herself understood, enlivening everyone in the process. I loved her sense of humor; I admired her gumption. Unconcerned about the opinion of others, she didn't show any of the hesitation I felt in unfamiliar circumstances. It was impossible to laugh at her; she was enjoying whatever predicament she was in just as much as the rest of us were. Her life up to now didn't sound all that exciting; she had taught English literature in the same New England boarding school for more than forty years. During that time, she also learned how to fly small airplanes. "I got my license, but I really wasn't very good," she said. "I was too apprehensive at the controls. I just wanted to see if I could do it." She also had been engaged. "It was during the Second World War, and my fiancé came down with tuberculosis. We wrote back and forth, but by the time he was released from the sanitarium, I'd lost interest. He married someone else." I couldn't imagine my life without a man somewhere, nor could I conceive of leaving my world behind at sixty-six to join the Peace Corps. Yet Phin had.

Daylight was fading. I was about to set off on my own rescue mission when I heard the downstairs door close.

"You wouldn't believe it, Mary," Phin said, adding her coat to the pile on the dining room table. "It is so dark back there, I don't know how these women find their houses. You'd think the city would light those narrow lanes."

"I was beginning to worry."

"Oh, no need for that. They took very good care of me. One of the women led me until my eyes got accustomed to the dimness. I thought her hand would be rough, but it was smooth and kind, just the right amount of friendliness."

This was pure Phin, taking her cues from things I wouldn't have noticed, relying on the senses of sight, touch, and perception rather than what she heard.

"We went through a door," she continued, "down a few steps, across a courtyard about as big as a handkerchief, up some mud steps, under a curtain, and into a room where I could hardly see; then up some more steps to a tiny room that was oh, so dark." Phin paused, looking around our living room at the shadows our lamps were throwing on the walls.

"Mary, do you remember how excited the rubbish lady was when she found that piece of broken window in our trash? It couldn't have been more than six inches long, but somehow she fit it into her wall. The only light in the room comes in through that wedge of glass."

I had never imagined that life could be so small, so basic, even here. We were so profligate, yet our waste was the difference between a little light and total darkness for this woman.

"Even with that sliver of light," Phin said, "it took awhile for my eyes to adjust. Everything in her tiny room was neat. The floor was as clean as a mud floor can be, and either rags or clothes hung over a pole at the top of one of the beds. Finally,

I saw the rubbish woman lying on a pallet against a wall. She didn't get up, but I could tell she was glad I was there."

"Does she still have a fever? Maybe we should get Dr. Azari to visit her." It was rumored that Dr. Azari and his wife were once imprisoned for Communist activities. Perhaps he wouldn't mind tending to Phin's friend.

"Her hand and forehead were cool to the touch. Let's wait. We'll call in Dr. Azari if your turkey soup doesn't do the trick."

During dinner our conversation drifted off into plans for follow-up visits, extra blankets, more soup. Soon it was time to flick off the living room lights and adjourn to our own private spaces, Phin to study written Persian and I to write to my parents.

Two days later, Phin and I were invited by her friend Mrs. Nouri to a celebration commemorating Reza Shah's banning of the veil, the edict of *kashf-e hijab*. We were outside looking for a taxi when Phin pointed across the street. "She's back," she said. Sultana, the rubbish lady, was bent over the water pump, washing her clothes.

Food for Thought

Letter home

When I begin to like the taste of rosewater in everything I eat, I'll know it's time to come home.

A warm breeze ruffled the Iranian flag flying over the Iran Air terminal as Mr. Sayeed-Nejad, Mr. Sanaati, and the Kerman volunteers waited with Fred for the plane that would carry him out of Kerman. I shifted from one foot to the other, half-listening while he bantered back and forth with the two Iranians.

Fred's two years in the Peace Corps were finished. When I first arrived, each day was an eternity; I would be in Iran forever. But I had checked the calendar. It was January, Fred was leaving, and in June, five months away, I would too.

If I went home, how would I use all the Iran savvy I'd accumulated? It was Ramadan, the Muslim month of fasting. Days before, I'd watched the grocer swirl pretzel-shaped streams of sugary batter into a cauldron of boiling oil. He pulled the *zelubias* out with tongs when they solidified, placing a dozen translucent, amber confections in a paper cone. A favorite treat for breaking the fast, the year before they were too sticky sweet for my taste, but this time around I was the first in line. In the States next year, there wouldn't be any zelubias. Would I even know when it was Ramadan?

The whir of propellers drowned the conversation as Fred's plane taxied to a stop. Passengers hastened toward the terminal while airport staff pulled their luggage from the aircraft. Then the process reversed, men heaving trunks and suitcases onto the plane, the artifacts of Fred's life in Kerman stowed along with the rest. "Now boarding for Esfahan and Tehran," the Iran Air manager announced to the dozen waiting passengers. Fred shook hands with the members of his entourage. "Maybe I'll see you soon," he murmured, leaving his hand in mine a beat longer than the others. Then he was off, striding toward the plane, toward the future. I followed my group to the car, *he's gone, I'm on my own* thrumming in my head.

Just keep busy, I resolved again and again over the next few days. January was still dragging on when I agreed to join a cooking class after school three days a week. Gathering around a table with seven other teachers in Mayel High School's kitchen, I scribbled furiously as Mrs. Ardeshir, our chef, listed the ingredients for the food of the day:

> 1 sheet of gelatin
> ½ cup sugar
> ½ cup water
> 1 cup fruit juice.

Jell-O! I was taking a cooking class in Farsi to learn how to make Jell-O.

"But I thought we were going to make Persian food," I said after class.

"These women know how to prepare our dishes. They want to learn something different," Mrs. Ardeshir said. I decided to keep at it. The teachers were pleased I was there, I'd never made Jell-O from scratch, and I needed something to distract me.

But the class had not progressed past Jell-O when I found a reason to go to Tehran while Fred's group was mustering out. Away from stringent Kermani scrutiny, we had a wonderful few days. Before flying off to India and points east, he promised to come back through Iran for the No Ruz holidays beginning in late March. Then he'd be off to Washington for more interviews for the Peace Corps job in Iran. And this is where it got confusing. Would I be returning with him? Fred seemed so reluctant. Right then I wanted two things: to be with this intelligent, charismatic man, and to stay in Iran. Neither was in my control.

I didn't consider extending my Kerman stay. Graduate school, the only alternative I could see, belonged to another time and place, before the Peace Corps, before Fred. But studying Chinese history at Berkeley was still possible. I could use my termination pay from the Peace Corps for tuition. The American University in Beirut was another option. There, I could learn Arabic—shouldn't everyone know Arabic?—and be closer to Iran. Half-heartedly, I began the paperwork that could take me back to school, squeezing the applications in among English classes and clubs, visiting friends, and those cooking lessons.

Ramadan over, our group of budding chefs was free to sample its handiwork. Having mastered Jell-O, we moved on to pirozhki, a more complicated dish. "Maybe you've made this in America, Miss Mary," Mrs. Ardeshir said. I hadn't. The fried half-moons of meat-filled dough were not part of my mother's repertoire. "They're Polish," one of the women said. "No, they're Russian," said another. Whatever nationality they were, the pungent aroma of sautéed onions, ground lamb, and parsley made my stomach rumble with anticipation.

"What do you fix for dinner in Kerman?" Mrs. Ardeshir asked, wiping beads of perspiration from her brow with the back of her hand.

"Well, right now I'm preparing three kilos of beef for sauerbraten," I said, scrambling for the right words in Farsi. "I have to leave the meat in vinegar, wine, and onions for three days. Before our friends from out of town arrive, I'll cook it slowly for several hours. It should be delicious." The faces of my fellow chefs froze.

"It's not American," I said, as if this would make sauerbraten more appealing. "It's German. I found the recipe in a cookbook."

"We don't eat much beef here, and we certainly don't eat it sour. Perhaps you can make pirozhkis for them instead." Mrs. Ardeshir turned the dumplings over in the hot oil.

The tendrils that link east to west are delicate I realized, taking down ingredients and preparation instructions in English. A meat-filled pastry could be a bridge, but sauerbraten was diving into the deep end of the divide.

The class moved on to Persian sweets. As the weeks passed, I added *loz-e nargil* (coconut diamonds) and *pufak*, a coconut meringue, to my recipe notebook, noting the amounts in *seers*, a traditional Iranian measure.

"When I first came to Iran," I said to Phin, who was sampling the meringue, "I knew if I started to like the sweets here it would be time to go home. Now I'm worried. This pufak is pretty good."

No, I wasn't ready to leave. My rhythms were slowing, allowing me to savor each moment. The chasm of difference between the Kermanis and me, the walls separating me from those around me no longer seemed so imposing

Mother Nature wasn't cooperating when the calendar announced spring. Chill winds whipped my coat around as I made the daily mail run to the Office of Education. Fred, writing from New Delhi, Agra, and finally Katmandu, seemed disengaged, his world expanding while I remained bound to Kerman's familiar routines. I was anxious for No Ruz to arrive so I could pull him back into my realm, reinforce our closeness, our shared experience of Iran.

We had been working up to No Ruz since the end of January, when half of Kerman had gathered in a field outside of town to witness *Jashn-e Sadeh*, the Festival of Fire the Zoroastrians celebrate fifty days before the Iranian New Year. Standing next to Mr. Sayeed-Nejad, I watched as men set an enormous pile of wood ablaze, hymns recited by priests of this venerable religion echoing through a tinny-sounding audio system. Mounted policemen kept the crowds back as the bonfire flamed to the skies, carrying upward all our hopes for the New Year.

Weeks later, just days before No Ruz, the chatter in the teachers' rooms was all about holiday cleaning, cooking, new clothing, gifts, visits. "Let's have a party for our dooreh before we leave town for the No Ruz break," I said to Phin. "Our friends remember our holidays. Let's celebrate theirs." We began our own rounds of shopping, cleaning, and cooking.

The day of the party, workmen in hand-woven moccasins and baggy pants were wielding shovels to prepare our street for paving. Skirting around the mounds of dirt in front of our apartment, the women approached our door in twos and threes, huffing and laughing their way to the second floor.

"Ohh, those steps are steep," Mrs. Nahidi said as she folded her chador, putting it on the dining room table next to a bowl of dyed Easter eggs. I was very fond of this perceptive English teacher who had taught me to look at my language from an Iranian perspective.

"Miss Phinney, how do you climb these stairs?" asked Mehri-khanum. Phin just smiled. Maybe she didn't understand Mehri's English; maybe such an obvious question wasn't worth an answer. Mehri was the only one of our group who was not a teacher. "My husband says I can go to the daneshsera when our children are older," she'd confided a few days before. "Then I can teach—just what I've always wanted to do."

The ladies easily negotiated the tangle of befarmayeeds at the living room entrance and sat down, some in the easy chairs we'd gotten from USAID, others in the director's chairs Betsy's Christopher had bought in Rezaiyeh. Mrs. Noruzi and Mrs. Farvahari perched on metal folding chairs that had traveled here with Betsy and me from the daneshsera. These two women could not have been more different. Mrs. Noruzi, a young, lively Tehrani, was in Kerman because her husband was stationed here with the military. Mrs. Farvahari, stolid and patient, was of the place; her Zoroastrian family was one of the city's oldest.

The conversation was cheerful as I passed tea and cherries, pistachios and tea, tea and apples, cookies and tea, pausing in front of each guest. She'd finally accept saying, "*Dast-e toon dard nakoneh*" ("May your hand not pain you"), or something equally polite. It all seemed so normal.

Remembering how unappreciated chocolate brownies were in this crowd, I was determined to try something Iranian for my food finale. With trepidation, I paused in front of Fereshteh-khanum, a plate of loz-e nargil, coconut treats from my cooking class in my hand. As a home economics teacher, I expected her to be my toughest critic; instead, she was a loyal friend.

"Look, look! Miss Mary's learned to make Kermani food!" she said, then primly refused the sweet several times before putting a piece on her plate.

"I wish I'd taken that cooking class," Maryam-khanum said, looking only a little uncomfortable in the soft easy chair. Maryam, tall, slender, and well-dressed, confused me. Without warning, she would transform from a sophisticated, westernized Iranian woman to a conservative, religious Kermani wife. But I knew I could count on her; she had made my New Year's phone call home possible.

Our guests were donning their chadors when Maryam asked if she might stay behind to speak with me. She had something personal she would like to discuss.

We sat on the director's chairs, making polite conversation. I was waiting for my guest to broach this important, personal topic when Phin appeared, a brass serving tray in hand. "Befarmayeed, befarmayeed," she said, offering tea first to

Maryam, then to me. She knew no important subject could be broached without a glass of tea. As Phin left the room, Maryam stirred lumps of sugar into the amber liquid and began.

"I've come as a *hastegaree*" ("go-between"), she said. "There is a gentleman, a very nice gentleman, a doctor, who wants your hand in marriage."

"Marry me? Someone wants to marry me? Really?" For months I had been waiting for a proposal of marriage, but this one, in Farsi yet, was totally unexpected.

Maryam assured me she was serious. She didn't know my suitor personally, didn't even know his name. The doctor was a friend of a friend whose opinions she respected. She was certain he would be a very good husband, well able to take care of me. His parents, she reported, would be happy to have an American daughter in the family. While we'd never met, we had seen each other, but Maryam didn't know where.

I had been in Iran too long to be disdainful of arranged marriages, but I had never considered myself a candidate. Maybe this doctor had always dreamed of having an American wife; surely, he didn't know about my involvements with Bill and Fred. But I chose to see his offer as an affirmation of my time in Kerman. Someone wanted me to stay.

Maryam sat very still, waiting for me to say something. I watched the lumps of sugar dissolve into a small mound in my glass of tea. Less than a year before, I'd been ready to give up, to leave Kerman. But the move out of the daneshsera and the presence of Phin had softened my image. Most significantly, Kerman had changed me.

Stretching my Farsi to new limits, I explained that my answer had to be no. I was very complimented by her efforts and his kind offer, but in my heart I knew I could not become an Iranian wife. Although I didn't want to leave Iran, living here forever, so far from my home, so far from my mother, was inconceivable. At last, missing mom had true resonance.

Talking over this remarkable development with Phin after Maryam left, we decided to save the poor doctor from embarrassment and not mention his proposal to any of our Iranian friends. We'd just laid out this plan of action when the doorbell rang. It was Mr. Sayeed-Nejad. His crutches grazed the mat on the floor as he swung into the living room and settled in a chair.

"Mary-jun, I was wondering how you answered Maryam-khanum."

"How did you know about this?"

"Everybody knows."

"Even the women who were here this afternoon?"

"Especially them."

Some secret. But not one of my friends ever mentioned the proposal, even to tease me. Marriage was no laughing matter.

What would have followed if I'd said I was interested? Mr. Sayeed-Nejad gave the standard reply. Maryam's inquiry was the informal asking. Had I answered affirmatively, I would have learned more about my suitor, even met him. If all went well, the formal asking would follow, the doctor and his family visiting me and my family, bearing gifts like clothing and shoes—shoes!—for everyone. At that time, we would become officially engaged.

But that never happened. I would leave Kerman as I had arrived, a single woman without visible family, an anomaly in the social fabric of the Iran I knew.

Khodahafez

*K*hodahafez, godspeed, goodbye. The weeks crept slowly on as the certainties in my life dissolved. I would be leaving Kerman in June, that was the only given.

The long-awaited No Ruz holidays, spent with Fred in Tehran, then Esfahan, were a huge letdown. I got sick, the weather was rainy and cold, and Fred was distracted. Back aching, fever raging, I crouched in the rear of the bus, fighting tears of frustration on the long ride back to Kerman. Fred headed to the States, first to Washington to finalize the Peace Corps Iran job, then home to California. Fall was months away. We would write.

But finally it was spring, a glorious time in Kerman. The heady aroma of roses filled the gardens and the bazaar exploded with the bounty of new fruits and vegetables. At dusk, young men paced to and fro under the streetlights, studying for their exams. I knew the girls at the daneshsera were keeping lonely moonlight vigils in the courtyard as they committed chapters of history, geometry, and English to heart.

Weekdays, I struggled to hold the attention of the seventh grade class I had inherited when its teacher was called away, but Fridays, the Muslim day of rest, were all mine. Kerman volunteers had fallen into a new routine: brunch. It started after the No Ruz holidays when one of Phin's students brought her a big fish from the distant Caspian Sea. Something had to be done fast. "You should barbeque it," said Tom Taaffe. He followed through by digging a pit in our courtyard, filling it with charcoal, brushing the fish with oil, and grilling it over the fire. Delicious! Fridays that followed featured omelets and sweet rolls; scrambled eggs with onions; and French toast, made from home-baked bread, the syrup a combination of blackberry jam and sugar water.

The mild weather lured us out of the city. One Friday afternoon in April, Mr. Sayeed-Nejad and Mr. Sanaati drove the Toms and me to Jupar, a town about twenty miles from Kerman. "The mountains of Jupar are famous for their wildlife," Mr. Sayeed-Nejad told us. I searched the landscape for signs of wild ass or ibex, but all I could see were the trails of a qanat, evidence of man, not beast. The lifelines of a village, these excavated underground channels brought spring water and snow melt from the mountains to irrigate the fields.

Driving through the valley, green with the crops of spring, we stopped at a spot where we could actually walk into the mouth of a qanat, the point where its water flowed into the fields. The entry was tall enough to stand in; taking off my shoes, I waded in the cool stream, minnow-sized fish flicking around my feet. Where on earth did they come from?

Jupar is home to a beautiful shrine erected to honor a brother of Imam Reza, one of Iran's most noted religious figures. Wearing my chador for the first time, I approached the sepulcher that dominated the shrine's inner sanctum. To my surprise, bits of brightly colored cloth dangled from the wrought iron gating.

"Women fasten them there to make their wishes come true," Mr. Sayeed-Nejad said. The tree of hope in Mr. Arjomand's village, where women lit candles and tied strips of material to its branches, flashed into my head. "Just superstition," Mr. Arjomand had said, but I'd been moved by the villagers' efforts to nourish this sacred symbol, and by the strength of their beliefs.

"Come on, Mary," Tom Sisul said. "There must be something you want." My face reddened as I fished in my pocketbook for a handkerchief. Trying to be casual, I approached the area, paused a minute, tied my own strip of cloth to a piece of iron work, and hurried back to our group.

"What did you wish for?" Tom Taaffe asked.

"World peace," I lied.

"This shrine will be draped in black in a few days," Mr. Sayeed-Nejad said as we left. "It's almost Moharram, the month we mourn the martyrdom of Hussein. The man buried here is his namesake."

The afternoon was deepening as we drove home, passing Mahan, Mr. Sayeed-Nejad's hometown. The tall minarets and rounded dome of Shah Ne'matollah Vali's mausoleum were backlit against the mountains at this, the most beautiful time of day. How breathtaking this dervish shrine appeared. The stark and the lush, contrasts that defined Iran for me, had never been more striking.

When Moharram began a few days later, from my balcony I could see three white prayer tents, their black flags flying. The loudspeaker from the nightly prayer meetings interrupted my sleep, just as it had the year before. Black dominated the bazaar—the shirts the men were wearing; the chadors of their wives; the flags, embroidered in reds and yellows, adorning every shop. As I left for school one morning, a man standing next to the bicycle shop was singing about the martyrdom of Hussein. A huge colored mural hung on the wall; as he chanted, he pointed out different characters in the story. Occasionally, he would pause to answer questions posed by a small boy. The audience, all in black, was entirely children.

The year before, on Chehlum, the most significant day of the mourning period, Fred and I had crept on our bellies to peek from my balcony at the procession passing down Cinema Nur Street. This year I felt more confident about my role as a nonbeliever, electing to stay inside at highly religious moments, not because it was dangerous, but because it was courteous. Was this the last time I would witness this drama?

View of the Shah Ne'matollah Vali shrine in Mahan.

Cooped up indoors, I forced myself to review the tests I had given my class the week before. The English language was a sore point with me these days. My sixty-two rambunctious seventh graders were failing. As I flipped through the exams, my heart sank. Red ink scarred their pages. These girls would have been better off with an Iranian teacher; they certainly could not have done worse. They might be singing "Ring Around the Rosie" with a lovely American accent, but this ability was not translating to the written page. And the written page was what counted. "My students are doing terribly, also. They are lazy. They don't study," Mrs. Nahidi tried to reassure me. But that didn't help. Now it was too late. If there had been an opportunity to lead these girls more responsibly, to be the kind of teacher students didn't want to disappoint, I had let it slip by. After nearly two years here, no one—not the students, not the teachers, not the director of education, and especially not me—saw my role as integral to the education of Kerman's girls. And these examinations, swimming in red, demonstrated how ineffective my classroom activities had been. If I had come to Iran only to improve the level of language learning, I should have stayed home.

Should we have stayed home? The Peace Corps asked this question, though they posed it a bit more subtly, during my group's three-day termination conference in May. It was the first time Iran 4 had assembled since arriving in the country twenty-one months earlier. Standing in the back of the room, I caught sight of Betsy. "Now here's a friendly face," I said, grabbing the chair next to her. We had met frequently in Tehran over the past nine months, but in this setting, among the rest of our group, I felt a special connection. The light brown curls escaping from her navy blue bandanna, the shirtwaist dress, the Dr. Scholl's clogs on her feet were all so familiar. But if Betsy was remarkably the same, the rest of us were not. Like me, many of the women had piled on the pounds, while some of the men were almost gaunt. Long hair, less hair, fat, thin, we had all changed. My thoughts drifted back to the young adventurers who gathered at Kennedy Airport all that time ago—fresh and determined, so certain we could make a difference, though unsure what that meant. But in this room, almost two life-bending years later, our faces reflected the complex reality of attempting to integrate into another culture.

It was unclear if Peace Corps/Washington had a grasp on this reality. It was expedient for the American government to place more of the thousands drawn to Peace Corps service in a host country like Iran. A large country, it was deemed politically stable, the Peace Corps was well-established there, and the shah's government welcoming. The benefit of an increasing American presence on the USSR's southern border was unspoken but understood. But the effect of adding to the Peace Corps numbers in Iran was unknown. Kerman province, home to seven volunteers, was expecting sixteen by September.

Still, they were indications that the Peace Corps was listening. Its training staff made efforts to mitigate culture shock for new volunteers. At the Peace Corps' behest, I had written to a woman named Dorothy, training at the University of Texas, who would arrive in Kerman just as I was leaving. Advising her to bring a good cookbook and lots of underwear, I also tried to prepare her for the reality of being a single woman in my town. "Things can't possibly be as restrictive for women in Kerman as you make them sound," Dorothy wrote back.

How did we contribute to our communities, the de-briefers from Peace Corps/Washington wanted to know. With those failing exams of my students fresh in mind, I could hardly champion the success of the English language program. But I, like many in Iran 4, had been determined to counter the image of the "ugly American." As a woman unfettered by a chador, I hoped my presence would be seen as a positive harbinger of the future for Iranian women. Foreign but approachable, I infused a layer of the unknown into their lives. They also discovered that when Americans finally learned enough Farsi to have a conversation, they could be fun. But walking through the bazaar, my light brown hair brushing my shoulders, my bare legs exposed below my skirt, was I tearing down or confirming

Iranian stereotypes about wanton western women? How difficult it was to be effective under these conditions. Kermanis were understanding. What if I'd been in a less forgiving town? What if Alice Phinney had not been there to burnish my image?

"I don't think the Peace Corps should send unmarried women to Iran," I burst out during a discussion session at the conference. A murmur of agreement spread around the room. Our de-briefers looked puzzled.

"The bar is too high," a woman stationed in Qazvin chimed in. "There are so many things we can't do, so many places we can't go, so much criticism, even hostility, for simply being who we are." Hostile was an understatement. Rocks, slaps, name-calling, the stories went on. One woman—and she was married—had fought back. Standing her ground in the town of Khoy, she had knocked her assailant off of his bicycle and flung it into a watery jube. The Iranian men witnessing the event had clapped their approval. Betsy and I exchanged glances. We had been lucky to be stationed in friendly Kerman.

The real impact of my Peace Corps experience, the one I was certain about, was what had happened to me. I had learned so much—not the classroom type of education, but the kind that seeps in through the walls we have erected around us. Like many volunteers, I came to Iran expecting to be the teacher but ended up the student instead. Each volunteer had her own Iran—an experience unduplicated by any other volunteer. We would bring these Irans back to our country, our expanded worldviews providing new tools with which to examine our society and ourselves. In the process we might even illuminate other Americans.

Outside the conference sessions, we didn't spend much time worrying about what should have been. Post-Peace Corps plans bounced around Iran 4, surfacing at dinner, in the bazaar, in myriad carpet shops lining Ferdowsi Street as we focused on the future.

"I've got it all figured out," Betsy said over a chicken sandwich in the Peace Corps lounge. "I'm flying to Beirut; no more buses for me. I'm going to lie on the beach and get a great tan. Then it's off to Greece, Rome, and London. Want to come along?" No longer engaged to Christopher (he'd left Iran), she'd had a full schedule of teaching and socializing in Tehran. Listening to her, we could have been back in our room at the daneshsera, discussing our boyfriends and planning a trip to Yazd.

"Sounds pretty good to me, especially the part about lying on the beach. Let me think about it." There were so many plans swirling around I was reluctant to pick one. I wanted to be in the States by September. The fall semester at Berkeley started then, Fred left for Tehran then....

Back in Kerman I puzzled over my travel options, wishing someone would decide for me. At first, Fred's letters had been wistful. "I told the guys at the Peace Corps about you," he wrote from Washington. He misses me, I thought, he's making plans. But once officially hired by the Peace Corps and back home in California, the tenor changed. Full of parties, new people, and Johnny Walker scotch, his letters were notable for what they didn't say.

"How's Fred doing?" Tom Sisul asked as we perused letters from home in Mr. Sayeed-Nejad's office.

"He's having way too much fun."

Shoving my mail in my purse, I started for home, back on the shady side of the road to avoid the blistering June sun. If there had been a can in sight I would have kicked it all the way to Cinema Nur Street. Enough angst! I would wing my travel plans, latch on to some group going west when we left Iran. I skipped up the apartment stairs, grabbed all Fred's letters, and tossed them into the trunk that would wend its way by land and sea back to America in less than a month.

In the few weeks remaining, even ordinary events took on an extraordinary texture. Fereshteh, Mehri, and I were drinking tea and eating tiny boiled new potatoes in their garden when my friend's scarf slipped off her head, revealing gold earrings peeking through her flattened curls. Every female in Kerman had pierced ears. Even Mehri's baby girl had tiny turquoise stones on each lobe. Back home at Bloom Township High School or the University of Illinois, no one's ears were pierced. Yet it was so attractive, so *not* American. Pierced ears would add an aura of other-worldliness to my demeanor, announce that I was not the same person who left two years earlier.

"Should I get my ears pierced?" I asked.

"You would look so pretty," said Mehri-khanum.

"Be sure the person who does it is careful," said Fereshteh. "It's easy to get infections."

"Could you pierce them for me?"

"No. I'd be afraid."

Pierced ears were still on my mind that evening at my adult English class.

"My husband could do it for you," Mrs. Azari said when I raised the question. The other women looked askance. A man piercing someone's ears? "No, I'm serious. He's a doctor. He won't allow infections."

It was settled. Two evenings later, I rang the bell at the Azari gate. After the requisite glass of tea, Mrs. Azari propped my head against a pillow and her husband shot each ear with Novocain.

"It won't hurt a bit," he said.

"Ouch." The medicine stung.

"Be sure you put the needle in straight," Mrs. Azari said. "One of my ear pierces is crooked."

Using coarse white thread, the doctor drew the sterile needle through each lobe several times and tied the loops together. "Come back in a few days when the holes are almost healed, and I'll put your earrings in for you," he said.

My earlobes were the talk of the classrooms the next few days.

"Miss Mary, you're a Kermani now."

"My baby sister's ears look just like yours."

"Be sure to get good gold earrings, Miss Mary. The others will hurt your ears."

Days later, I was back at the Azaris', simple eighteen-karat gold earrings in hand. The doctor cut the threads, pulling them gently from each lobe. Then he pushed the thick loops I had brought through the holes. Ouch! "You must pull them in and out often," Mrs. Azari said, "otherwise the hole will close."

I admired my sophisticated self frequently in the mirror during the days that followed. My pierced ears and gold earrings were just the right touch. "She's different," they would announce to the people back home. But they sent the opposite message to my Iranian friends. "Now you look like a Kermani woman. Why do you have to leave?"

Packing and shopping filled the rest of my time. After spending months trying to buy the perfect Kerman carpet for my parents, a small navy rug with a flowered medallion lay on top of Fred's letters in my trunk, ready for its long trip to Homewood. I scoured the bazaar for mementos of Iran, wishing that Kerman had a better selection, regretting I had not bought more in Esfahan or Tehran. A week to go, my bags were almost packed when Phin came bustling up the stairs.

"You've got a telegram," she said, breathing heavily from the climb. "It's from the Peace Corps." I scanned the piece of paper she handed me.

"They're asking me to train new volunteers at the University of Texas this summer. The program starts in a couple of weeks. I have to let them know right away."

"Are you going to do it? I think you'd be good."

"I don't know. This changes everything."

The morning I left Kerman to head for Texas, I wandered through the apartment. I had packed the red printed Esfahani bedspread, so my bed looked naked. My red leather camel saddle was also in the trunk, but the director's chairs remained. The Iran Air posters of historic sites of Persia were still on my wall, but the woven Shiraz belt that had hung below was coming home with me. Not much in the refrigerator now, someone else would do the shopping. Picking up Willy, I carried him purring into the dark blue room that had been mine those first months in the apartment. That room was one thing I would not miss—practically the only thing. I checked out the bathroom to be sure the hole to the well was covered; I wouldn't want the new volunteer to fall into it. Willy jumped from my arms when I sat down to go through my pocketbook for the third time. Passport, residence permit, cash were all there. Outside on the balcony, I watched the women at the pump across the street. How extraordinary, but how normal it had been to see them at work in this public place. The mountains beyond, so outstanding at sunset, were hazy this time of day. I was about to go back inside when the Office of Education

Land Rover pulled up in front of our building. "Miss Phinney and I will be right down," I called to the driver. Pocketbook slung over my shoulder, suitcases at my side, I stooped to pick up Willy one last time. "I'll miss you, kitty," I whispered into his white fur.

I drove down Cinema Nur Street in style that last day.

"They paved the street in my honor," I said to Mr. Sayeed-Nejad, who was sitting beside Tom Sisul in the front seat of the Land Rover.

"Yeah," said Tom Taaffe. "You think things never change in Kerman, but they do."

But some things stayed the same: a small boy, holding a bunch of alfalfa just out of reach, led his flock down the newly paved road; a donkey pulling a cart managed to escape his owner, his loud brays announcing how pleased he was; men and boys, the tails of their suit jackets flapping, wove their bicycles in and out of the thin stream of cars; women in light-colored chadors, their shopping baskets loaded with fresh fruit and vegetables, hurried to their homes secluded behind the adobe walls that lined the streets.

Our little group waited in the shade of the passenger terminal for the Kerman-bound passengers to de-plane the Iran Air DC6 that would take me to Tehran, the only stop on my way to Homewood, from where I would later travel to Texas. The Toms weren't hurrying home, so I was leaving alone. We didn't say very much. What could we say? There was a chance I would meet the other volunteers again. We all lived on the same continent. But what about Mr. Sayeed-Nejad? This slender man with dancing eyes stood apart from all the other Iranians I knew. Curious, understanding, strict, funny, proper, he had made my life in Kerman possible.

"Mary-jun," I'm going to miss you." Mr. Sayeed-Nejad took my hand. "Why do you have to leave just when you've become a human being?"

I couldn't answer. It was time to go. Tears pouring down my cheeks, my fingers brushed a gold earring as I headed across the dirt runway, waving goodbye.

Epilogue

Once you have traveled, the voyage never ends,
but is played out over and over again in the
quietest chambers. The mind can never break
off from the journey. —*Pat Conroy*

I ran had not seen the last of me. Fred and I married, but rather than return to the Middle East as a Peace Corps field officer, he entered a doctoral program in Persian literature at the University of Michigan. While in Ann Arbor, I earned a library science degree, and daughter Ellen was born. In 1970, we went back to Iran, this time to Tehran, where Fred did research for his dissertation, and I put my library degree to work at a UNESCO-affiliated adult literacy institute. I would parlay that experience to head unique libraries in Ann Arbor and New York City. In the midst of our Iran stay, son Joe arrived in a Tehran hospital. We returned to the United States in 1974. The regime of Shah Mohammad Reza Pahlavi was severely challenged in the years that followed, leading to his hasty departure from the country in January 1979; two weeks later, Ayatollah Ruhollah Khomeini returned to Iran from exile, becoming the Supreme Leader of the Islamic Republic of Iran.

When we met at a New York City reunion of our Peace Corps/Iran group in 1984, my first roommate in Kerman, Betsy Burlingham, was a Montessori teacher in an Arlington, Virginia, public elementary school where the majority of the students are English Language Learners." She taught there for thirty-eight years. Tom Taaffe, then a hospital administrator in western North Carolina, attended the reunion with his wife,

Ann, who had volunteered in Yazd. Drawn to the far north, Tom Sisul became a special education teacher in Talkeetna, Alaska. He, Tom, Ann, and I took part in a reunion of Peace Corps/Iran volunteers in Portland, Oregon in 2011. Tom Taaffe died in 2015. Overall, the Peace Corps was in Iran for fourteen years; more than 1700 Americans served as volunteers there.

Alice Phinney extended her stay in Kerman for an additional year. Back in Massachusetts, she was employed for years by the local senior citizen center. When I visited her in 1983, she was driving the only three-wheeled moped in the town of West Wareham. Alice died in 2000 at the age of 101. After more than a decade of marriage, Fred and I divorced. A computer programmer when he retired, he lives with his wife in California's Bay Area. To my chagrin, over the years I lost contact with the Iranian friends who shared my life there in such wonderful ways.

A ninth floor apartment overlooking the Hudson River in Manhattan has been home to my husband Richard and me for more than thirty years. It is the closest I can come to living in a leafy green tree in the middle of an island, like I longed for that hot, long-ago summer in Kerman.

Words, Terms, and Expressions

aash reshteh: soup with noodles

agha, agha-ye: mister

Ahura Mazda: name of the Zoroastrian creator or god

USAID: Agency for International Development (U.S.)

aid-e shoma mobarak: happy New Year, happy holiday

Alhamdulillah: God be praised

Ali, ca. 600-661 AD: first imam of Shi'ism; son-in-law of Mohammad, the Prophet of Islam

Ashura: day commemorating the martyrdom of Hussein in Karbala, 680 AD

bachaha: children; also a term of endearment

Bahmanyar, d. 1067 AD: famed Iranian student of Avicenna for whom a girls' high school in Kerman was named

Baluchis: tribal people from southeastern Iran, Pakistan, and Afghanistan

bandar: port

befarmayeed: polite expression: you first, help yourself, etc.

bod-gir: chimney-like structure that captures wind to cool a room

CENTO: Central Treaty Organization, 1955-1979, comprised of Turkey, Iran, Pakistan, and the United Kingdom. The U.S. was an associate member

chador: veil worn by women, draping from the top of the head
   to the ground

chashm: I'll do what you say

chesre: Kerman herb used in *aash*

Cinema Nur: name of a movie theater

daneshsera: place of learning; institution of higher education

Dasht-e Kavir: Great Salt Desert

Dasht-e Lut: desert north of Kerman; one of the driest, hot-
   test places on earth

dooreh: circle of friends who meet regularly

Edareh Farhang: Office of Education

Farsi: official language of Iran; synonymous with "Persian" in
   English

Ferdowsi, ca. 935-1026 AD: author of the *Shahnameh*, Iran's
   epic poem; name of a street in Tehran

fesenjan: sauce made with ground walnuts and pomegranate
   syrup, served over rice, often with chicken

Hussein, ca. 626-680 AD: son of Ali, grandson of
   Mohammad; martyred in 680 AD

imam: spiritual and political successor to Mohammad

imam-zadeh: immediate descendent of a Shi'a imam

jalabiyah: robe; a traditional Arab garment

jube: channel for water running alongside a street

jun: dear

khanum: miss, Mrs.

khodahafez: goodbye

khoresh: stew served over rice; there are many varieties

kolompeh: date-filled pastry, a specialty of Kerman

kucheh: narrow, wall-lined lane or alley

madresseh: religious school (*madrasah* in Arabic)

Maidun-e shah: Shah Square

meeram: I am going

Mihan Tour: a bus company

Moharram: month in Arab lunar calendar when Hussein was martyred

Mohammad, 570-632 AD: founder of the religion of Islam; accepted by Muslims as the last of the prophets of God

No Ruz: Iranian New Year; it begins on the vernal equinox

noon: bread

Ob-e Hussein Abad: water from a spring named for Hussein

Parveen Etesami, 1907-1941: noted woman poet for whom a girls' high school in Kerman was named

Persian (language): synonymous with Farsi

qanat: underground water channel for irrigation

Ramadan: month of fasting for Muslims

rial: currency of Iran

salaam alaikum: greeting: peace be upon you

sangyak: bread baked on stones

SAVAK: acronym for the shah's secret police

seen: letter of Persian alphabet equivalent to "s"

Shah Abbas: shah of the Safavid dynasty who ruled from 1571 to 1629 AD

Shah Ne'matollah Vali, ca. 1331-1431 AD: a Sufi dervish whose shrine is in the town of Mahan

Shahnameh: epic poem of Iran, written by Ferdowsi between 977 and 1010 AD

Shi'a: branch of Islam whose adherents hold Ali to be the successor to Mohammad

sofreh: cloth laid on the floor for meals

sumac: spice in Middle Eastern cuisine

ta'arof: system of ritualized polite exchanges

takrar konid: repeat

TBT: a bus company

toman: unit of Iranian currency equaling ten rials

zir shalvari: pajama-style men's pants worn under street clothing and while relaxing

Zoroastrianism: one of the world's oldest monotheistic religions, dating to at least the fifth century BC.

About This Book

My writing instructor, Veronica Golos, had a standing order to her students: If you start to explain to the class what you've written, you must toss a quarter into the jar. Let your writing speak for itself. But, Veronica, sometimes...

Tossing in a handful of quarters: This book is a memoir, a memoir in that it's what I carry with me about my time in the Peace Corps in Iran more than fifty years ago. Do I remember everyone's name? No. Most remain the same, but some are changed because I don't remember them. Others are changed because I do. And then there's the person who wished to remain anonymous.

There's a lot of dialog in this memoir, used because it conveys the feelings I was experiencing and the personalities of the individuals in my story. The conversations are created, not reproduced; it is my hope that they portray the situations where they appear accurately and convincingly.

Acknowledgments

Living in a society so different from my own, among kind, understanding Iranians, shaped the way I view the world. It could have remained just that, a seminal part of my young life not widely shared with others. But my father stepped in, encouraging me to write about my time in Iran. Maurice Beckett is gone, but I took his advice.

So many individuals helped and inspired me while I worked on this book. Several of us from Veronica Golos's writing class, "Memoirs from the Middle," formed our own writing group, first with Veronica as our teacher, then on our own, "channeling" Veronica when we needed inspiration. Working alongside these thoughtful, supportive women has been a privilege. They read and reread chapters and versions of the manuscript, not once but many times. Gerri Marielle, Susan Ades Stone, Grace Kennan Warnecke, and Rosanne Weston know my book almost as well as I do. I am extremely grateful for their input.

I am also indebted to those who invested their time and thought reading versions of the manuscript. Judi Andrews, Alison Clement, Gail Persky, Ananda Reese, Carole Rosenthal, Rhoda Tagliacozzo, and Genna Wangsness made cogent suggestions that I attempted to implement. Marcia Croll and I held weekly telephone discussions of each new chapter. My children, thoughtful readers themselves, had unique insights into some of book's main characters. Jenny Burman, my conscientious copyeditor, corrected inconsistencies as she helped prepare the manuscript for publication.

Friends and colleagues who have lived in Iran contributed enormously to the book. Betsy Burlingham shared the wonderful pictures she took and helped clarify events we had shared. Phyllis Dillon's evocative photographs of Kerman helped focus my memory. Tom Klobe graciously allowed me to use his map of Iran, adapting it to a Kerman setting. I thank Wendy Coyle for assisting with Persian language issues. Responsibility for any errors in this memoir rests with me.

My friends were there when I needed them. Members of my thoughtful and encouraging proprioceptive writing group—Brenda Kaulbach, Gerri Marielle, and Fran Sullivan—knew just what to say when I couldn't find the right words. Charles

Persky's insights into the strengths and pitfalls of the memoir genre were most helpful. Deirdre Lawrence, a fellow librarian, motivated me to get the book out of my computer and into the public eye.

Peace Corps Iran has reentered my life in recent years, holding its first reunion in Portland, Oregon in 2011. John Krauskopf's session for writers drew me to the conference with the opportunity to debut a chapter from my memoir. This led to several years of involvement with Peace Corps Iran Association and the dedicated individuals who lead it. Enriched by this experience, my perspective of Iran during the 1960s has broadened.

While I worked on the book, my husband, Richard Marks, listened to me go on and on about Iran. He perused various chapters, advising me on the best approach to the story. He helped with words, with time, with patience. He printed photos and altered maps. His optimism kept me going. This book is dedicated to him.

Credits

El Anatsui quotation: The Brooklyn Museum exhibition "Gravity and Grace: Monumental Works by El Anatsui"
Map: Tom Klobe
Photographs: Betsy Burlingham

The Author

Mary Dana Marks served as a Peace Corps volunteer in Kerman, Iran from 1964-66. After earning a master's degree in library science from the University of Michigan, she returned to Iran where she worked as librarian of the UNESCO-affiliated International Institute for Adult Literacy Methods in Tehran and taught English as a second language. She and her family left Iran five years before its 1979 revolution. Marks spent most of her career as library director for the Museum of the American Indian in New York. Editor of the award-winning *Native America in the Twentieth Century: An Encyclopedia*, she lives with her husband in New York City.

CPSIA information can be obtained
at www.ICGtesting.com
Printed in the USA
LVOW03s0024201217
560341LV00012B/381/P